The Baker Street Four, Vol. 3

Written by **J. B. DJIAN** and **OLIVIER LEGRAND**

Art by **DAVID ETIEN**

INSIGHT COMICS

San Rafael, California

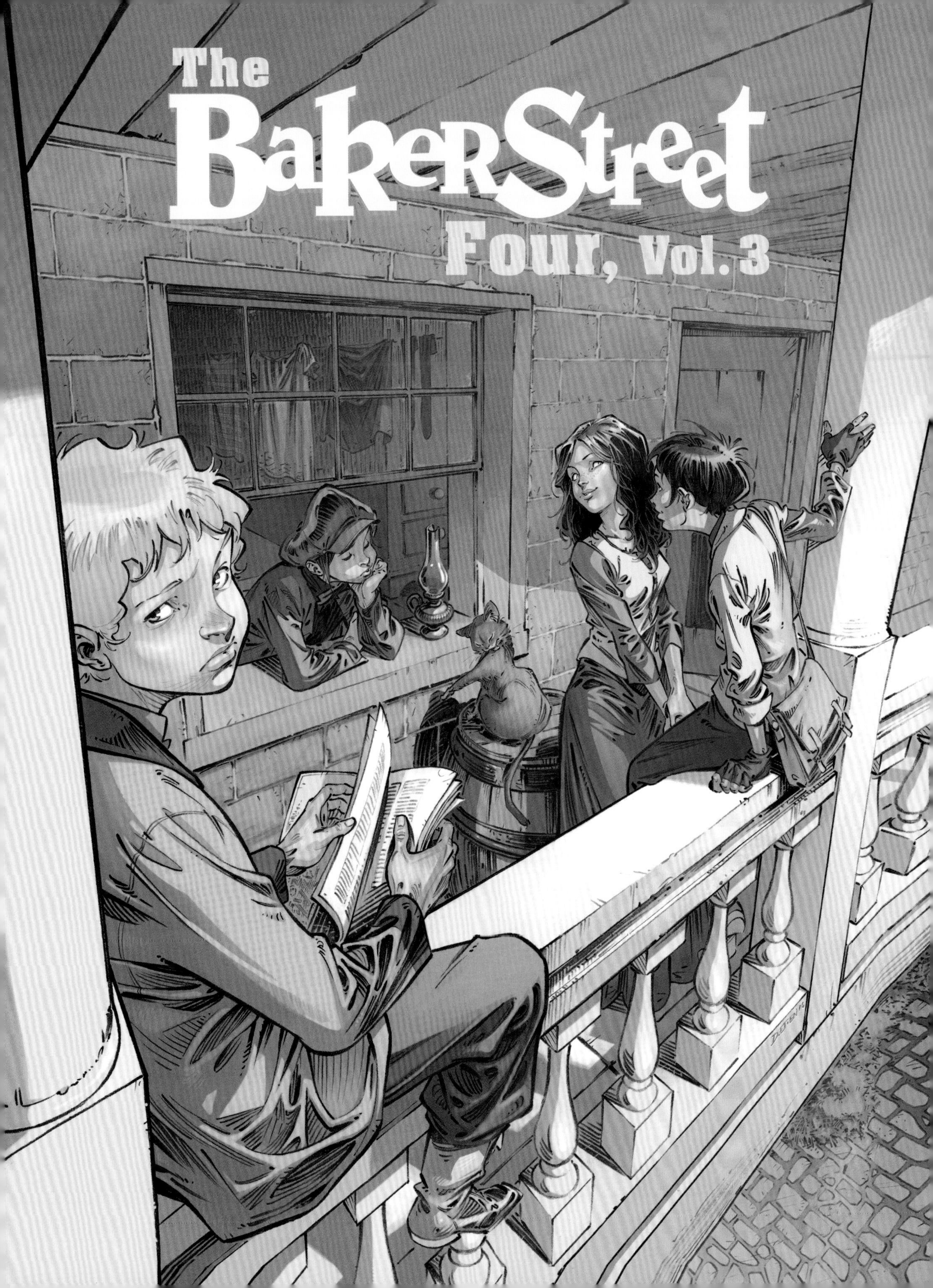
The
Baker Street
Four, Vol. 3

Moriarty's Successors

"It is the unofficial force,
the Baker Street Irregulars."

— Sherlock Holmes

ARTHUR CONAN DOYLE,
The Sign of the Four

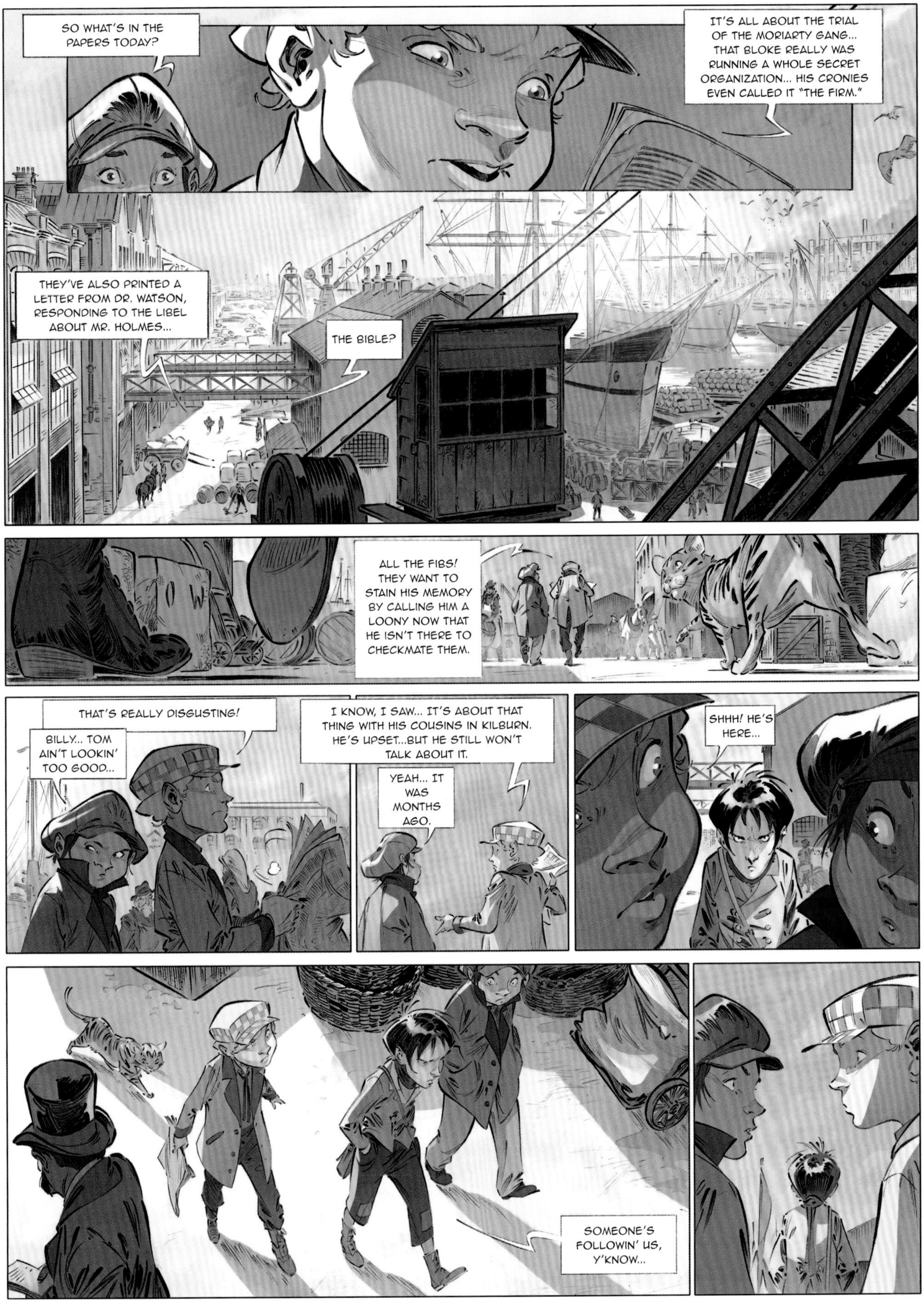
SO WHAT'S IN THE PAPERS TODAY?
IT'S ALL ABOUT THE TRIAL OF THE MORIARTY GANG... THAT BLOKE REALLY WAS RUNNING A WHOLE SECRET ORGANIZATION... HIS CRONIES EVEN CALLED IT "THE FIRM."
THEY'VE ALSO PRINTED A LETTER FROM DR. WATSON, RESPONDING TO THE LIBEL ABOUT MR. HOLMES...
THE BIBLE?
ALL THE FIBS! THEY WANT TO STAIN HIS MEMORY BY CALLING HIM A LOONY NOW THAT HE ISN'T THERE TO CHECKMATE THEM.
THAT'S REALLY DISGUSTING!
BILLY... TOM AIN'T LOOKIN' TOO GOOD...
I KNOW, I SAW... IT'S ABOUT THAT THING WITH HIS COUSINS IN KILBURN. HE'S UPSET...BUT HE STILL WON'T TALK ABOUT IT.
YEAH... IT WAS MONTHS AGO.
SHHH! HE'S HERE...
SOMEONE'S FOLLOWIN' US, Y'KNOW...

TALL THIN FELLA IN A BOWLER WITH A MOUSTACHE. LOOKS LIKE A COPPER...

D'YA REALLY THINK HE'S AFTER US?

LET'S TURN RIGHT AT THE NEXT CORNER AND BACK 'ROUND THE WAREHOUSE. THEN WE'LL KNOW...

WE KNOW THE ROPES, BILLY FLETCHER!

HE'S GONE... MAYBE YOU WERE WRONG?

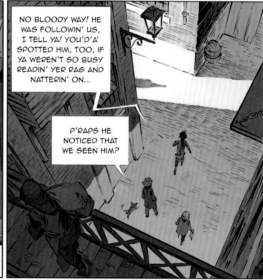

NO BLOODY WAY! HE WAS FOLLOWIN' US, I TELL YA! YOU'D'A' SPOTTED HIM, TOO, IF YA WEREN'T SO BUSY READIN' YER RAG AND NATTERIN' ON...

P'RAPS HE NOTICED THAT WE SEEN HIM?

YES, I DID...

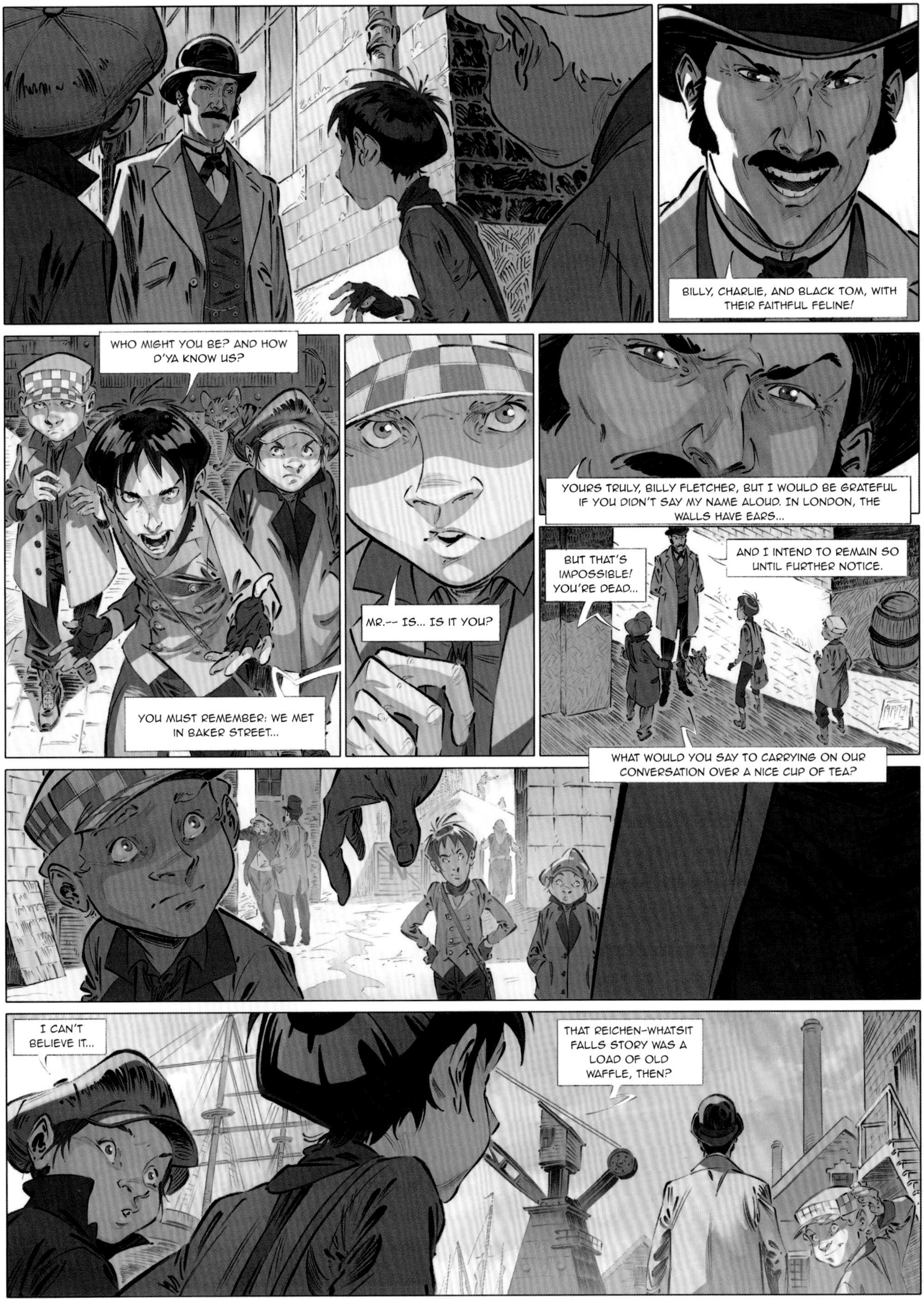
BILLY, CHARLIE, AND BLACK TOM, WITH THEIR FAITHFUL FELINE!
WHO MIGHT YOU BE? AND HOW D'YA KNOW US?
YOU MUST REMEMBER: WE MET IN BAKER STREET...
MR.-- IS... IS IT YOU?
YOURS TRULY, BILLY FLETCHER, BUT I WOULD BE GRATEFUL IF YOU DIDN'T SAY MY NAME ALOUD. IN LONDON, THE WALLS HAVE EARS...
BUT THAT'S IMPOSSIBLE! YOU'RE DEAD...
AND I INTEND TO REMAIN SO UNTIL FURTHER NOTICE.
WHAT WOULD YOU SAY TO CARRYING ON OUR CONVERSATION OVER A NICE CUP OF TEA?
I CAN'T BELIEVE IT...
THAT REICHEN-WHATSIT FALLS STORY WAS A LOAD OF OLD WAFFLE, THEN?

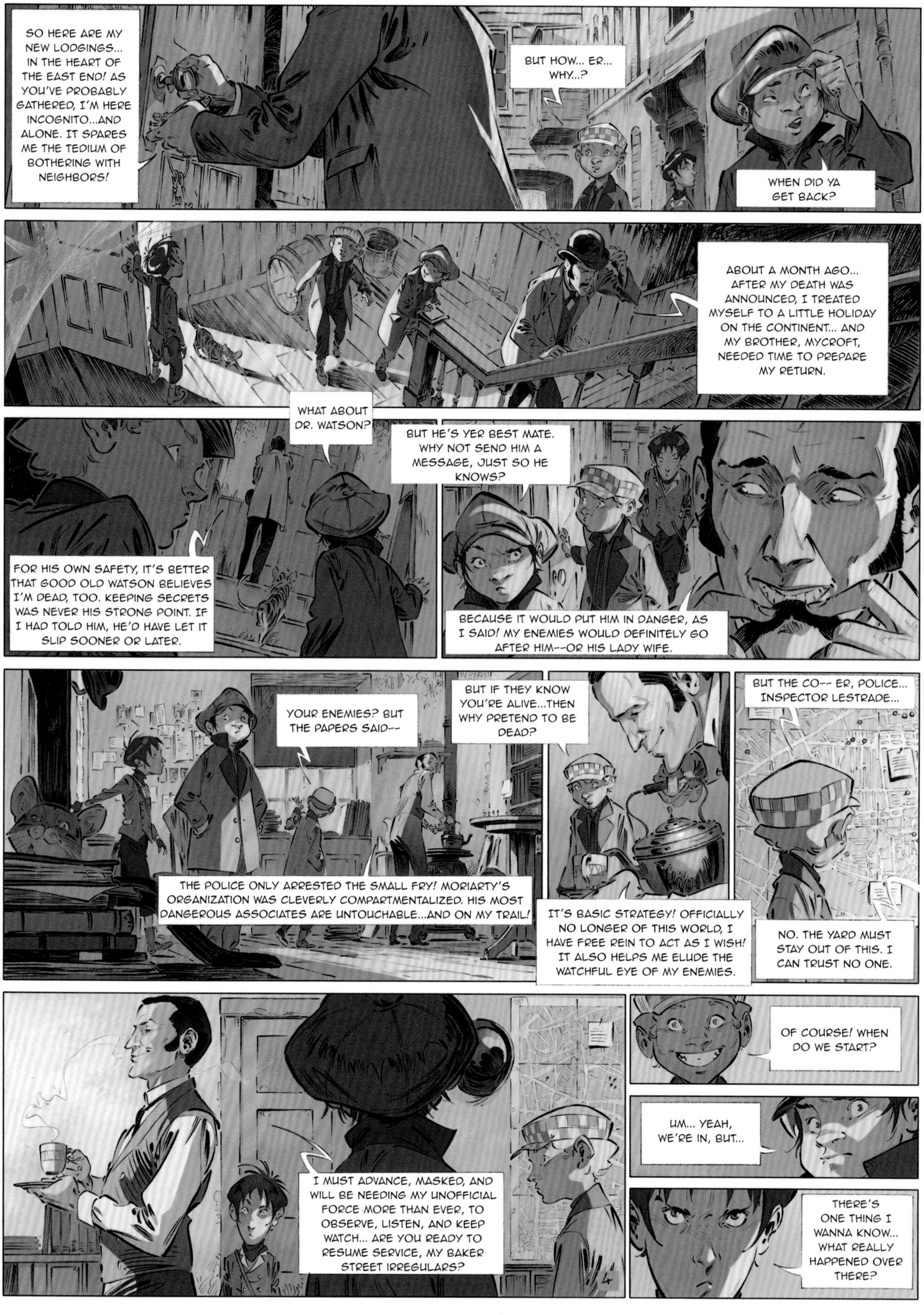
SO HERE ARE MY NEW LODGINGS... IN THE HEART OF THE EAST END! AS YOU'VE PROBABLY GATHERED, I'M HERE INCOGNITO...AND ALONE. IT SPARES ME THE TEDIUM OF BOTHERING WITH NEIGHBORS!
BUT HOW... ER... WHY...?
WHEN DID YA GET BACK?
ABOUT A MONTH AGO... AFTER MY DEATH WAS ANNOUNCED, I TREATED MYSELF TO A LITTLE HOLIDAY ON THE CONTINENT... AND MY BROTHER, MYCROFT, NEEDED TIME TO PREPARE MY RETURN.
WHAT ABOUT DR. WATSON?
FOR HIS OWN SAFETY, IT'S BETTER THAT GOOD OLD WATSON BELIEVES I'M DEAD, TOO. KEEPING SECRETS WAS NEVER HIS STRONG POINT. IF I HAD TOLD HIM, HE'D HAVE LET IT SLIP SOONER OR LATER.
BUT HE'S YER BEST MATE. WHY NOT SEND HIM A MESSAGE, JUST SO HE KNOWS?
BECAUSE IT WOULD PUT HIM IN DANGER, AS I SAID! MY ENEMIES WOULD DEFINITELY GO AFTER HIM--OR HIS LADY WIFE.
YOUR ENEMIES? BUT THE PAPERS SAID--
THE POLICE ONLY ARRESTED THE SMALL FRY! MORIARTY'S ORGANIZATION WAS CLEVERLY COMPARTMENTALIZED. HIS MOST DANGEROUS ASSOCIATES ARE UNTOUCHABLE...AND ON MY TRAIL!
BUT IF THEY KNOW YOU'RE ALIVE...THEN WHY PRETEND TO BE DEAD?
IT'S BASIC STRATEGY! OFFICIALLY NO LONGER OF THIS WORLD, I HAVE FREE REIN TO ACT AS I WISH! IT ALSO HELPS ME ELUDE THE WATCHFUL EYE OF MY ENEMIES.
BUT THE CO-- ER, POLICE... INSPECTOR LESTRADE...
NO. THE YARD MUST STAY OUT OF THIS. I CAN TRUST NO ONE.
I MUST ADVANCE, MASKED, AND WILL BE NEEDING MY UNOFFICIAL FORCE MORE THAN EVER, TO OBSERVE, LISTEN, AND KEEP WATCH... ARE YOU READY TO RESUME SERVICE, MY BAKER STREET IRREGULARS?
OF COURSE! WHEN DO WE START?
UM... YEAH, WE'RE IN, BUT...
THERE'S ONE THING I WANNA KNOW... WHAT REALLY HAPPENED OVER THERE?

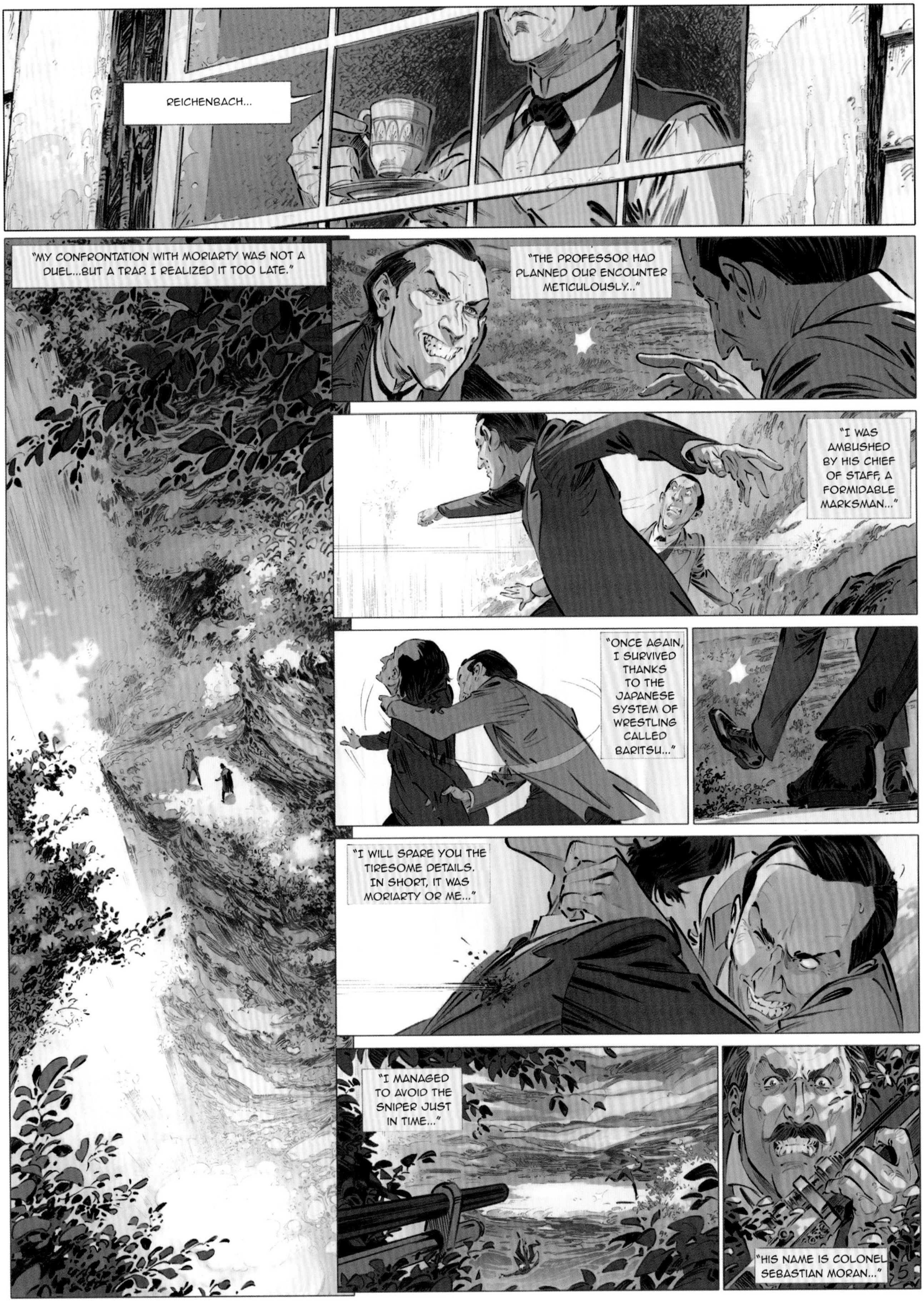
REICHENBACH...
"MY CONFRONTATION WITH MORIARTY WAS NOT A DUEL...BUT A TRAP. I REALIZED IT TOO LATE."
"THE PROFESSOR HAD PLANNED OUR ENCOUNTER METICULOUSLY..."
"I WAS AMBUSHED BY HIS CHIEF OF STAFF, A FORMIDABLE MARKSMAN..."
"ONCE AGAIN, I SURVIVED THANKS TO THE JAPANESE SYSTEM OF WRESTLING CALLED BARITSU..."
"I WILL SPARE YOU THE TIRESOME DETAILS. IN SHORT, IT WAS MORIARTY OR ME..."
"I MANAGED TO AVOID THE SNIPER JUST IN TIME..."
"HIS NAME IS COLONEL SEBASTIAN MORAN..."

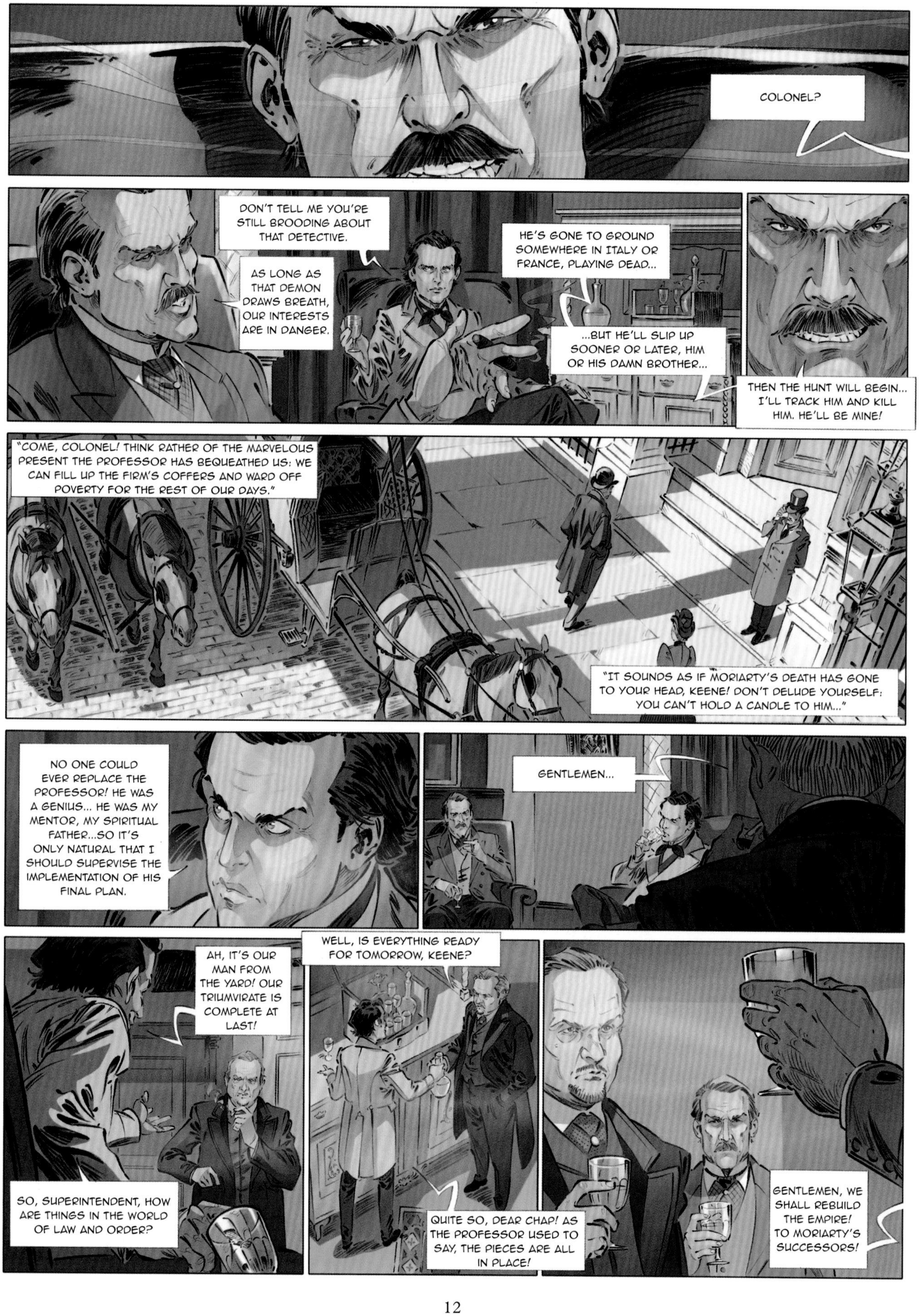
COLONEL?
DON'T TELL ME YOU'RE STILL BROODING ABOUT THAT DETECTIVE.
AS LONG AS THAT DEMON DRAWS BREATH, OUR INTERESTS ARE IN DANGER.
HE'S GONE TO GROUND SOMEWHERE IN ITALY OR FRANCE, PLAYING DEAD...
...BUT HE'LL SLIP UP SOONER OR LATER, HIM OR HIS DAMN BROTHER...
THEN THE HUNT WILL BEGIN... I'LL TRACK HIM AND KILL HIM. HE'LL BE MINE!
"COME, COLONEL! THINK RATHER OF THE MARVELOUS PRESENT THE PROFESSOR HAS BEQUEATHED US: WE CAN FILL UP THE FIRM'S COFFERS AND WARD OFF POVERTY FOR THE REST OF OUR DAYS."
"IT SOUNDS AS IF MORIARTY'S DEATH HAS GONE TO YOUR HEAD, KEENE! DON'T DELUDE YOURSELF: YOU CAN'T HOLD A CANDLE TO HIM..."
NO ONE COULD EVER REPLACE THE PROFESSOR! HE WAS A GENIUS... HE WAS MY MENTOR, MY SPIRITUAL FATHER...SO IT'S ONLY NATURAL THAT I SHOULD SUPERVISE THE IMPLEMENTATION OF HIS FINAL PLAN.
GENTLEMEN...
AH, IT'S OUR MAN FROM THE YARD! OUR TRIUMVIRATE IS COMPLETE AT LAST!
SO, SUPERINTENDENT, HOW ARE THINGS IN THE WORLD OF LAW AND ORDER?
WELL, IS EVERYTHING READY FOR TOMORROW, KEENE?
QUITE SO, DEAR CHAP! AS THE PROFESSOR USED TO SAY, THE PIECES ARE ALL IN PLACE!
GENTLEMEN, WE SHALL REBUILD THE EMPIRE! TO MORIARTY'S SUCCESSORS!

ARE THESE YOUR BAKER STREET FILES?

YES! I ASKED MYCROFT TO STORE THEM SAFELY WHILE I WAS OFF HUNTING MORIARTY, SO HIS ACCOMPLICES WOULDN'T SEIZE THEM DURING MY ABSENCE.

BIN SEEIN' YER BROTHER A LOT, THEN?

OH, NO! MORAN IS WATCHING HIM, IN THE HOPE OF FINDING ME! FORTUNATELY FOR MY BROTHER, HIS FAVORITE DIOGENES CLUB IS OFF-LIMITS TO THE COLONEL'S SPIES...

MYCROFT AND I COMMUNICATE DAILY VIA THE TIMES' CLASSIFIED ADVERTISEMENTS, IN A CODE WE INVENTED...BIDING OUR TIME TO BEAT MORAN AT HIS OWN GAME!

BUT AREN'T YOU GOING TO COME BACK ONE DAY? A TRIUMPHANT RETURN, I MEAN...

OF COURSE! BUT FIRST I MUST UNMASK AND NEUTRALIZE THE PROFESSOR'S HEIRS. I WILL NEVER BE ABLE TO ACT OPENLY WHILE THEY ARE STILL AT LARGE.

SO IT'S NOT JUST THIS MORAN, THEN?

MORIARTY HAD AT LEAST TWO MORE ASSOCIATES, BOTH AS UNTOUCHABLE AS THE COLONEL. ONE IS DESMOND KEENE, THE FIRM'S TREASURER AND THE PROFESSOR'S FORMER STUDENT. HIS MENTOR'S DEATH IS AN UNEXPECTED BOON.

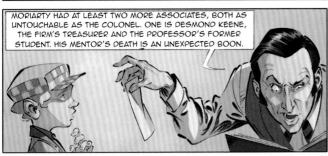

BUT I'LL NEVER LET A NEW NAPOLEON OF CRIME TAKE HIS PLACE.

AND YOUR VIOLIN?

IT'S AT BAKER STREET. I MISS IT, OF COURSE...BUT THE EAST END HAS EARS, AND A MENDELSSOHN CONCERTO MIGHT BE ENOUGH TO PUT MORAN'S AGENTS ON TO ME.

AND WHAT ABOUT YOUR OTHER, ER...HABIT?

YOU'VE BEEN READING TOO MANY OF WATSON'S STORIES! I HAVEN'T BEEN NEAR A SYRINGE SINCE REICHENBACH! THE CURRENT SITUATION IS SUPPLYING MY BRAIN WITH ALL THE STIMULATION IT NEEDS!

SO D'YA REALLY WANNA WORK FOR HIM AGAIN, TOM? I THOUGHT--

BEST JOB WE EVER HAD, AIN'T IT? AND HE'S ALWAYS BEEN FAIR TO US...

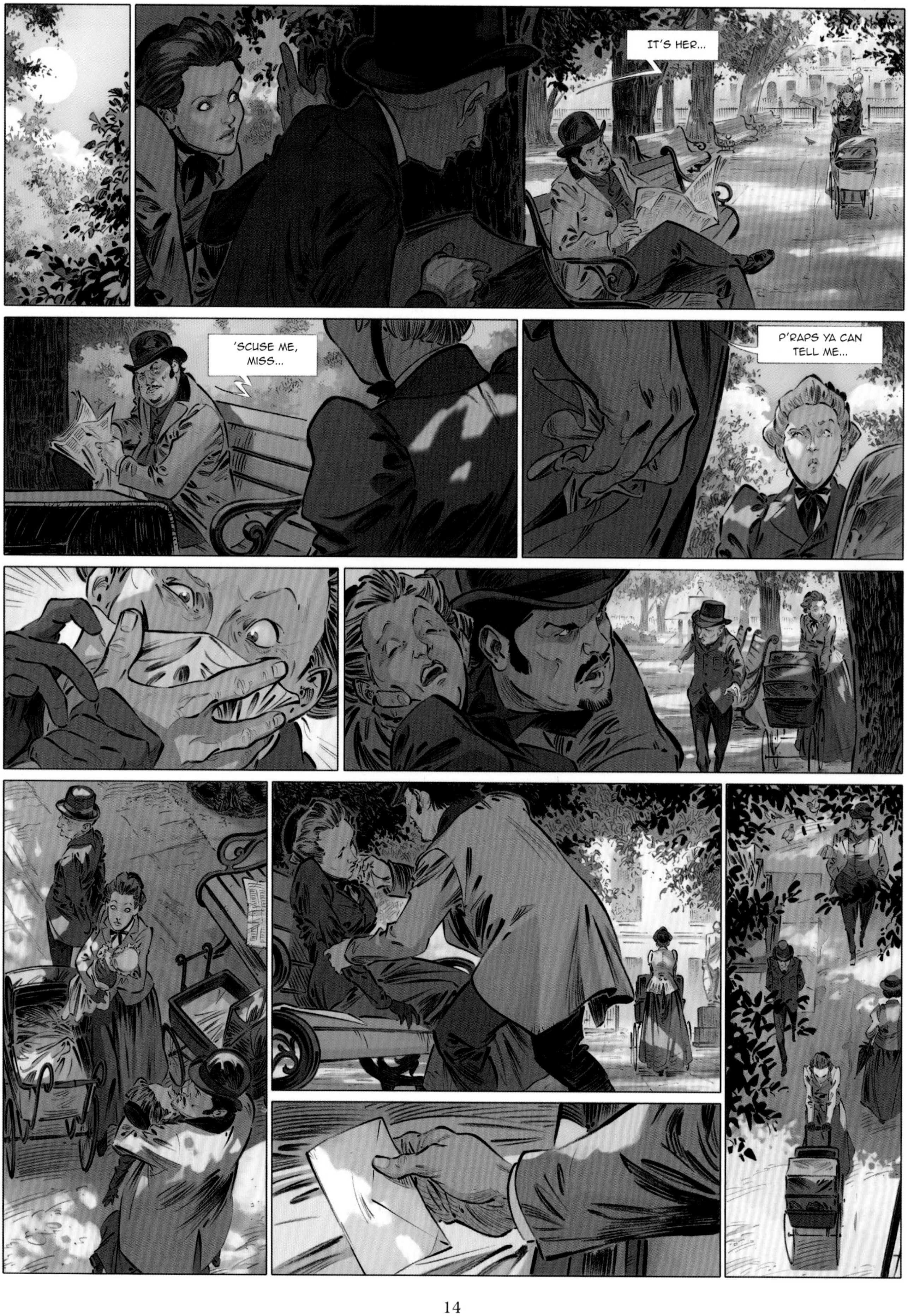
IT'S HER...
'SCUSE ME, MISS...
P'RAPS YA CAN TELL ME...

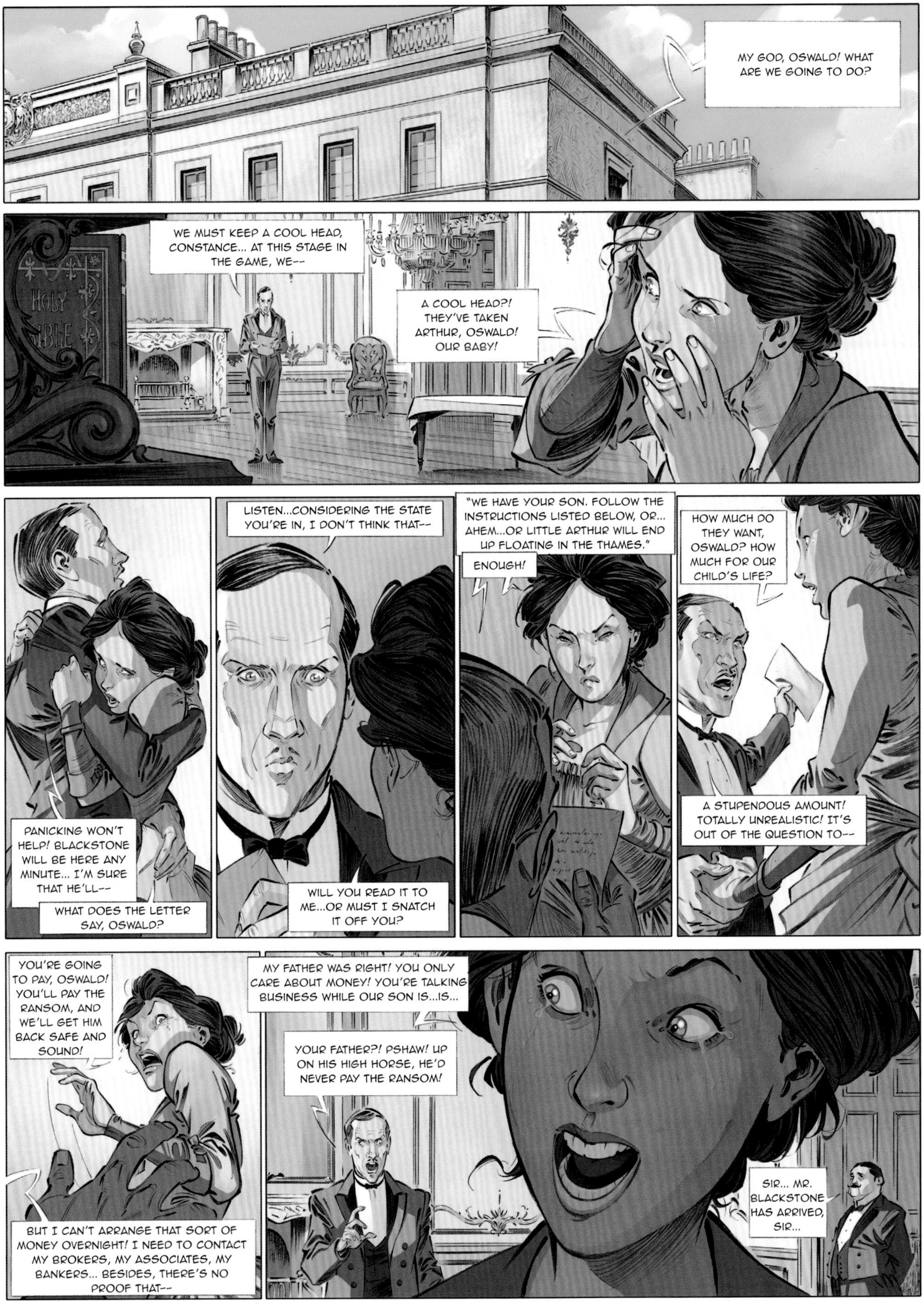
MY GOD, OSWALD! WHAT ARE WE GOING TO DO?
WE MUST KEEP A COOL HEAD, CONSTANCE... AT THIS STAGE IN THE GAME, WE--
A COOL HEAD?! THEY'VE TAKEN ARTHUR, OSWALD! OUR BABY!
HOLY BIBLE
PANICKING WON'T HELP! BLACKSTONE WILL BE HERE ANY MINUTE... I'M SURE THAT HE'LL--
WHAT DOES THE LETTER SAY, OSWALD?
LISTEN...CONSIDERING THE STATE YOU'RE IN, I DON'T THINK THAT--
WILL YOU READ IT TO ME...OR MUST I SNATCH IT OFF YOU?
"WE HAVE YOUR SON. FOLLOW THE INSTRUCTIONS LISTED BELOW, OR... AHEM...OR LITTLE ARTHUR WILL END UP FLOATING IN THE THAMES."
ENOUGH!
HOW MUCH DO THEY WANT, OSWALD? HOW MUCH FOR OUR CHILD'S LIFE?
A STUPENDOUS AMOUNT! TOTALLY UNREALISTIC! IT'S OUT OF THE QUESTION TO--
YOU'RE GOING TO PAY, OSWALD! YOU'LL PAY THE RANSOM, AND WE'LL GET HIM BACK SAFE AND SOUND!
BUT I CAN'T ARRANGE THAT SORT OF MONEY OVERNIGHT! I NEED TO CONTACT MY BROKERS, MY ASSOCIATES, MY BANKERS... BESIDES, THERE'S NO PROOF THAT--
MY FATHER WAS RIGHT! YOU ONLY CARE ABOUT MONEY! YOU'RE TALKING BUSINESS WHILE OUR SON IS...IS...
YOUR FATHER?! PSHAW! UP ON HIS HIGH HORSE, HE'D NEVER PAY THE RANSOM!
SIR... MR. BLACKSTONE HAS ARRIVED, SIR...

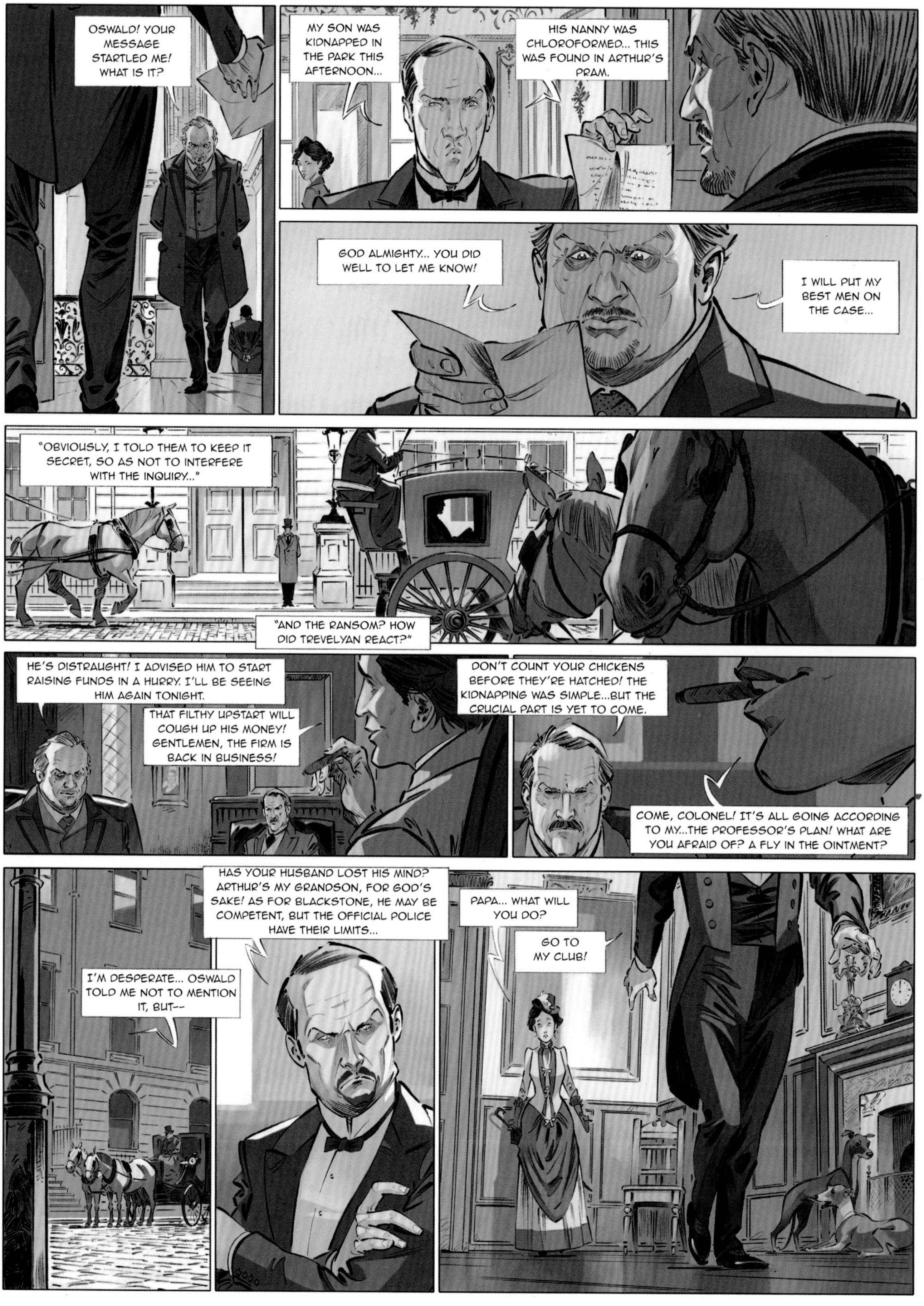
OSWALD! YOUR MESSAGE STARTLED ME! WHAT IS IT?
MY SON WAS KIDNAPPED IN THE PARK THIS AFTERNOON...
HIS NANNY WAS CHLOROFORMED... THIS WAS FOUND IN ARTHUR'S PRAM.
GOD ALMIGHTY... YOU DID WELL TO LET ME KNOW!
I WILL PUT MY BEST MEN ON THE CASE...
"OBVIOUSLY, I TOLD THEM TO KEEP IT SECRET, SO AS NOT TO INTERFERE WITH THE INQUIRY..."
"AND THE RANSOM? HOW DID TREVELYAN REACT?"
HE'S DISTRAUGHT! I ADVISED HIM TO START RAISING FUNDS IN A HURRY. I'LL BE SEEING HIM AGAIN TONIGHT.
THAT FILTHY UPSTART WILL COUGH UP HIS MONEY! GENTLEMEN, THE FIRM IS BACK IN BUSINESS!
DON'T COUNT YOUR CHICKENS BEFORE THEY'RE HATCHED! THE KIDNAPPING WAS SIMPLE...BUT THE CRUCIAL PART IS YET TO COME.
COME, COLONEL! IT'S ALL GOING ACCORDING TO MY...THE PROFESSOR'S PLAN! WHAT ARE YOU AFRAID OF? A FLY IN THE OINTMENT?
I'M DESPERATE... OSWALD TOLD ME NOT TO MENTION IT, BUT--
HAS YOUR HUSBAND LOST HIS MIND? ARTHUR'S MY GRANDSON, FOR GOD'S SAKE! AS FOR BLACKSTONE, HE MAY BE COMPETENT, BUT THE OFFICIAL POLICE HAVE THEIR LIMITS...
PAPA... WHAT WILL YOU DO?
GO TO MY CLUB!

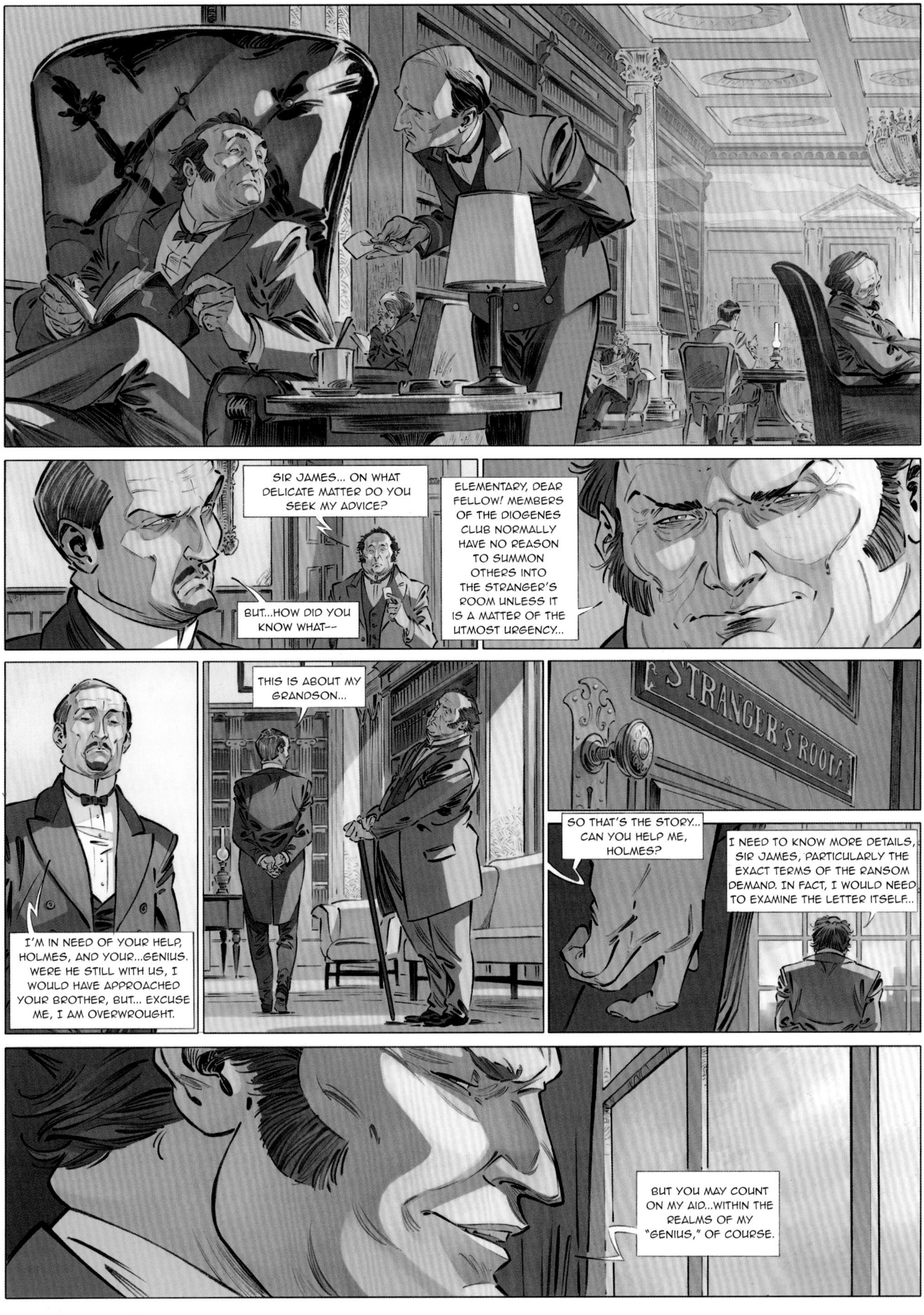
SIR JAMES... ON WHAT DELICATE MATTER DO YOU SEEK MY ADVICE?
BUT...HOW DID YOU KNOW WHAT--
ELEMENTARY, DEAR FELLOW! MEMBERS OF THE DIOGENES CLUB NORMALLY HAVE NO REASON TO SUMMON OTHERS INTO THE STRANGER'S ROOM UNLESS IT IS A MATTER OF THE UTMOST URGENCY...
I'M IN NEED OF YOUR HELP, HOLMES, AND YOUR...GENIUS. WERE HE STILL WITH US, I WOULD HAVE APPROACHED YOUR BROTHER, BUT... EXCUSE ME, I AM OVERWROUGHT.
THIS IS ABOUT MY GRANDSON...
STRANGER'S ROOM
SO THAT'S THE STORY... CAN YOU HELP ME, HOLMES?
I NEED TO KNOW MORE DETAILS, SIR JAMES, PARTICULARLY THE EXACT TERMS OF THE RANSOM DEMAND. IN FACT, I WOULD NEED TO EXAMINE THE LETTER ITSELF...
BUT YOU MAY COUNT ON MY AID...WITHIN THE REALMS OF MY "GENIUS," OF COURSE.

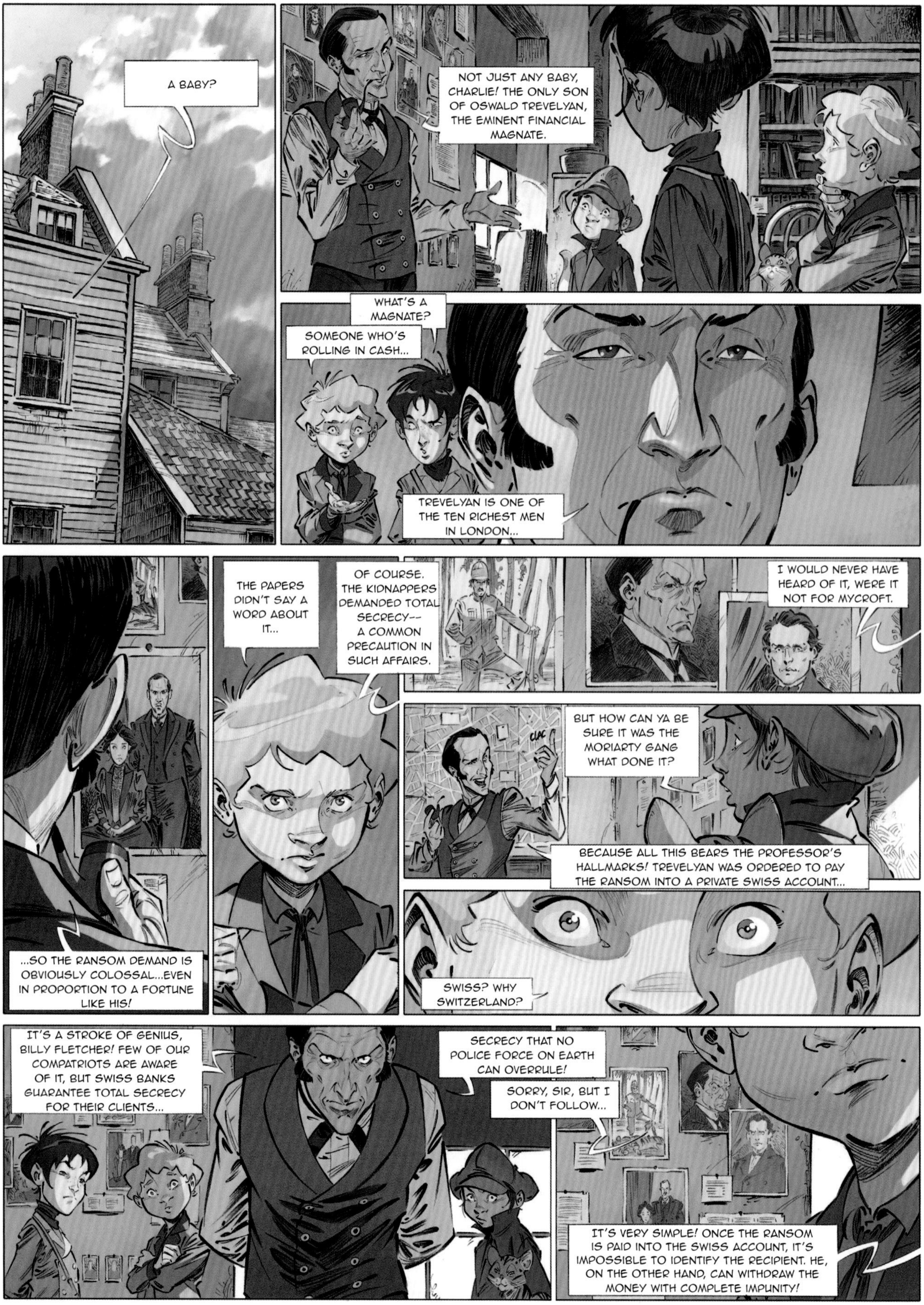

A BABY?
NOT JUST ANY BABY, CHARLIE! THE ONLY SON OF OSWALD TREVELYAN, THE EMINENT FINANCIAL MAGNATE.
WHAT'S A MAGNATE?
SOMEONE WHO'S ROLLING IN CASH...
TREVELYAN IS ONE OF THE TEN RICHEST MEN IN LONDON...
...SO THE RANSOM DEMAND IS OBVIOUSLY COLOSSAL...EVEN IN PROPORTION TO A FORTUNE LIKE HIS!
THE PAPERS DIDN'T SAY A WORD ABOUT IT...
OF COURSE. THE KIDNAPPERS DEMANDED TOTAL SECRECY-- A COMMON PRECAUTION IN SUCH AFFAIRS.
I WOULD NEVER HAVE HEARD OF IT, WERE IT NOT FOR MYCROFT.
BUT HOW CAN YA BE SURE IT WAS THE MORIARTY GANG WHAT DONE IT?
CLAC
BECAUSE ALL THIS BEARS THE PROFESSOR'S HALLMARKS! TREVELYAN WAS ORDERED TO PAY THE RANSOM INTO A PRIVATE SWISS ACCOUNT...
SWISS? WHY SWITZERLAND?
IT'S A STROKE OF GENIUS, BILLY FLETCHER! FEW OF OUR COMPATRIOTS ARE AWARE OF IT, BUT SWISS BANKS GUARANTEE TOTAL SECRECY FOR THEIR CLIENTS...
SECRECY THAT NO POLICE FORCE ON EARTH CAN OVERRULE!
SORRY, SIR, BUT I DON'T FOLLOW...
IT'S VERY SIMPLE! ONCE THE RANSOM IS PAID INTO THE SWISS ACCOUNT, IT'S IMPOSSIBLE TO IDENTIFY THE RECIPIENT. HE, ON THE OTHER HAND, CAN WITHDRAW THE MONEY WITH COMPLETE IMPUNITY!

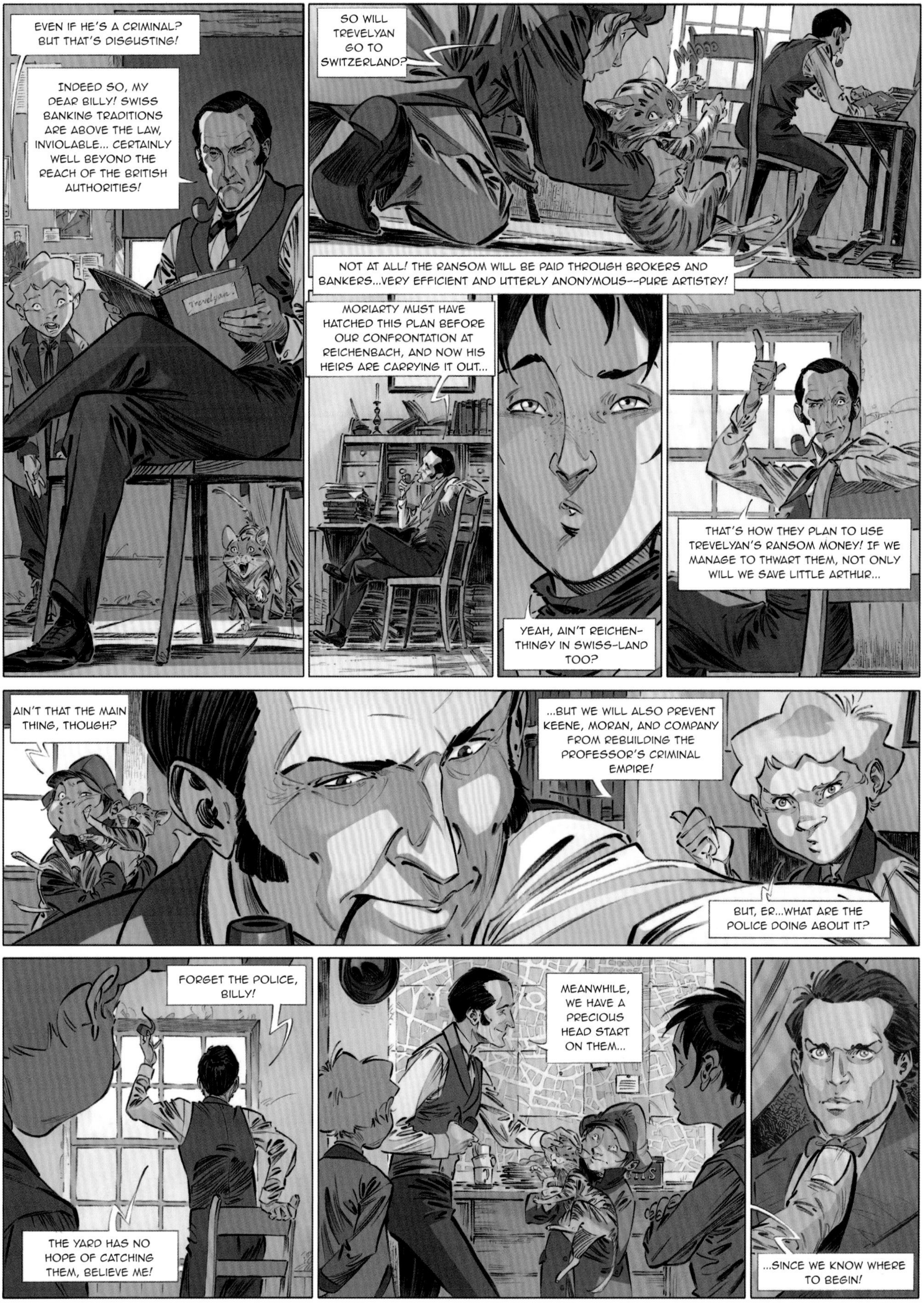
EVEN IF HE'S A CRIMINAL? BUT THAT'S DISGUSTING!
INDEED SO, MY DEAR BILLY! SWISS BANKING TRADITIONS ARE ABOVE THE LAW, INVIOLABLE... CERTAINLY WELL BEYOND THE REACH OF THE BRITISH AUTHORITIES!
SO WILL TREVELYAN GO TO SWITZERLAND?
NOT AT ALL! THE RANSOM WILL BE PAID THROUGH BROKERS AND BANKERS...VERY EFFICIENT AND UTTERLY ANONYMOUS--PURE ARTISTRY!
MORIARTY MUST HAVE HATCHED THIS PLAN BEFORE OUR CONFRONTATION AT REICHENBACH, AND NOW HIS HEIRS ARE CARRYING IT OUT...
YEAH, AIN'T REICHEN-THINGY IN SWISS-LAND TOO?
THAT'S HOW THEY PLAN TO USE TREVELYAN'S RANSOM MONEY! IF WE MANAGE TO THWART THEM, NOT ONLY WILL WE SAVE LITTLE ARTHUR...
AIN'T THAT THE MAIN THING, THOUGH?
...BUT WE WILL ALSO PREVENT KEENE, MORAN, AND COMPANY FROM REBUILDING THE PROFESSOR'S CRIMINAL EMPIRE!
BUT, ER...WHAT ARE THE POLICE DOING ABOUT IT?
FORGET THE POLICE, BILLY!
THE YARD HAS NO HOPE OF CATCHING THEM, BELIEVE ME!
MEANWHILE, WE HAVE A PRECIOUS HEAD START ON THEM...
...SINCE WE KNOW WHERE TO BEGIN!

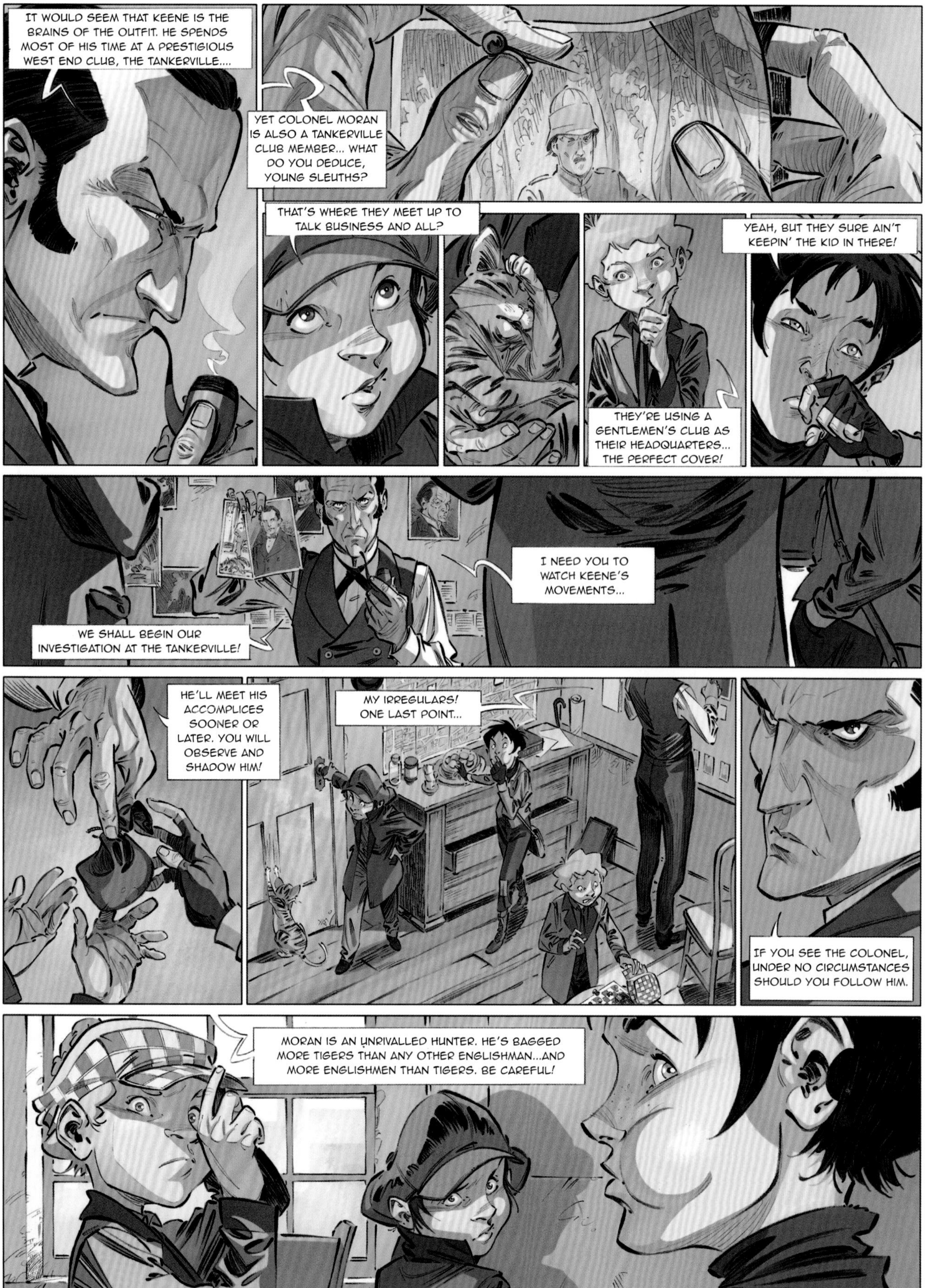
IT WOULD SEEM THAT KEENE IS THE BRAINS OF THE OUTFIT. HE SPENDS MOST OF HIS TIME AT A PRESTIGIOUS WEST END CLUB, THE TANKERVILLE....
YET COLONEL MORAN IS ALSO A TANKERVILLE CLUB MEMBER... WHAT DO YOU DEDUCE, YOUNG SLEUTHS?
THAT'S WHERE THEY MEET UP TO TALK BUSINESS AND ALL?
THEY'RE USING A GENTLEMEN'S CLUB AS THEIR HEADQUARTERS... THE PERFECT COVER!
YEAH, BUT THEY SURE AIN'T KEEPIN' THE KID IN THERE!
WE SHALL BEGIN OUR INVESTIGATION AT THE TANKERVILLE!
I NEED YOU TO WATCH KEENE'S MOVEMENTS...
HE'LL MEET HIS ACCOMPLICES SOONER OR LATER. YOU WILL OBSERVE AND SHADOW HIM!
MY IRREGULARS! ONE LAST POINT...
IF YOU SEE THE COLONEL, UNDER NO CIRCUMSTANCES SHOULD YOU FOLLOW HIM.
MORAN IS AN UNRIVALLED HUNTER. HE'S BAGGED MORE TIGERS THAN ANY OTHER ENGLISHMAN...AND MORE ENGLISHMEN THAN TIGERS. BE CAREFUL!

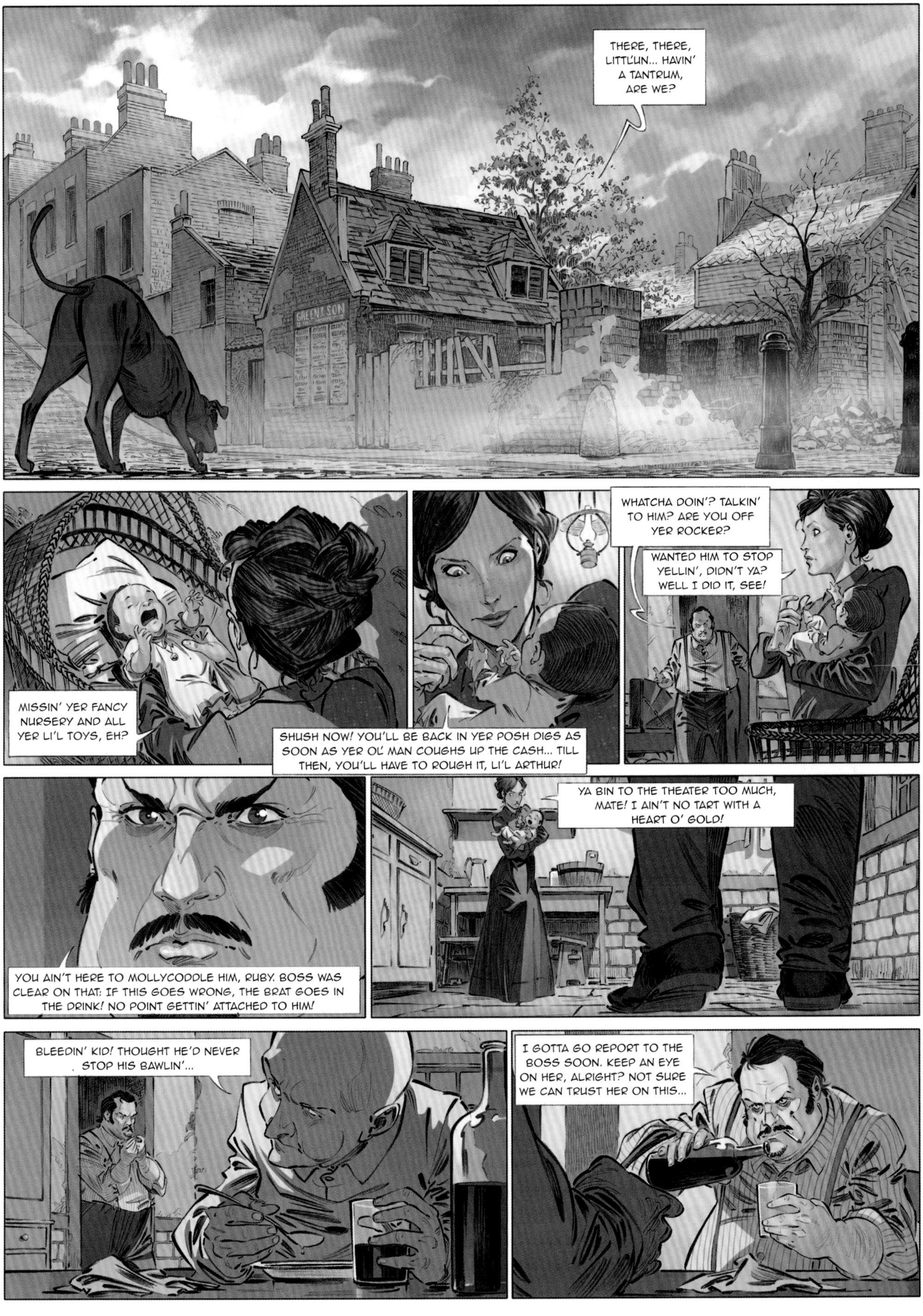
THERE, THERE, LITTL'UN... HAVIN' A TANTRUM, ARE WE?
MISSIN' YER FANCY NURSERY AND ALL YER LI'L TOYS, EH?
SHUSH NOW! YOU'LL BE BACK IN YER POSH DIGS AS SOON AS YER OL' MAN COUGHS UP THE CASH... TILL THEN, YOU'LL HAVE TO ROUGH IT, LI'L ARTHUR!
WHATCHA DOIN'? TALKIN' TO HIM? ARE YOU OFF YER ROCKER?
WANTED HIM TO STOP YELLIN', DIDN'T YA? WELL I DID IT, SEE!
YOU AIN'T HERE TO MOLLYCODDLE HIM, RUBY. BOSS WAS CLEAR ON THAT: IF THIS GOES WRONG, THE BRAT GOES IN THE DRINK! NO POINT GETTIN' ATTACHED TO HIM!
YA BIN TO THE THEATER TOO MUCH, MATE! I AIN'T NO TART WITH A HEART O' GOLD!
BLEEDIN' KID! THOUGHT HE'D NEVER STOP HIS BAWLIN'...
I GOTTA GO REPORT TO THE BOSS SOON. KEEP AN EYE ON HER, ALRIGHT? NOT SURE WE CAN TRUST HER ON THIS...

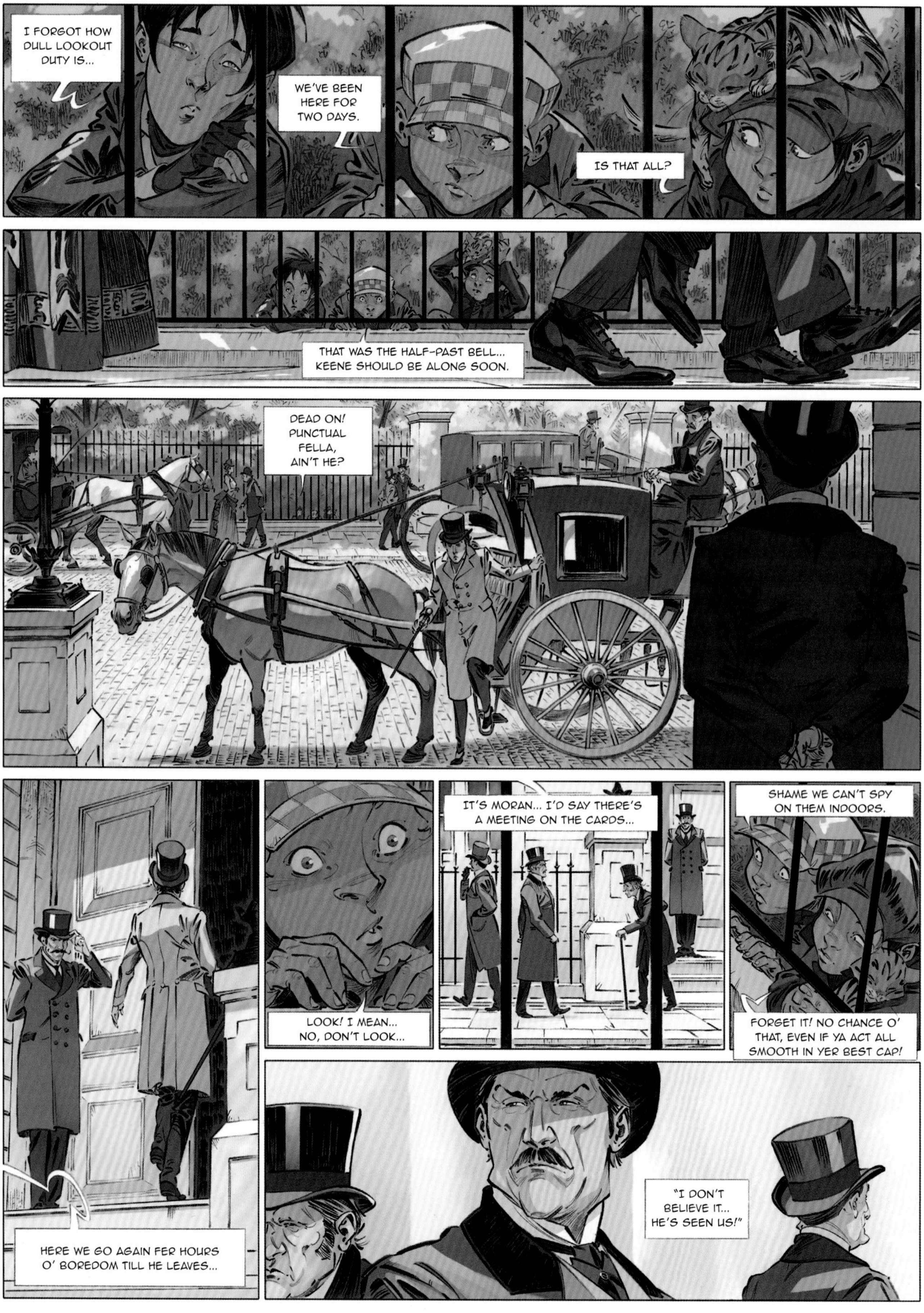
I FORGOT HOW DULL LOOKOUT DUTY IS...
WE'VE BEEN HERE FOR TWO DAYS.
IS THAT ALL?
THAT WAS THE HALF-PAST BELL... KEENE SHOULD BE ALONG SOON.
DEAD ON! PUNCTUAL FELLA, AIN'T HE?
HERE WE GO AGAIN FER HOURS O' BOREDOM TILL HE LEAVES...
LOOK! I MEAN... NO, DON'T LOOK...
IT'S MORAN... I'D SAY THERE'S A MEETING ON THE CARDS...
SHAME WE CAN'T SPY ON THEM INDOORS.
FORGET IT! NO CHANCE O' THAT, EVEN IF YA ACT ALL SMOOTH IN YER BEST CAP!
"I DON'T BELIEVE IT... HE'S SEEN US!"

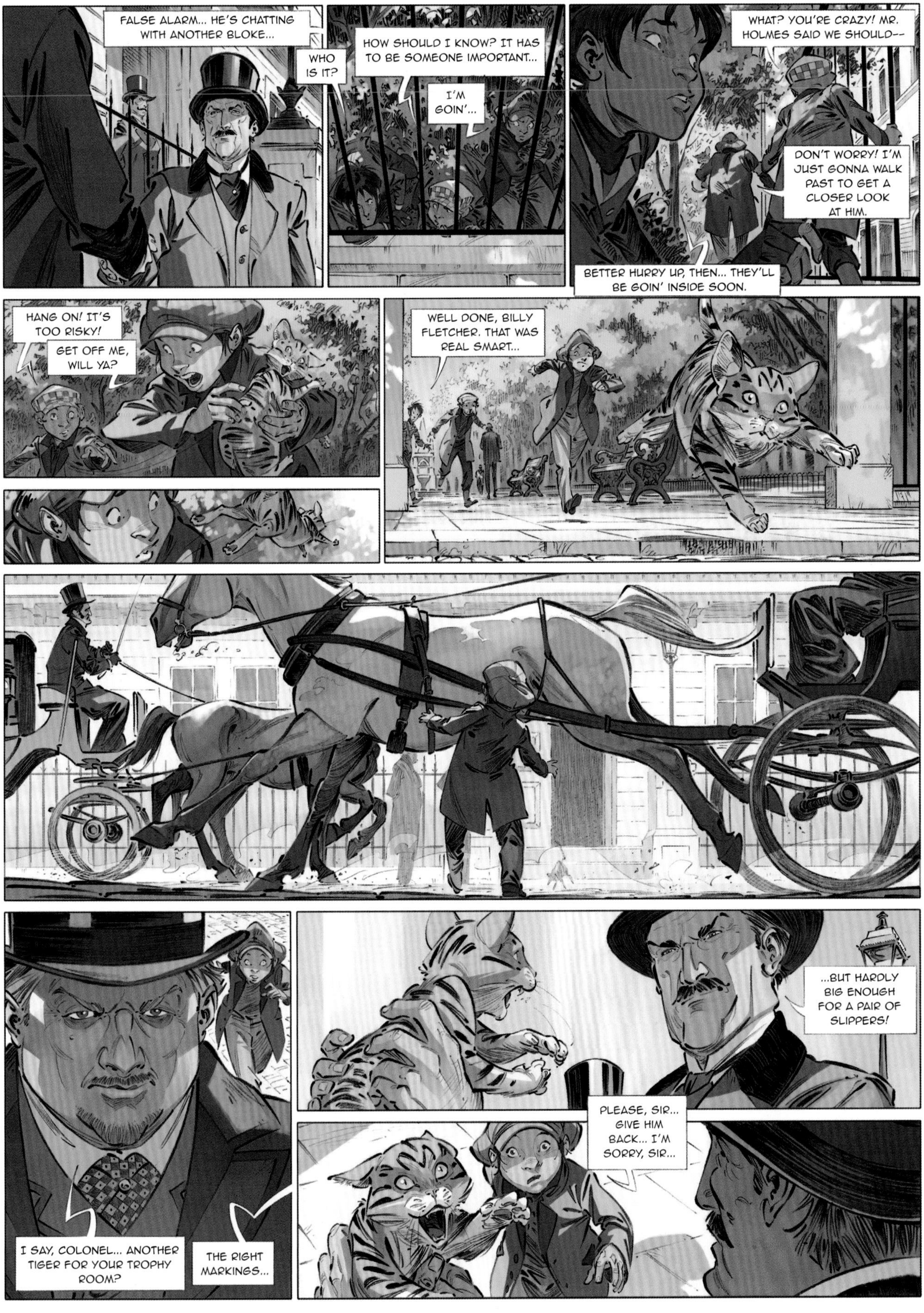

FALSE ALARM... HE'S CHATTING WITH ANOTHER BLOKE...
WHO IS IT?
HOW SHOULD I KNOW? IT HAS TO BE SOMEONE IMPORTANT...
I'M GOIN'...
WHAT? YOU'RE CRAZY! MR. HOLMES SAID WE SHOULD--
DON'T WORRY! I'M JUST GONNA WALK PAST TO GET A CLOSER LOOK AT HIM.
BETTER HURRY UP, THEN... THEY'LL BE GOIN' INSIDE SOON.
HANG ON! IT'S TOO RISKY!
GET OFF ME, WILL YA?
WELL DONE, BILLY FLETCHER. THAT WAS REAL SMART...
...BUT HARDLY BIG ENOUGH FOR A PAIR OF SLIPPERS!
I SAY, COLONEL... ANOTHER TIGER FOR YOUR TROPHY ROOM?
THE RIGHT MARKINGS...
PLEASE, SIR... GIVE HIM BACK... I'M SORRY, SIR...

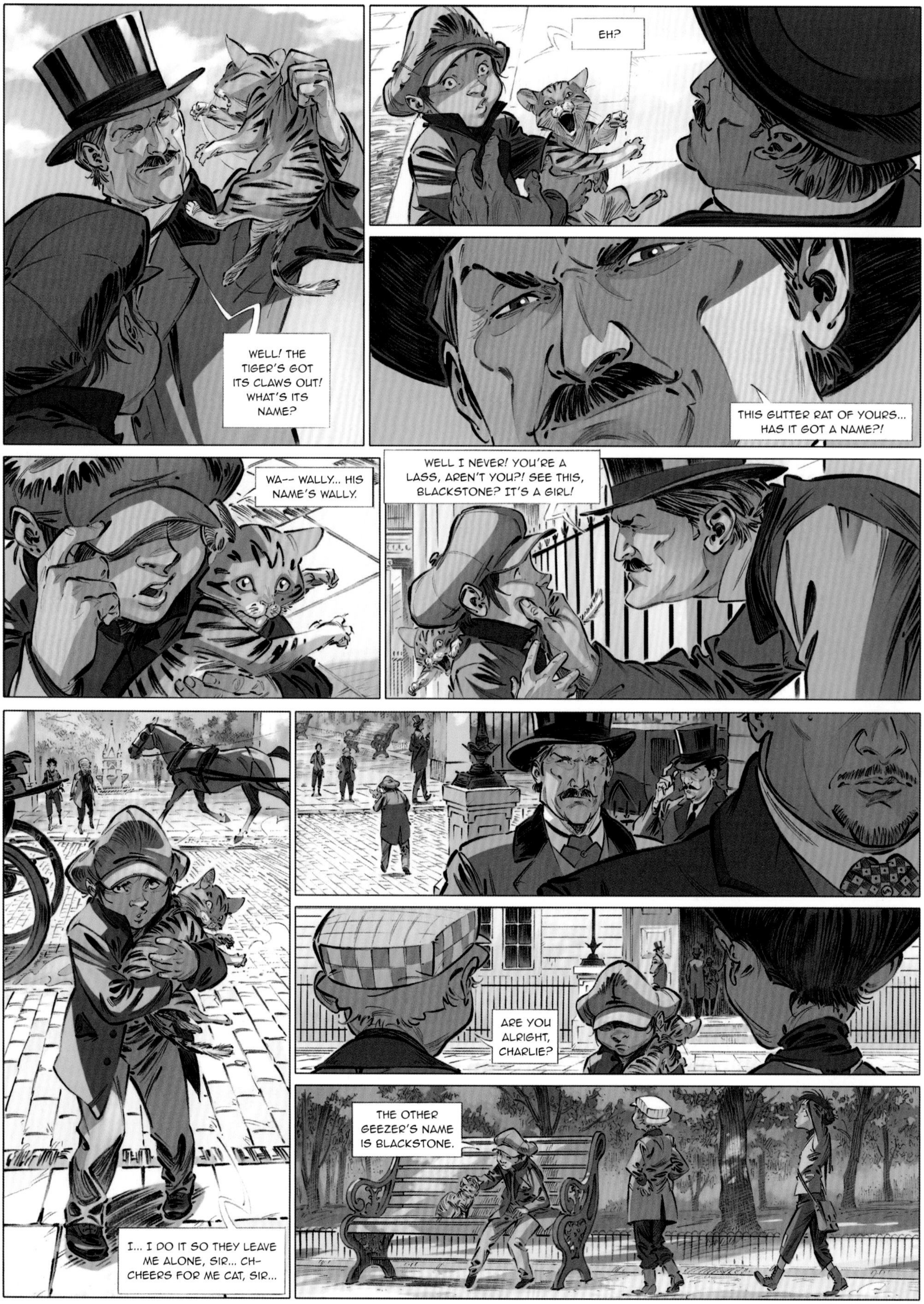

WELL! THE TIGER'S GOT ITS CLAWS OUT! WHAT'S ITS NAME?
EH?
THIS GUTTER RAT OF YOURS... HAS IT GOT A NAME?!
WA-- WALLY... HIS NAME'S WALLY.
WELL I NEVER! YOU'RE A LASS, AREN'T YOU?! SEE THIS, BLACKSTONE? IT'S A GIRL!
I... I DO IT SO THEY LEAVE ME ALONE, SIR... CH-CHEERS FOR ME CAT, SIR...
ARE YOU ALRIGHT, CHARLIE?
THE OTHER GEEZER'S NAME IS BLACKSTONE.

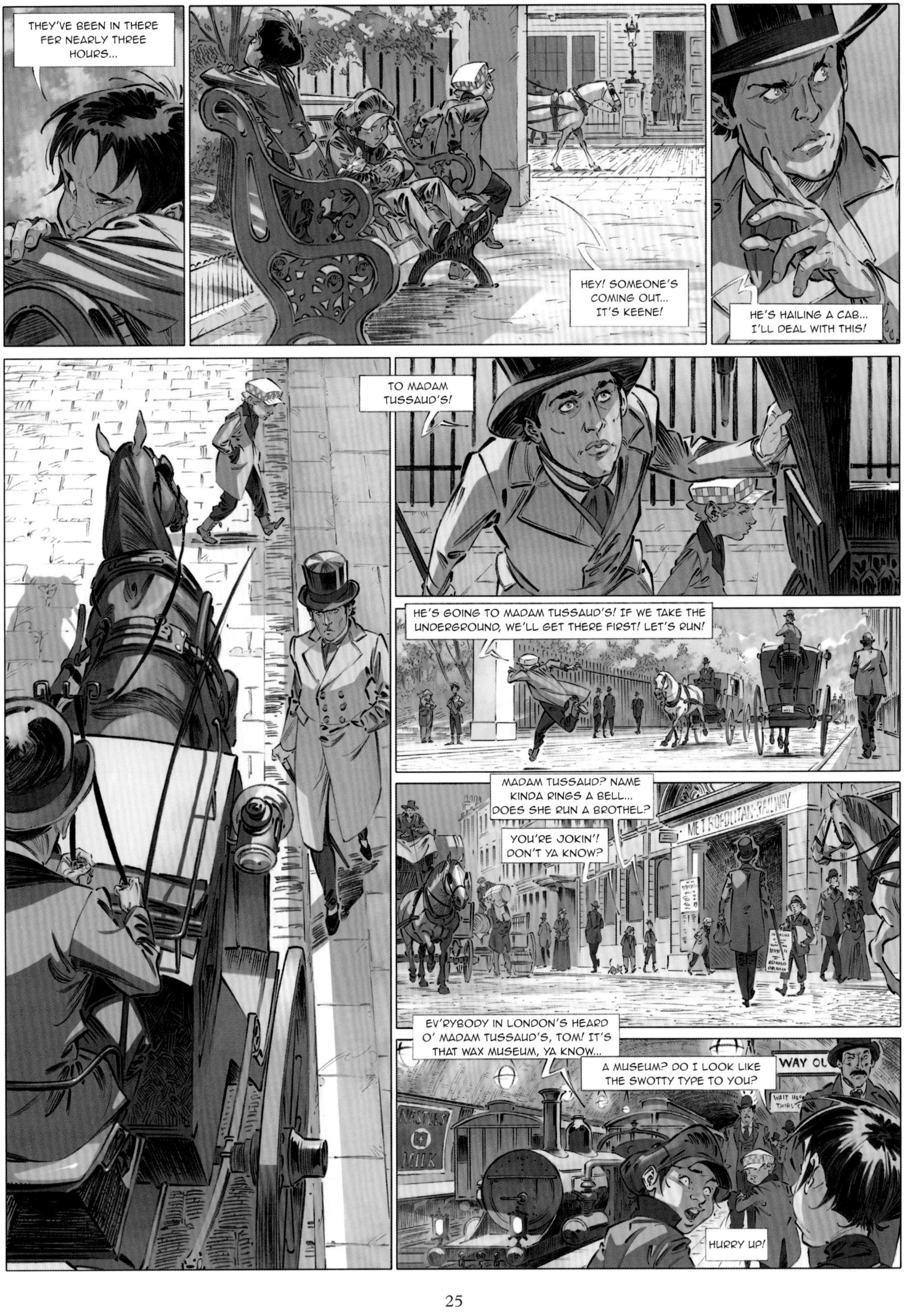
THEY'VE BEEN IN THERE FER NEARLY THREE HOURS...
HEY! SOMEONE'S COMING OUT... IT'S KEENE!
HE'S HAILING A CAB... I'LL DEAL WITH THIS!
TO MADAM TUSSAUD'S!
HE'S GOING TO MADAM TUSSAUD'S! IF WE TAKE THE UNDERGROUND, WE'LL GET THERE FIRST! LET'S RUN!
MADAM TUSSAUD? NAME KINDA RINGS A BELL... DOES SHE RUN A BROTHEL?
YOU'RE JOKIN'! DON'T YA KNOW?
METROPOLITAN RAILWAY
EV'RYBODY IN LONDON'S HEARD O' MADAM TUSSAUD'S, TOM! IT'S THAT WAX MUSEUM, YA KNOW...
A MUSEUM? DO I LOOK LIKE THE SWOTTY TYPE TO YOU?
HURRY UP!

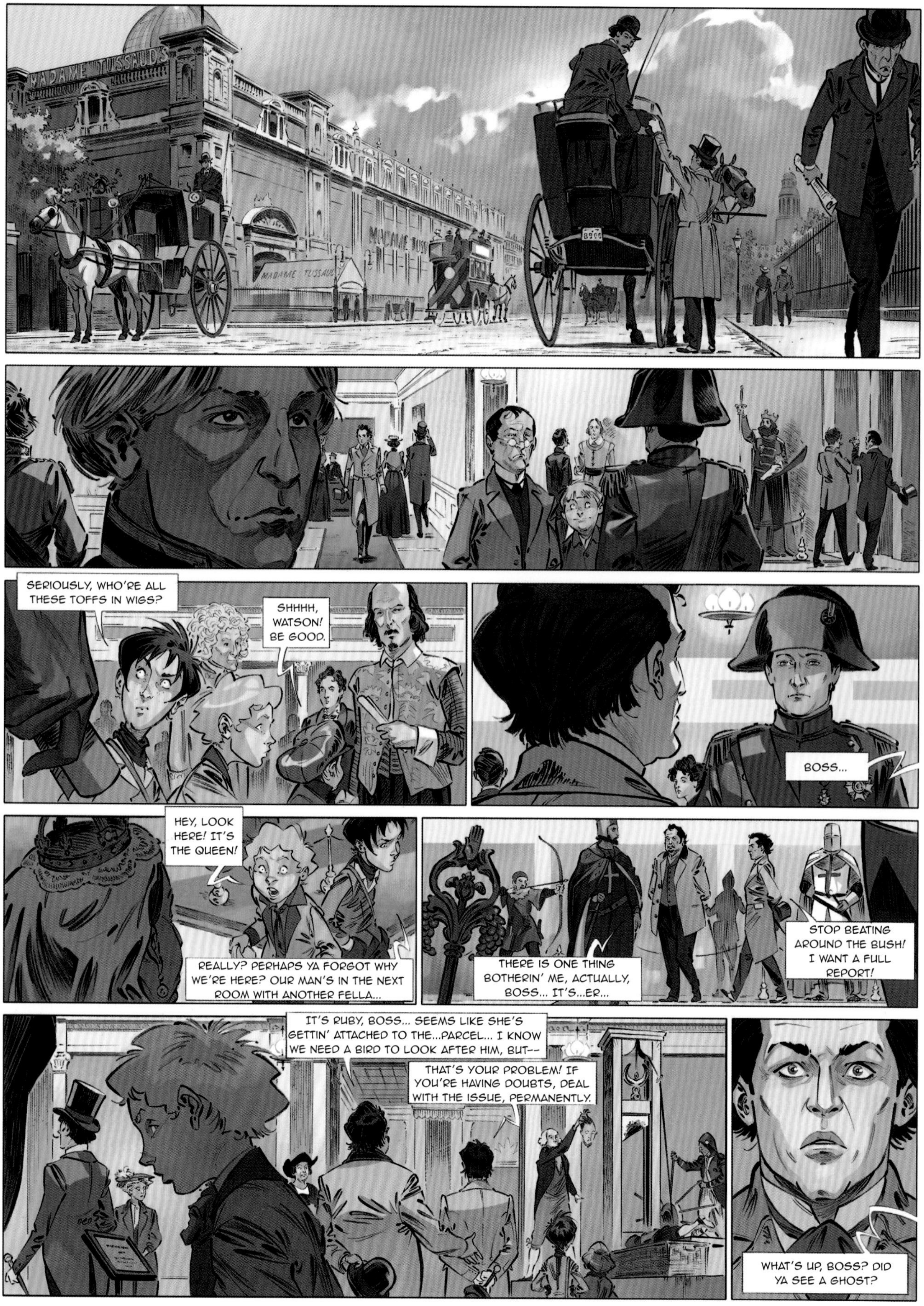
SERIOUSLY, WHO'RE ALL THESE TOFFS IN WIGS?
SHHHH, WATSON! BE GOOD.
BOSS...
HEY, LOOK HERE! IT'S THE QUEEN!
REALLY? PERHAPS YA FORGOT WHY WE'RE HERE? OUR MAN'S IN THE NEXT ROOM WITH ANOTHER FELLA...
THERE IS ONE THING BOTHERIN' ME, ACTUALLY, BOSS... IT'S...ER...
STOP BEATING AROUND THE BUSH! I WANT A FULL REPORT!
IT'S RUBY, BOSS... SEEMS LIKE SHE'S GETTIN' ATTACHED TO THE...PARCEL... I KNOW WE NEED A BIRD TO LOOK AFTER HIM, BUT--
THAT'S YOUR PROBLEM! IF YOU'RE HAVING DOUBTS, DEAL WITH THE ISSUE, PERMANENTLY.
WHAT'S UP, BOSS? DID YA SEE A GHOST?

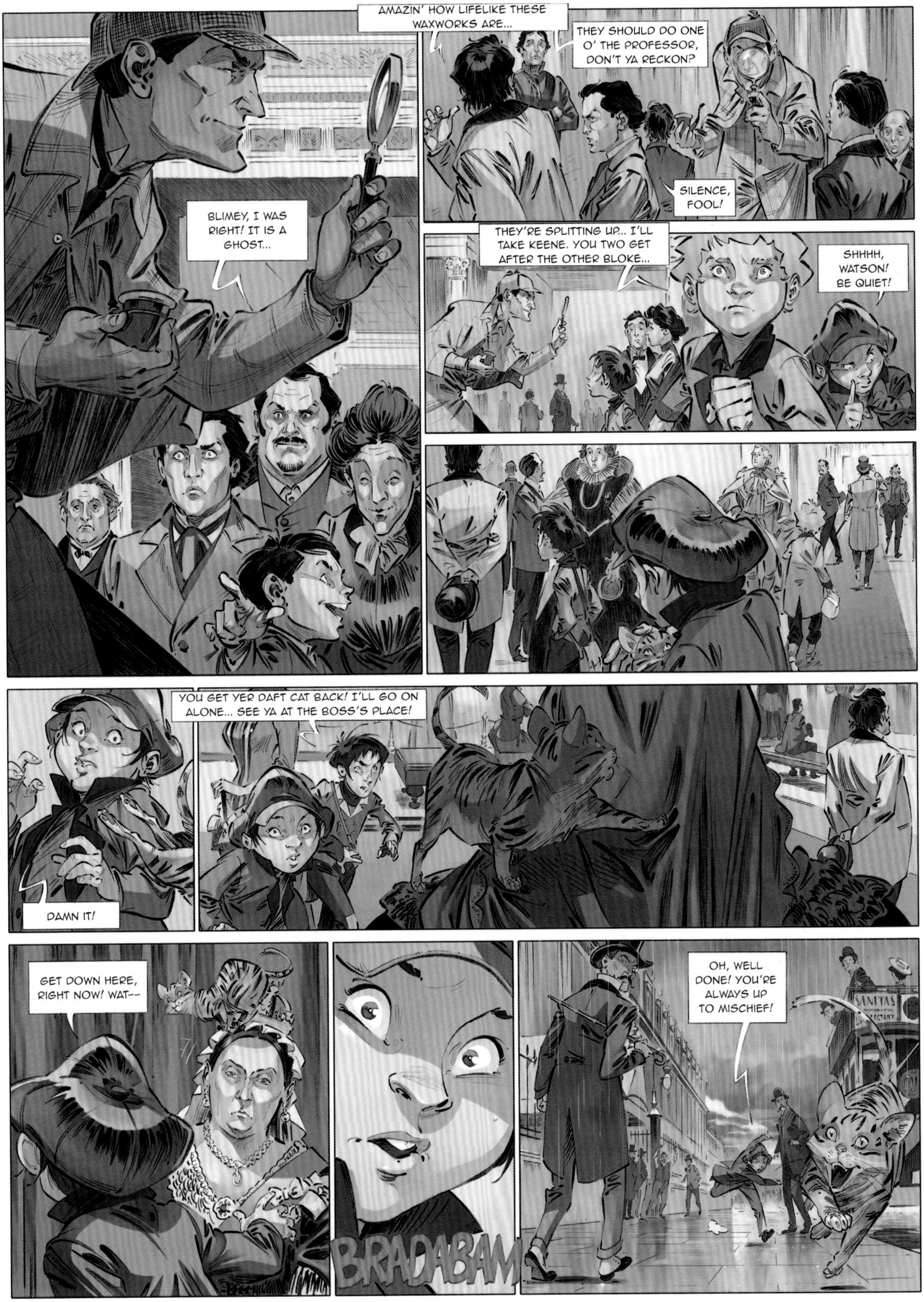
BLIMEY, I WAS RIGHT! IT IS A GHOST...
AMAZIN' HOW LIFELIKE THESE WAXWORKS ARE...
THEY SHOULD DO ONE O' THE PROFESSOR, DON'T YA RECKON?
SILENCE, FOOL!
THEY'RE SPLITTING UP... I'LL TAKE KEENE. YOU TWO GET AFTER THE OTHER BLOKE...
SHHHH, WATSON! BE QUIET!
DAMN IT!
YOU GET YER DAFT CAT BACK! I'LL GO ON ALONE... SEE YA AT THE BOSS'S PLACE!
GET DOWN HERE, RIGHT NOW! WAT--
BRADABAM
OH, WELL DONE! YOU'RE ALWAYS UP TO MISCHIEF!

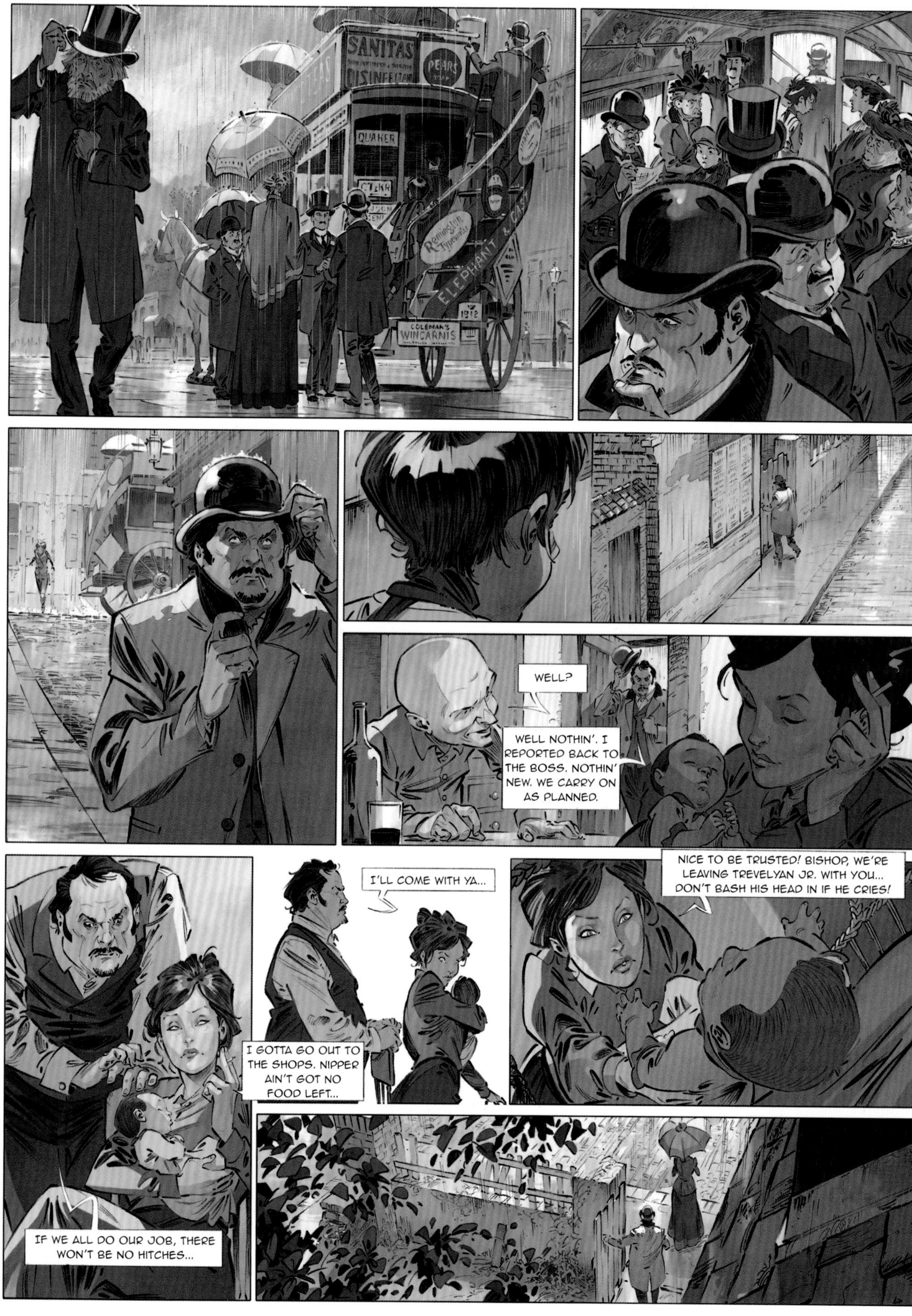
SANITAS
PEARS
QUAKER
ELEPHANT & CASTLE
COLEMAN'S
WINCARNIS
WELL?
WELL NOTHIN'. I REPORTED BACK TO THE BOSS. NOTHIN' NEW. WE CARRY ON AS PLANNED.
IF WE ALL DO OUR JOB, THERE WON'T BE NO HITCHES...
I GOTTA GO OUT TO THE SHOPS. NIPPER AIN'T GOT NO FOOD LEFT...
I'LL COME WITH YA...
NICE TO BE TRUSTED! BISHOP, WE'RE LEAVING TREVELYAN JR. WITH YOU... DON'T BASH HIS HEAD IN IF HE CRIES!

ANYWAY, AFTER THAT, KEENE WENT BACK TO THE TANKERVILLE...

...AND, ER, CHARLIE AND I DECIDED WE'D BETTER COME AND GIVE YOU A REPORT...

THIS BLACKSTONE CHAP THAT CHARLIE SAW CHATTING TO MORAN... DO YOU KNOW HIM?

YES, I DO... BUT I WILL EXPLORE THAT AVENUE MYSELF.

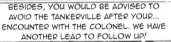

BESIDES, YOU WOULD BE ADVISED TO AVOID THE TANKERVILLE AFTER YOUR... ENCOUNTER WITH THE COLONEL. WE HAVE ANOTHER LEAD TO FOLLOW UP!

YEAH... WELL, I HOPE TOM'S HAVIN' BETTER LUCK THAN US...

THE MAN'S REFERENCE TO A "PARCEL" IMPLIES THAT WE'RE ON THE RIGHT TRACK!

AS TO THE MYSTERIOUS RUBY...

I THINK I KNOW WHO SHE IS...

I FOLLOWED THAT FELLA TO A HOUSE IN THE EAST END, NOT TOO FAR FROM HERE...

HE CAME OUT AGAIN WITH A PRETTY CLASSY REDHEAD...

AND YA RECKON SHE'S THIS RUBY?

GOOD NICKNAME FER A REDHEAD, AIN'T IT?

DID THEY VISIT A CHEMIST'S, OR BUY SOME MILK, PERHAPS?

THEY DID A BIT O' SHOPPIN', THEN WENT BACK. I WAS STARTIN' TO BLOODY FREEZE, SO I GAVE UP...

YEAH--BOTH... HOW DID YA GUESS?

MILK! THAT MEANS THE TREVELYAN BABY'S IN THERE!

DON'T JUMP TO CONCLUSIONS, MASTER FLETCHER!

BUT IT WOULD BE WISE TO KEEP A CLOSER WATCH ON THAT HOUSE AND ITS OCCUPANTS.

YOU WILL BEGIN YOUR SURVEILLANCE TONIGHT. MEANWHILE, I WILL GO AND SEE THE TEARFUL PARENTS. TIME FOR SPECIAL BRANCH TO MAKE AN APPEARANCE!

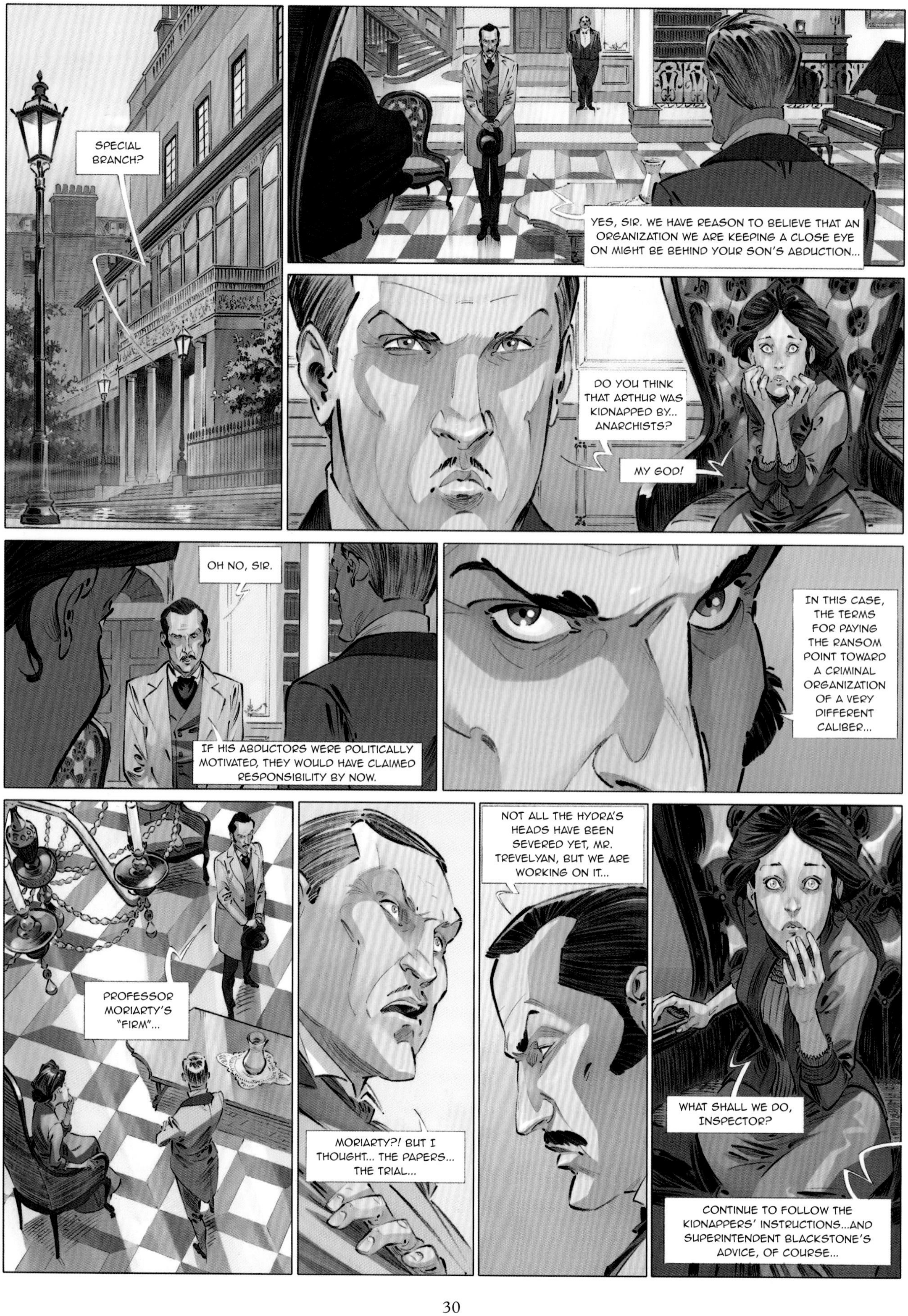
SPECIAL BRANCH?
YES, SIR. WE HAVE REASON TO BELIEVE THAT AN ORGANIZATION WE ARE KEEPING A CLOSE EYE ON MIGHT BE BEHIND YOUR SON'S ABDUCTION...
DO YOU THINK THAT ARTHUR WAS KIDNAPPED BY... ANARCHISTS?
MY GOD!
OH NO, SIR.
IF HIS ABDUCTORS WERE POLITICALLY MOTIVATED, THEY WOULD HAVE CLAIMED RESPONSIBILITY BY NOW.
IN THIS CASE, THE TERMS FOR PAYING THE RANSOM POINT TOWARD A CRIMINAL ORGANIZATION OF A VERY DIFFERENT CALIBER...
PROFESSOR MORIARTY'S "FIRM"...
MORIARTY?! BUT I THOUGHT... THE PAPERS... THE TRIAL...
NOT ALL THE HYDRA'S HEADS HAVE BEEN SEVERED YET, MR. TREVELYAN, BUT WE ARE WORKING ON IT...
WHAT SHALL WE DO, INSPECTOR?
CONTINUE TO FOLLOW THE KIDNAPPERS' INSTRUCTIONS...AND SUPERINTENDENT BLACKSTONE'S ADVICE, OF COURSE...

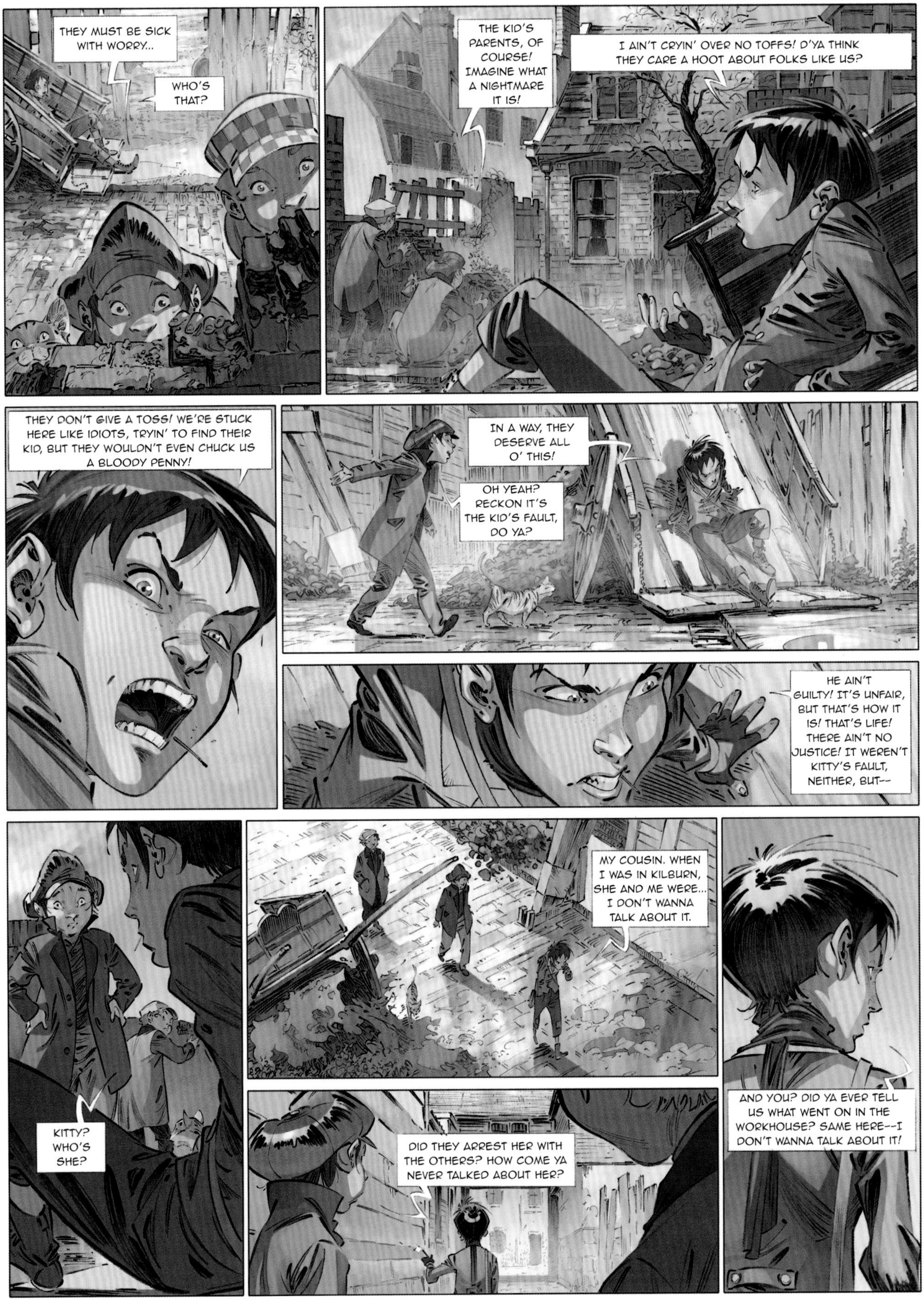
THEY MUST BE SICK WITH WORRY...
WHO'S THAT?
THE KID'S PARENTS, OF COURSE! IMAGINE WHAT A NIGHTMARE IT IS!
I AIN'T CRYIN' OVER NO TOFFS! D'YA THINK THEY CARE A HOOT ABOUT FOLKS LIKE US?
THEY DON'T GIVE A TOSS! WE'RE STUCK HERE LIKE IDIOTS, TRYIN' TO FIND THEIR KID, BUT THEY WOULDN'T EVEN CHUCK US A BLOODY PENNY!
IN A WAY, THEY DESERVE ALL O' THIS!
OH YEAH? RECKON IT'S THE KID'S FAULT, DO YA?
HE AIN'T GUILTY! IT'S UNFAIR, BUT THAT'S HOW IT IS! THAT'S LIFE! THERE AIN'T NO JUSTICE! IT WEREN'T KITTY'S FAULT, NEITHER, BUT--
KITTY? WHO'S SHE?
MY COUSIN. WHEN I WAS IN KILBURN, SHE AND ME WERE... I DON'T WANNA TALK ABOUT IT.
DID THEY ARREST HER WITH THE OTHERS? HOW COME YA NEVER TALKED ABOUT HER?
AND YOU? DID YA EVER TELL US WHAT WENT ON IN THE WORKHOUSE? SAME HERE--I DON'T WANNA TALK ABOUT IT!

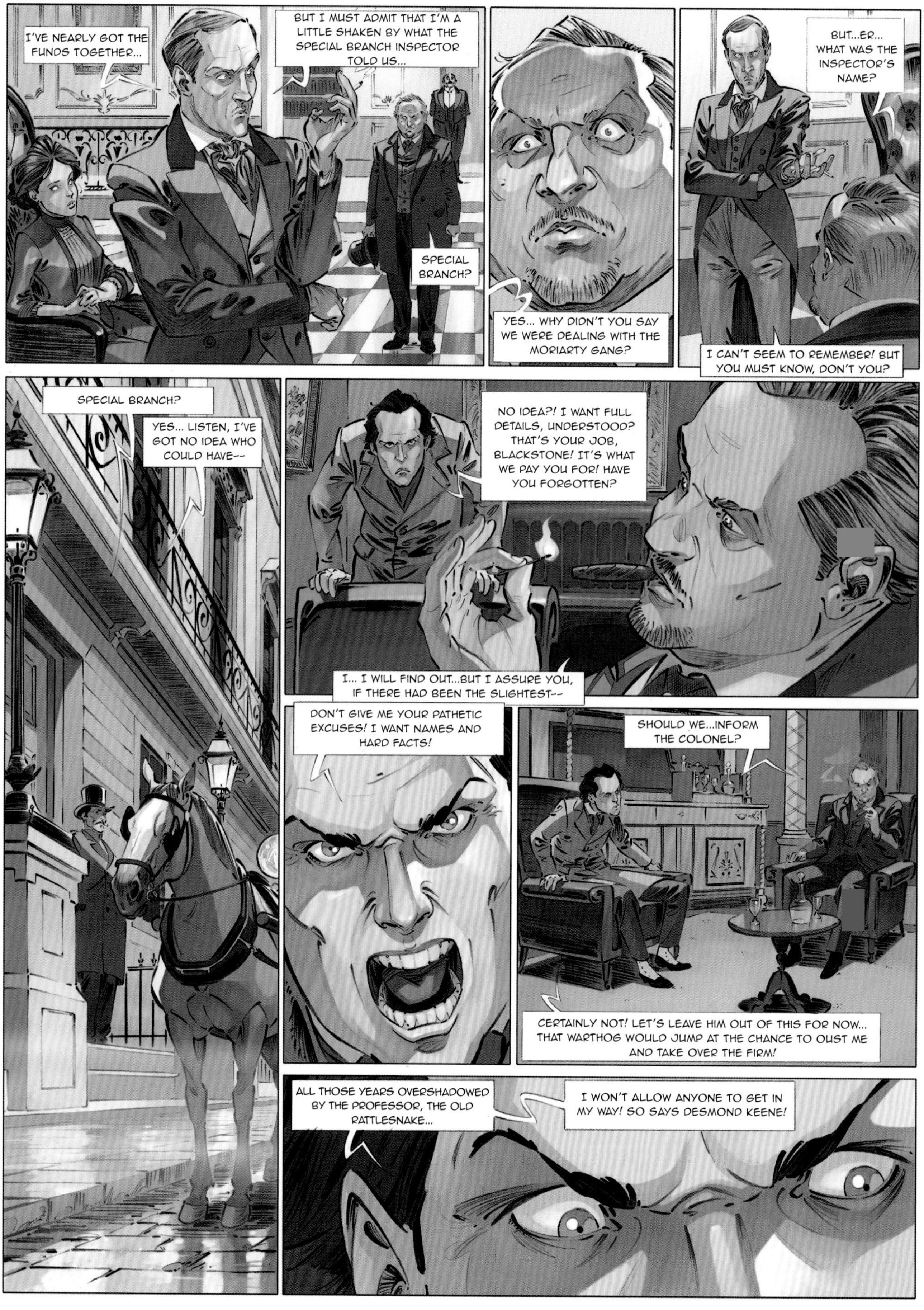
I'VE NEARLY GOT THE FUNDS TOGETHER...
BUT I MUST ADMIT THAT I'M A LITTLE SHAKEN BY WHAT THE SPECIAL BRANCH INSPECTOR TOLD US...
SPECIAL BRANCH?
YES... WHY DIDN'T YOU SAY WE WERE DEALING WITH THE MORIARTY GANG?
BUT...ER... WHAT WAS THE INSPECTOR'S NAME?
I CAN'T SEEM TO REMEMBER! BUT YOU MUST KNOW, DON'T YOU?
SPECIAL BRANCH?
YES... LISTEN, I'VE GOT NO IDEA WHO COULD HAVE--
NO IDEA?! I WANT FULL DETAILS, UNDERSTOOD? THAT'S YOUR JOB, BLACKSTONE! IT'S WHAT WE PAY YOU FOR! HAVE YOU FORGOTTEN?
I... I WILL FIND OUT...BUT I ASSURE YOU, IF THERE HAD BEEN THE SLIGHTEST--
DON'T GIVE ME YOUR PATHETIC EXCUSES! I WANT NAMES AND HARD FACTS!
SHOULD WE...INFORM THE COLONEL?
CERTAINLY NOT! LET'S LEAVE HIM OUT OF THIS FOR NOW... THAT WARTHOG WOULD JUMP AT THE CHANCE TO OUST ME AND TAKE OVER THE FIRM!
ALL THOSE YEARS OVERSHADOWED BY THE PROFESSOR, THE OLD RATTLESNAKE...
I WON'T ALLOW ANYONE TO GET IN MY WAY! SO SAYS DESMOND KEENE!

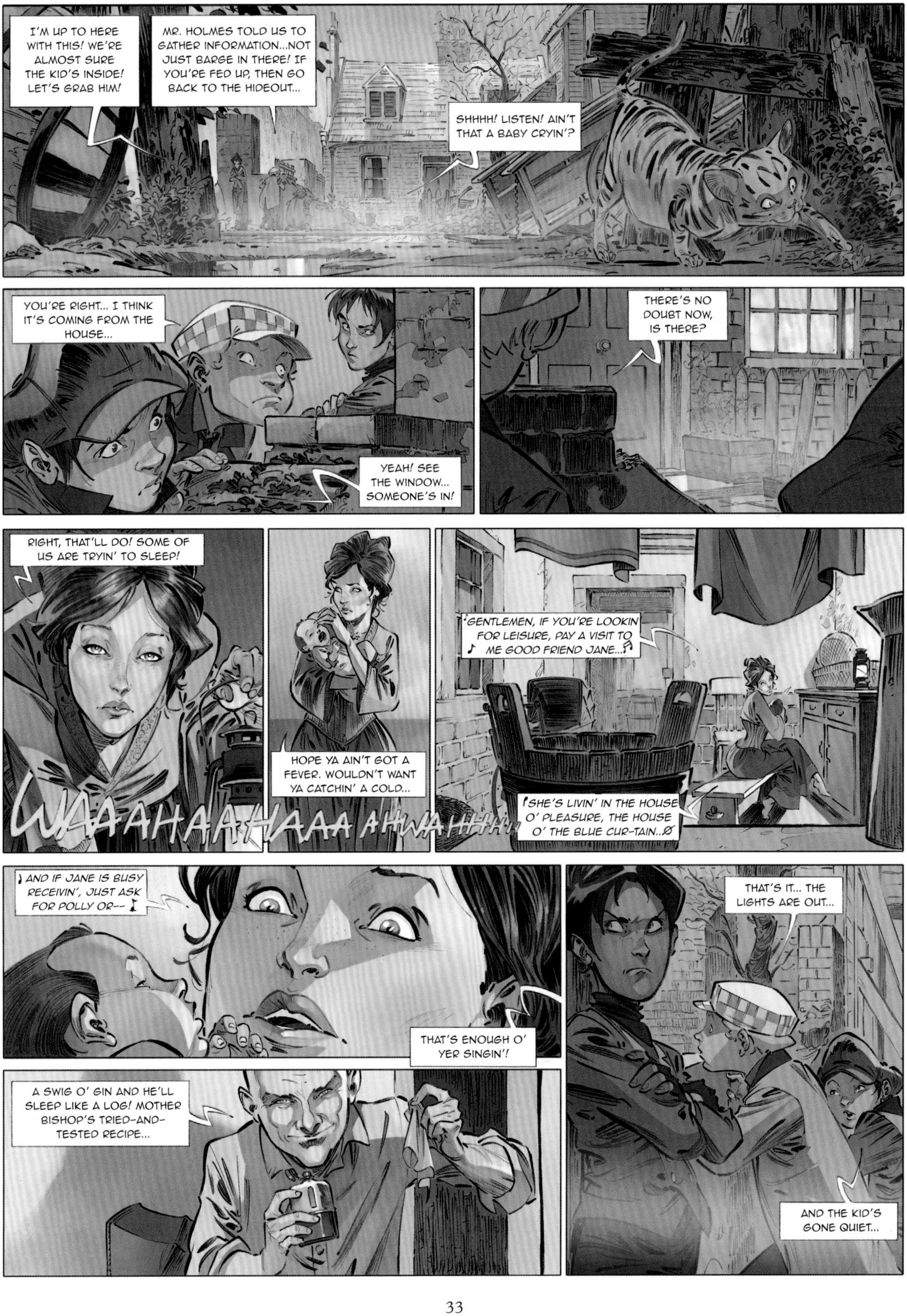
I'M UP TO HERE WITH THIS! WE'RE ALMOST SURE THE KID'S INSIDE! LET'S GRAB HIM!
MR. HOLMES TOLD US TO GATHER INFORMATION...NOT JUST BARGE IN THERE! IF YOU'RE FED UP, THEN GO BACK TO THE HIDEOUT...
SHHHH! LISTEN! AIN'T THAT A BABY CRYIN'?
YOU'RE RIGHT... I THINK IT'S COMING FROM THE HOUSE...
YEAH! SEE THE WINDOW... SOMEONE'S IN!
THERE'S NO DOUBT NOW, IS THERE?
RIGHT, THAT'LL DO! SOME OF US ARE TRYIN' TO SLEEP!
WAAAHAAAHAAA AHWAHHHH
HOPE YA AIN'T GOT A FEVER. WOULDN'T WANT YA CATCHIN' A COLD...
GENTLEMEN, IF YOU'RE LOOKIN FOR LEISURE, PAY A VISIT TO ME GOOD FRIEND JANE...
SHE'S LIVIN' IN THE HOUSE O' PLEASURE, THE HOUSE O' THE BLUE CUR-TAIN...
AND IF JANE IS BUSY RECEIVIN', JUST ASK FOR POLLY OR--
THAT'S ENOUGH O' YER SINGIN'!
A SWIG O' GIN AND HE'LL SLEEP LIKE A LOG! MOTHER BISHOP'S TRIED-AND-TESTED RECIPE...
THAT'S IT... THE LIGHTS ARE OUT...
AND THE KID'S GONE QUIET...

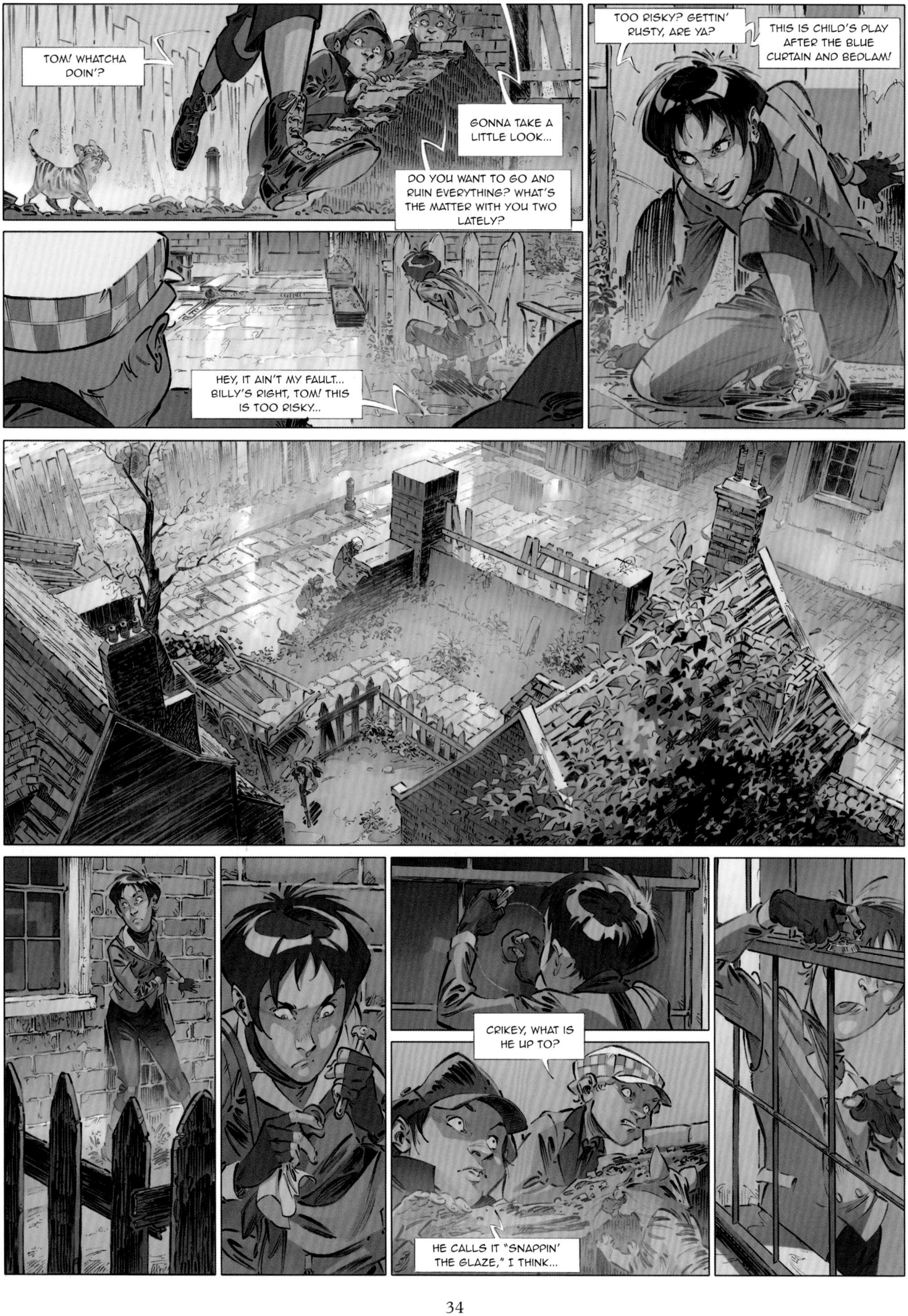
TOM! WHATCHA DOIN'?
GONNA TAKE A LITTLE LOOK...
DO YOU WANT TO GO AND RUIN EVERYTHING? WHAT'S THE MATTER WITH YOU TWO LATELY?
HEY, IT AIN'T MY FAULT... BILLY'S RIGHT, TOM! THIS IS TOO RISKY...
TOO RISKY? GETTIN' RUSTY, ARE YA?
THIS IS CHILD'S PLAY AFTER THE BLUE CURTAIN AND BEDLAM!
CRIKEY, WHAT IS HE UP TO?
HE CALLS IT "SNAPPIN' THE GLAZE," I THINK...

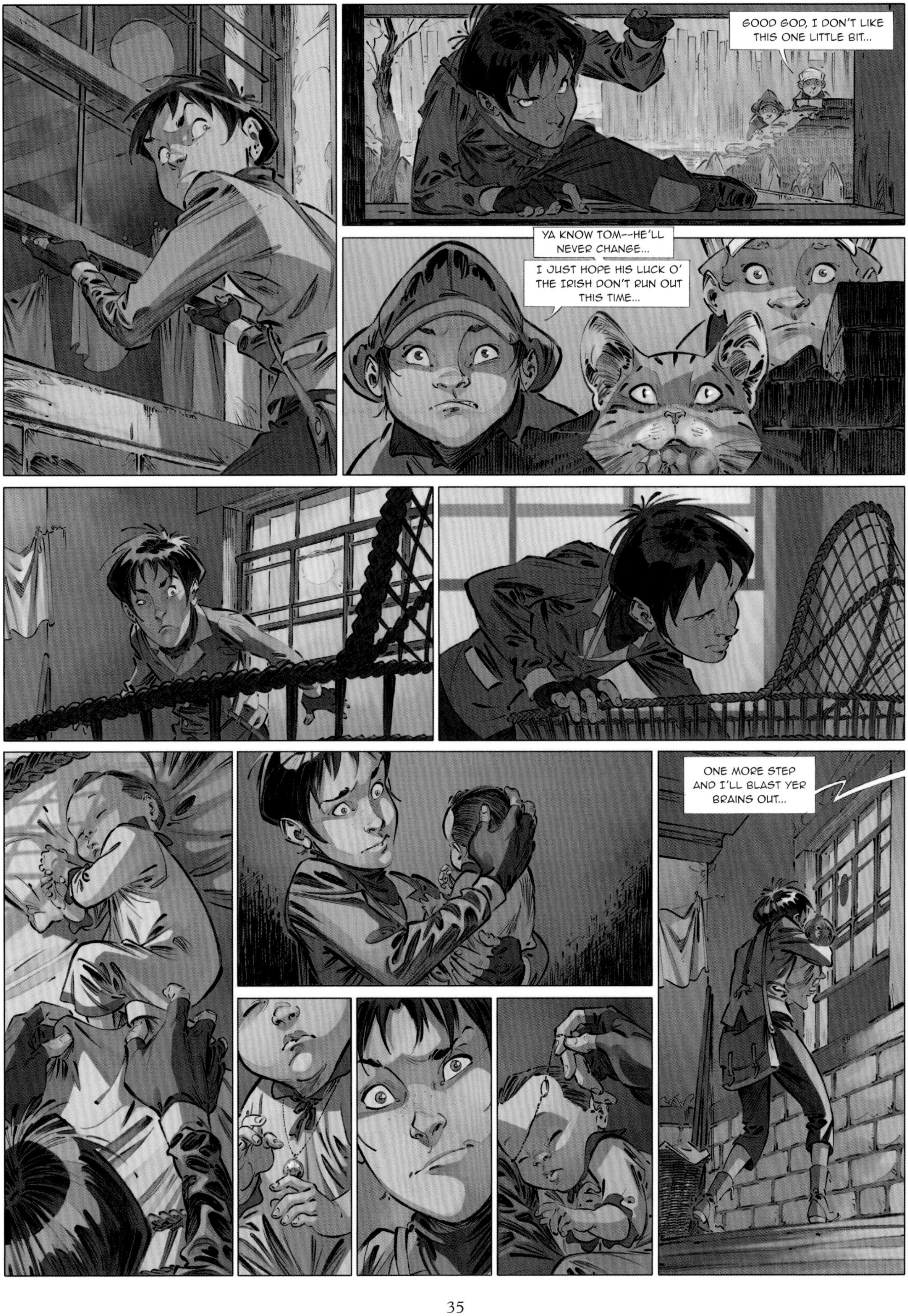
GOOD GOD, I DON'T LIKE THIS ONE LITTLE BIT...
YA KNOW TOM--HE'LL NEVER CHANGE...
I JUST HOPE HIS LUCK O' THE IRISH DON'T RUN OUT THIS TIME...
ONE MORE STEP AND I'LL BLAST YER BRAINS OUT...

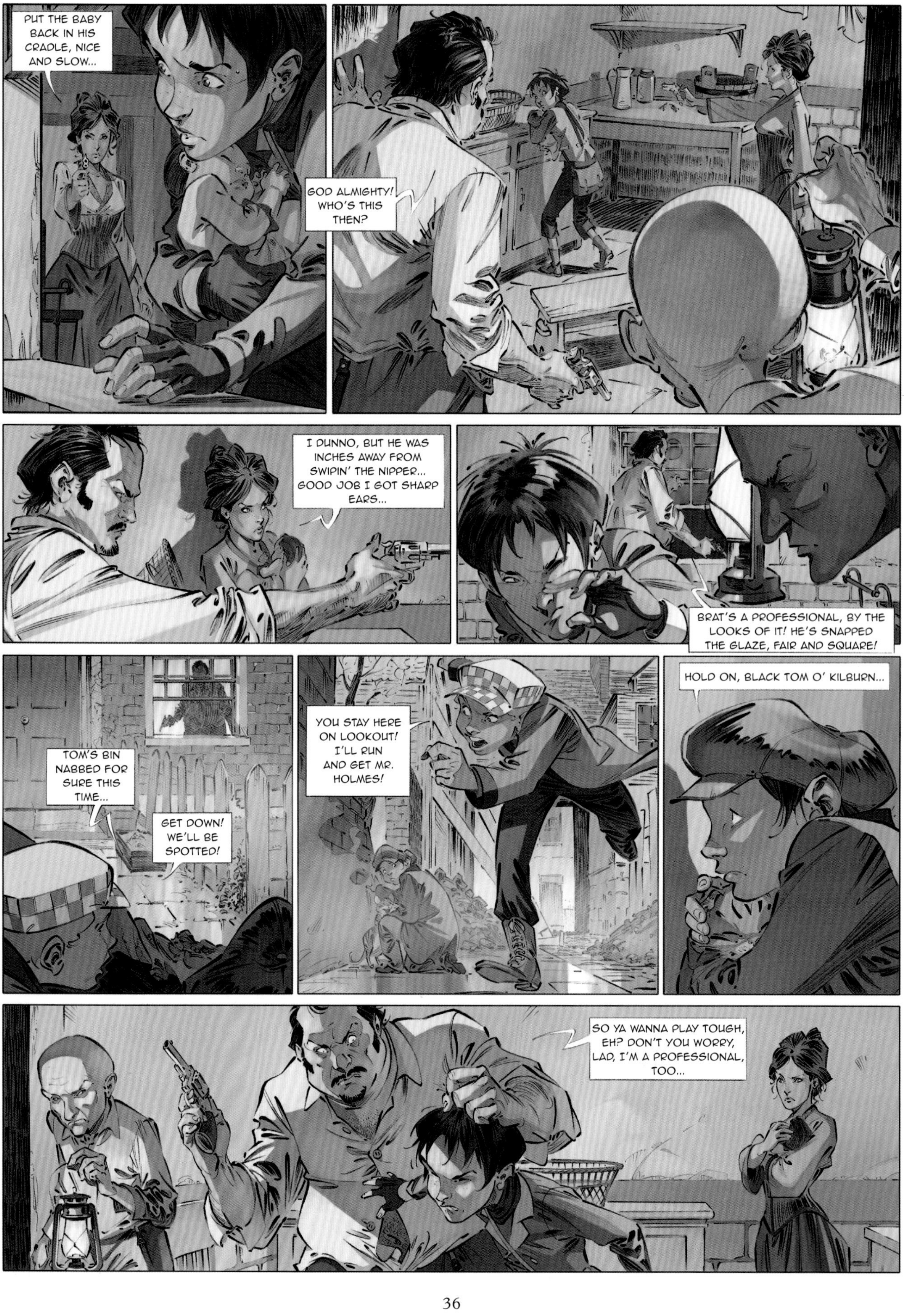
PUT THE BABY BACK IN HIS CRADLE, NICE AND SLOW...
GOD ALMIGHTY! WHO'S THIS THEN?
I DUNNO, BUT HE WAS INCHES AWAY FROM SWIPIN' THE NIPPER... GOOD JOB I GOT SHARP EARS...
BRAT'S A PROFESSIONAL, BY THE LOOKS OF IT! HE'S SNAPPED THE GLAZE, FAIR AND SQUARE!
TOM'S BIN NABBED FOR SURE THIS TIME...
GET DOWN! WE'LL BE SPOTTED!
YOU STAY HERE ON LOOKOUT! I'LL RUN AND GET MR. HOLMES!
HOLD ON, BLACK TOM O' KILBURN...
SO YA WANNA PLAY TOUGH, EH? DON'T YOU WORRY, LAD, I'M A PROFESSIONAL, TOO...

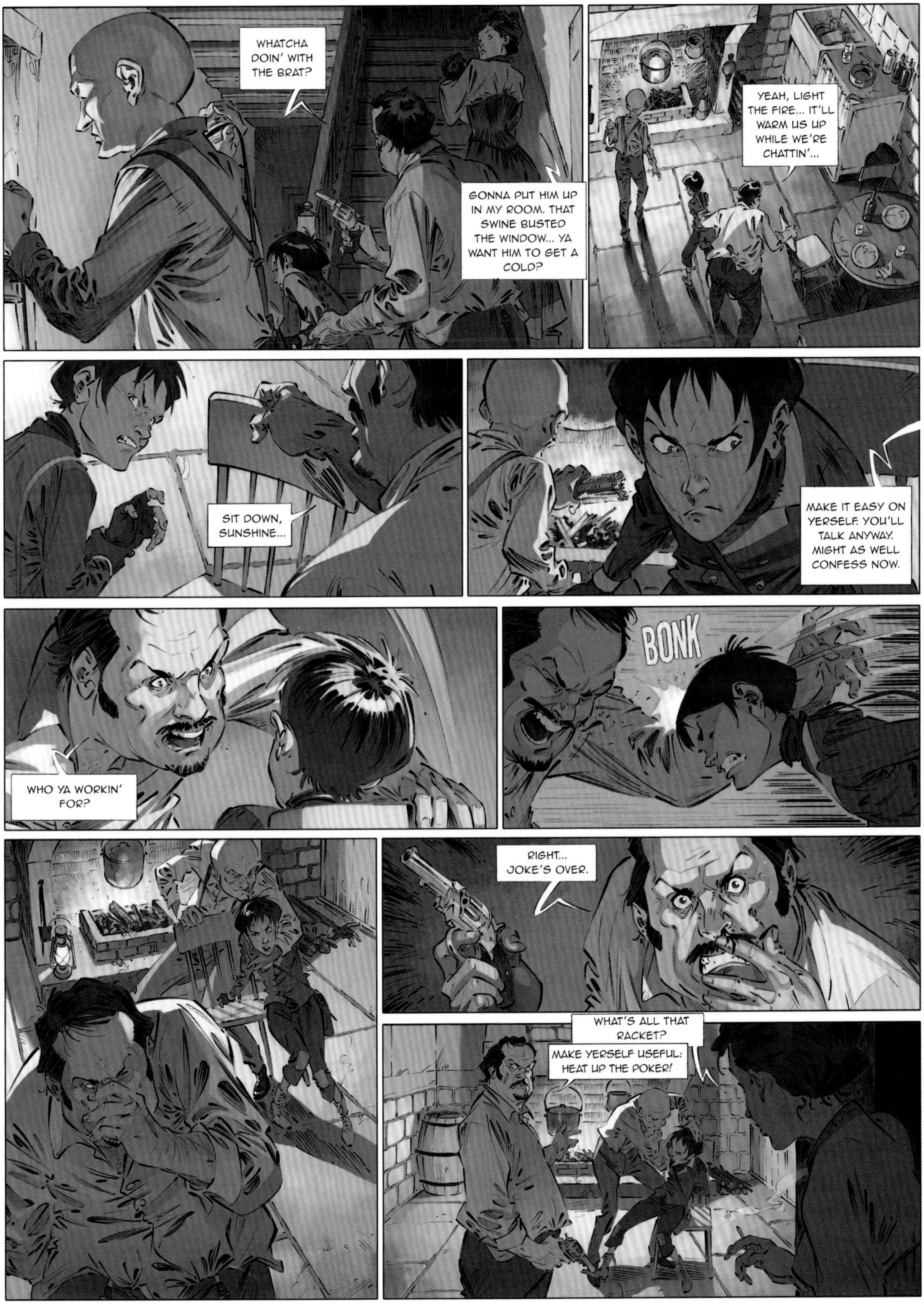
WHATCHA DOIN' WITH THE BRAT?
GONNA PUT HIM UP IN MY ROOM. THAT SWINE BUSTED THE WINDOW... YA WANT HIM TO GET A COLD?
YEAH, LIGHT THE FIRE... IT'LL WARM US UP WHILE WE'RE CHATTIN'...
SIT DOWN, SUNSHINE...
MAKE IT EASY ON YERSELF. YOU'LL TALK ANYWAY. MIGHT AS WELL CONFESS NOW.
WHO YA WORKIN' FOR?
BONK
RIGHT... JOKE'S OVER.
WHAT'S ALL THAT RACKET?
MAKE YERSELF USEFUL: HEAT UP THE POKER!

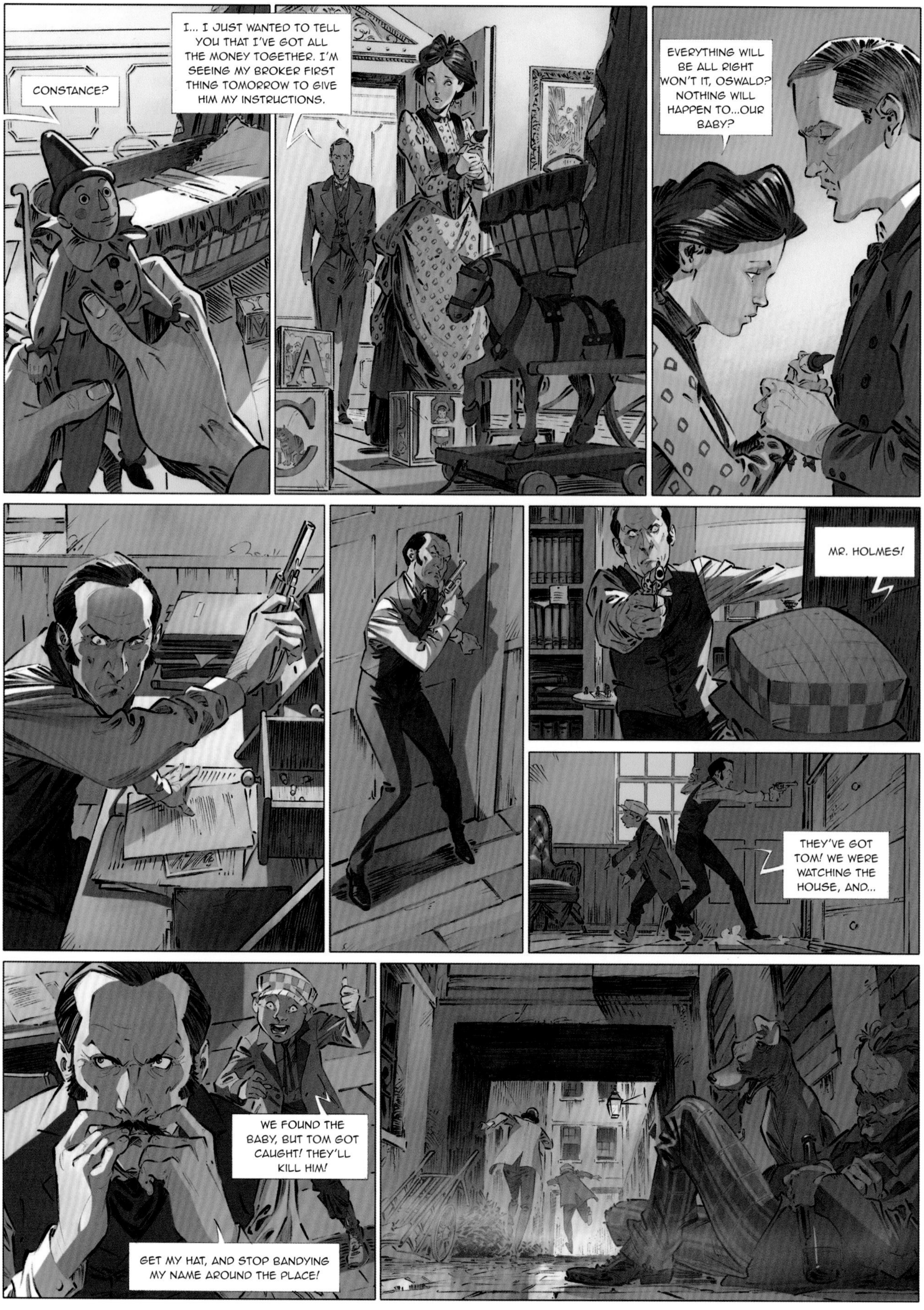
CONSTANCE?
I... I JUST WANTED TO TELL YOU THAT I'VE GOT ALL THE MONEY TOGETHER. I'M SEEING MY BROKER FIRST THING TOMORROW TO GIVE HIM MY INSTRUCTIONS.
EVERYTHING WILL BE ALL RIGHT WON'T IT, OSWALD? NOTHING WILL HAPPEN TO...OUR BABY?
MR. HOLMES!
THEY'VE GOT TOM! WE WERE WATCHING THE HOUSE, AND...
WE FOUND THE BABY, BUT TOM GOT CAUGHT! THEY'LL KILL HIM!
GET MY HAT, AND STOP BANDYING MY NAME AROUND THE PLACE!

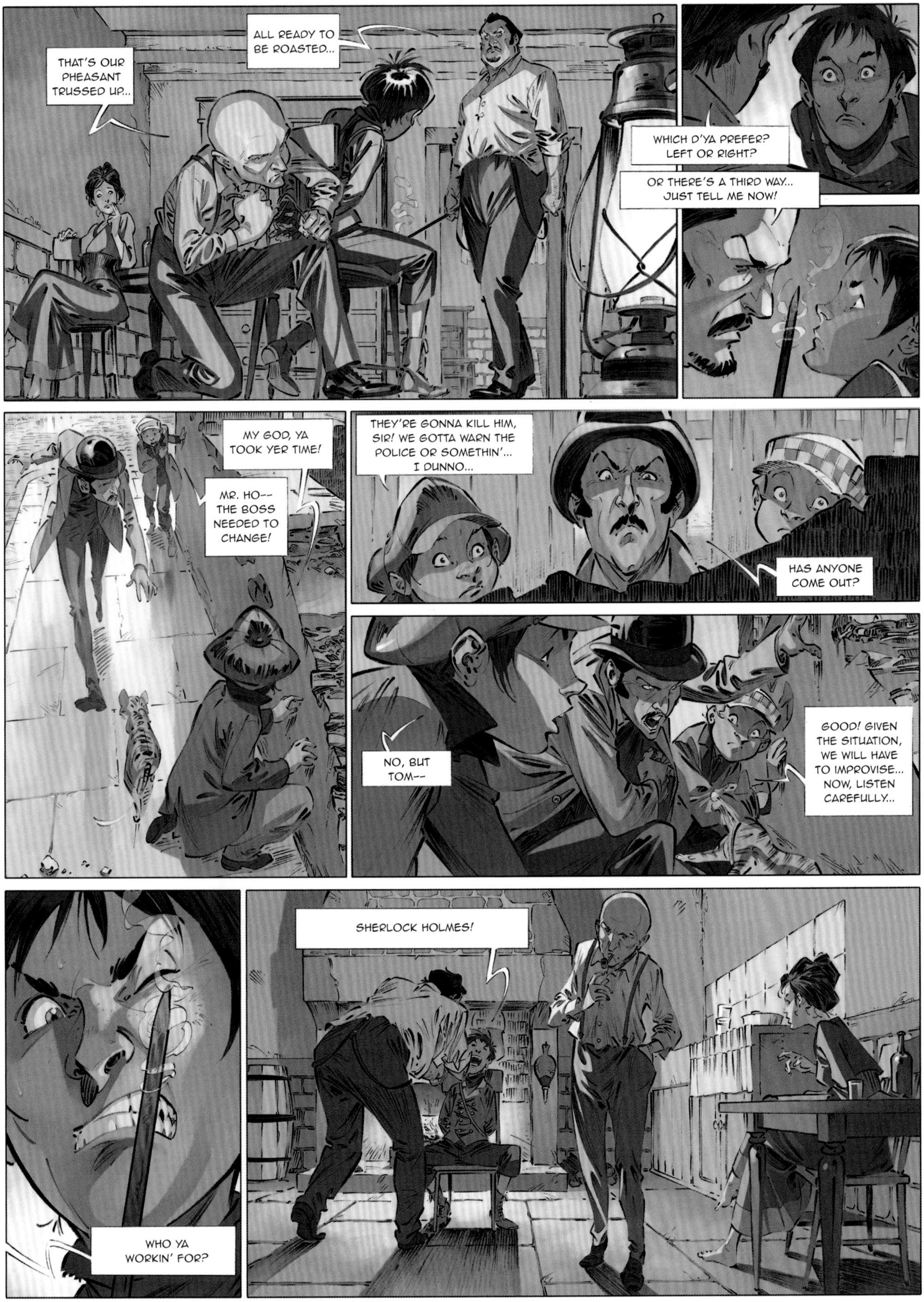
THAT'S OUR PHEASANT TRUSSED UP...
ALL READY TO BE ROASTED...
WHICH D'YA PREFER? LEFT OR RIGHT?
OR THERE'S A THIRD WAY... JUST TELL ME NOW!
MY GOD, YA TOOK YER TIME!
MR. HO-- THE BOSS NEEDED TO CHANGE!
THEY'RE GONNA KILL HIM, SIR! WE GOTTA WARN THE POLICE OR SOMETHIN'... I DUNNO...
HAS ANYONE COME OUT?
NO, BUT TOM--
GOOD! GIVEN THE SITUATION, WE WILL HAVE TO IMPROVISE... NOW, LISTEN CAREFULLY...
WHO YA WORKIN' FOR?
SHERLOCK HOLMES!

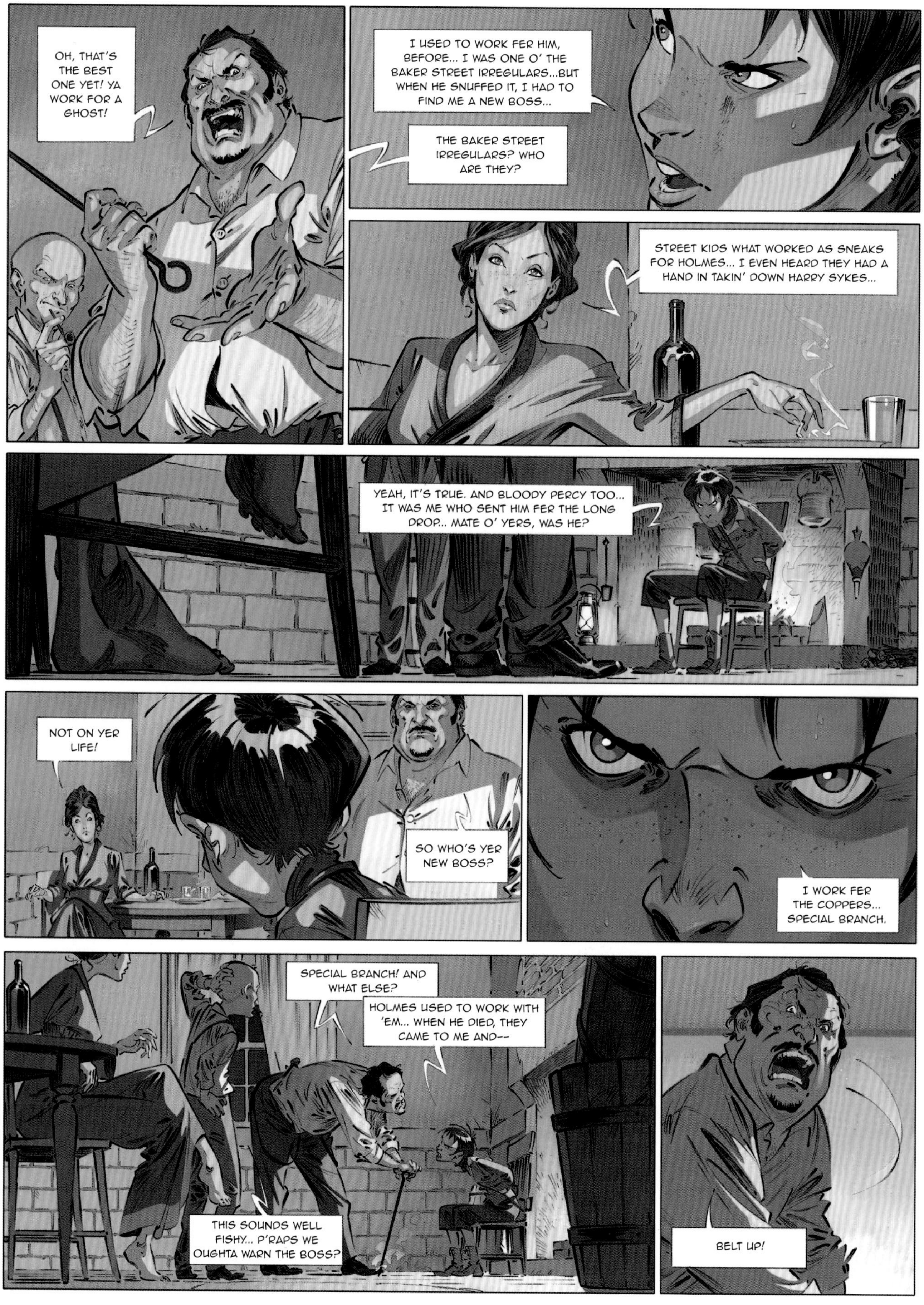
OH, THAT'S THE BEST ONE YET! YA WORK FOR A GHOST!
I USED TO WORK FER HIM, BEFORE... I WAS ONE O' THE BAKER STREET IRREGULARS...BUT WHEN HE SNUFFED IT, I HAD TO FIND ME A NEW BOSS...
THE BAKER STREET IRREGULARS? WHO ARE THEY?
STREET KIDS WHAT WORKED AS SNEAKS FOR HOLMES... I EVEN HEARD THEY HAD A HAND IN TAKIN' DOWN HARRY SYKES...
YEAH, IT'S TRUE. AND BLOODY PERCY TOO... IT WAS ME WHO SENT HIM FER THE LONG DROP... MATE O' YERS, WAS HE?
NOT ON YER LIFE!
SO WHO'S YER NEW BOSS?
I WORK FER THE COPPERS... SPECIAL BRANCH.
SPECIAL BRANCH! AND WHAT ELSE?
HOLMES USED TO WORK WITH 'EM... WHEN HE DIED, THEY CAME TO ME AND--
THIS SOUNDS WELL FISHY... P'RAPS WE OUGHTA WARN THE BOSS?
BELT UP!

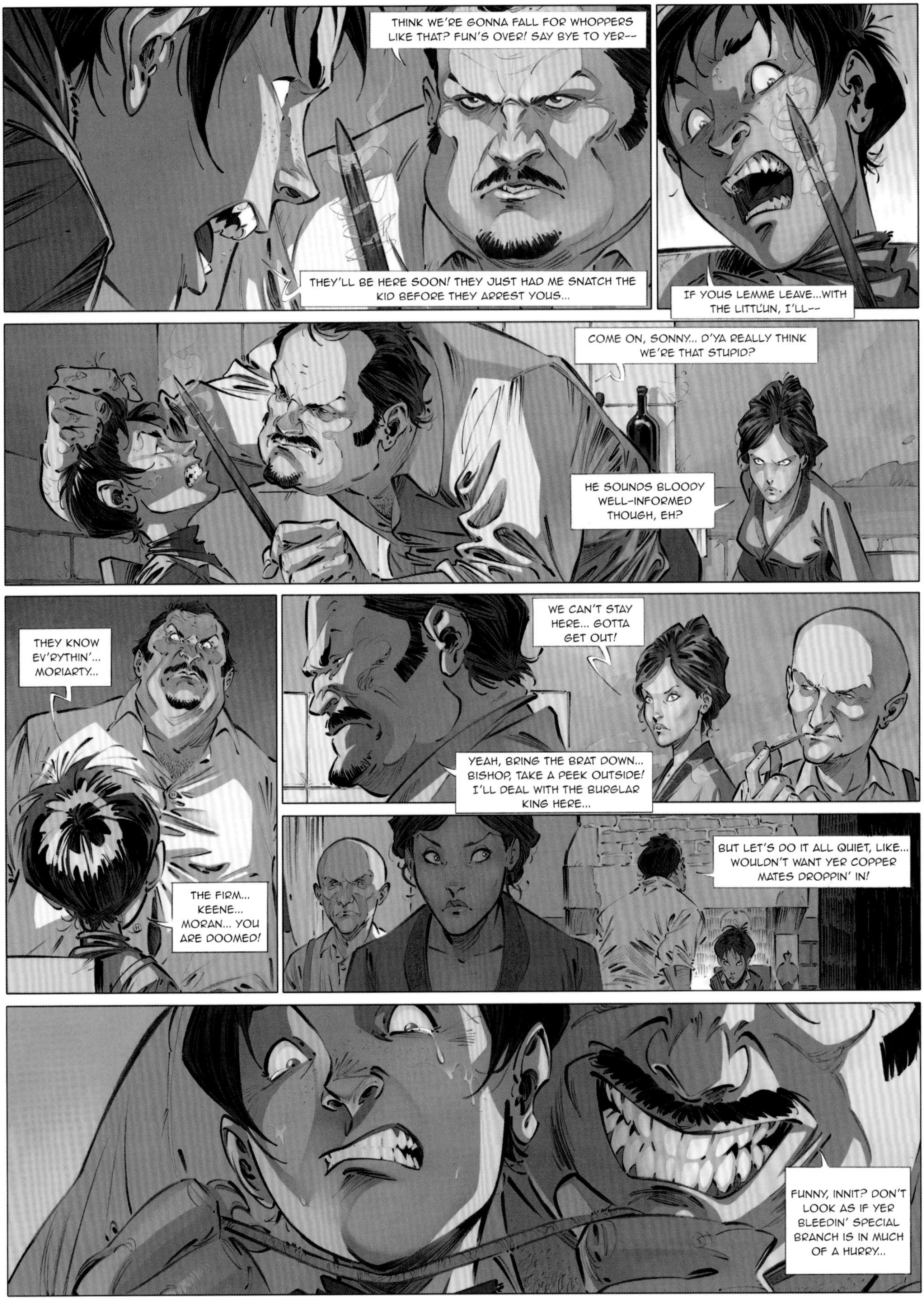
THINK WE'RE GONNA FALL FOR WHOPPERS LIKE THAT? FUN'S OVER! SAY BYE TO YER--
THEY'LL BE HERE SOON! THEY JUST HAD ME SNATCH THE KID BEFORE THEY ARREST YOUS...
IF YOUS LEMME LEAVE...WITH THE LITTL'UN, I'LL--
COME ON, SONNY... D'YA REALLY THINK WE'RE THAT STUPID?
HE SOUNDS BLOODY WELL-INFORMED THOUGH, EH?
THEY KNOW EV'RYTHIN'... MORIARTY...
THE FIRM... KEENE... MORAN... YOU ARE DOOMED!
WE CAN'T STAY HERE... GOTTA GET OUT!
YEAH, BRING THE BRAT DOWN... BISHOP, TAKE A PEEK OUTSIDE! I'LL DEAL WITH THE BURGLAR KING HERE...
BUT LET'S DO IT ALL QUIET, LIKE... WOULDN'T WANT YER COPPER MATES DROPPIN' IN!
FUNNY, INNIT? DON'T LOOK AS IF YER BLEEDIN' SPECIAL BRANCH IS IN MUCH OF A HURRY...

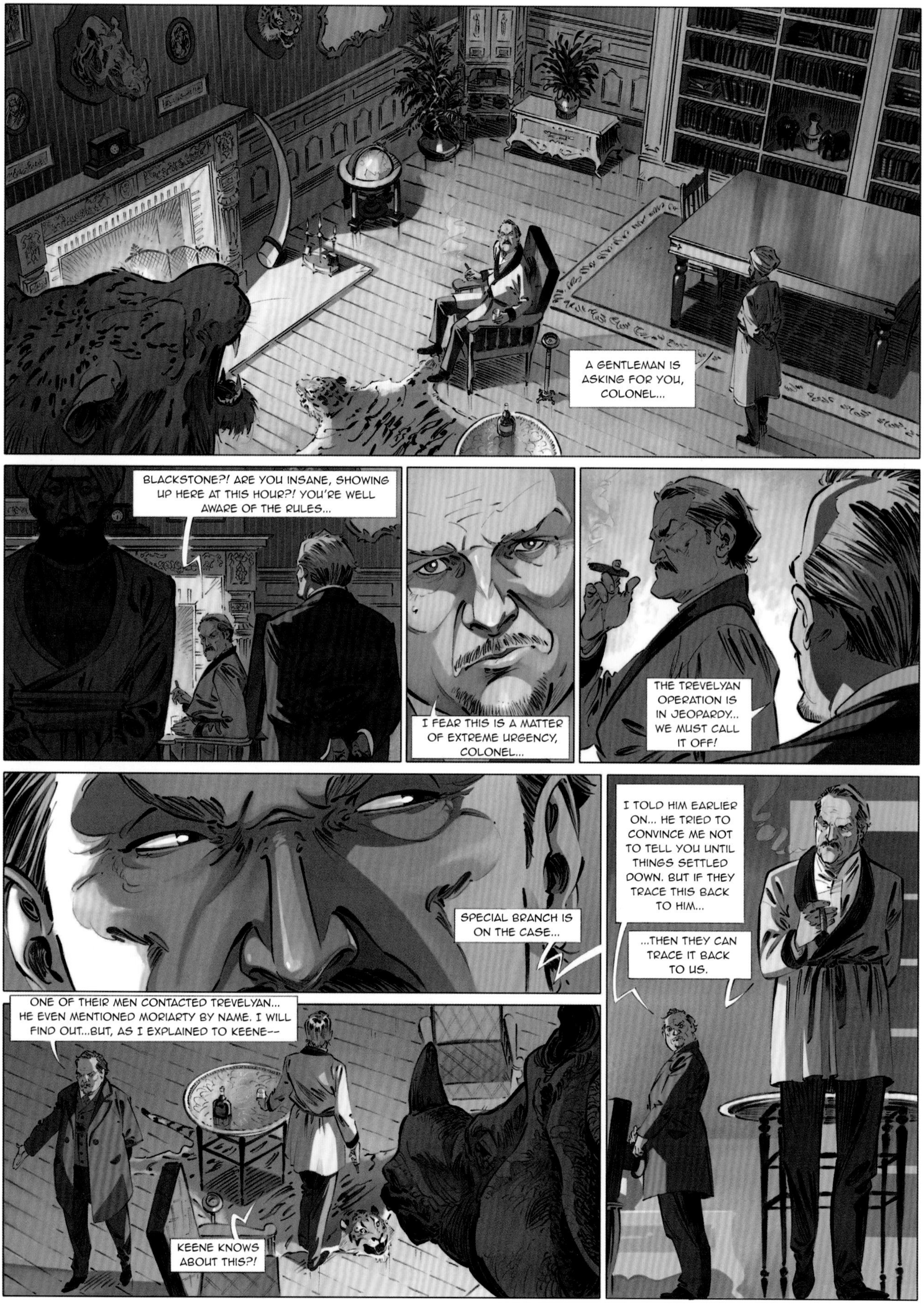

A GENTLEMAN IS ASKING FOR YOU, COLONEL...
BLACKSTONE?! ARE YOU INSANE, SHOWING UP HERE AT THIS HOUR?! YOU'RE WELL AWARE OF THE RULES...
I FEAR THIS IS A MATTER OF EXTREME URGENCY, COLONEL...
THE TREVELYAN OPERATION IS IN JEOPARDY... WE MUST CALL IT OFF!
SPECIAL BRANCH IS ON THE CASE...
I TOLD HIM EARLIER ON... HE TRIED TO CONVINCE ME NOT TO TELL YOU UNTIL THINGS SETTLED DOWN. BUT IF THEY TRACE THIS BACK TO HIM...
...THEN THEY CAN TRACE IT BACK TO US.
ONE OF THEIR MEN CONTACTED TREVELYAN... HE EVEN MENTIONED MORIARTY BY NAME. I WILL FIND OUT...BUT, AS I EXPLAINED TO KEENE--
KEENE KNOWS ABOUT THIS?!

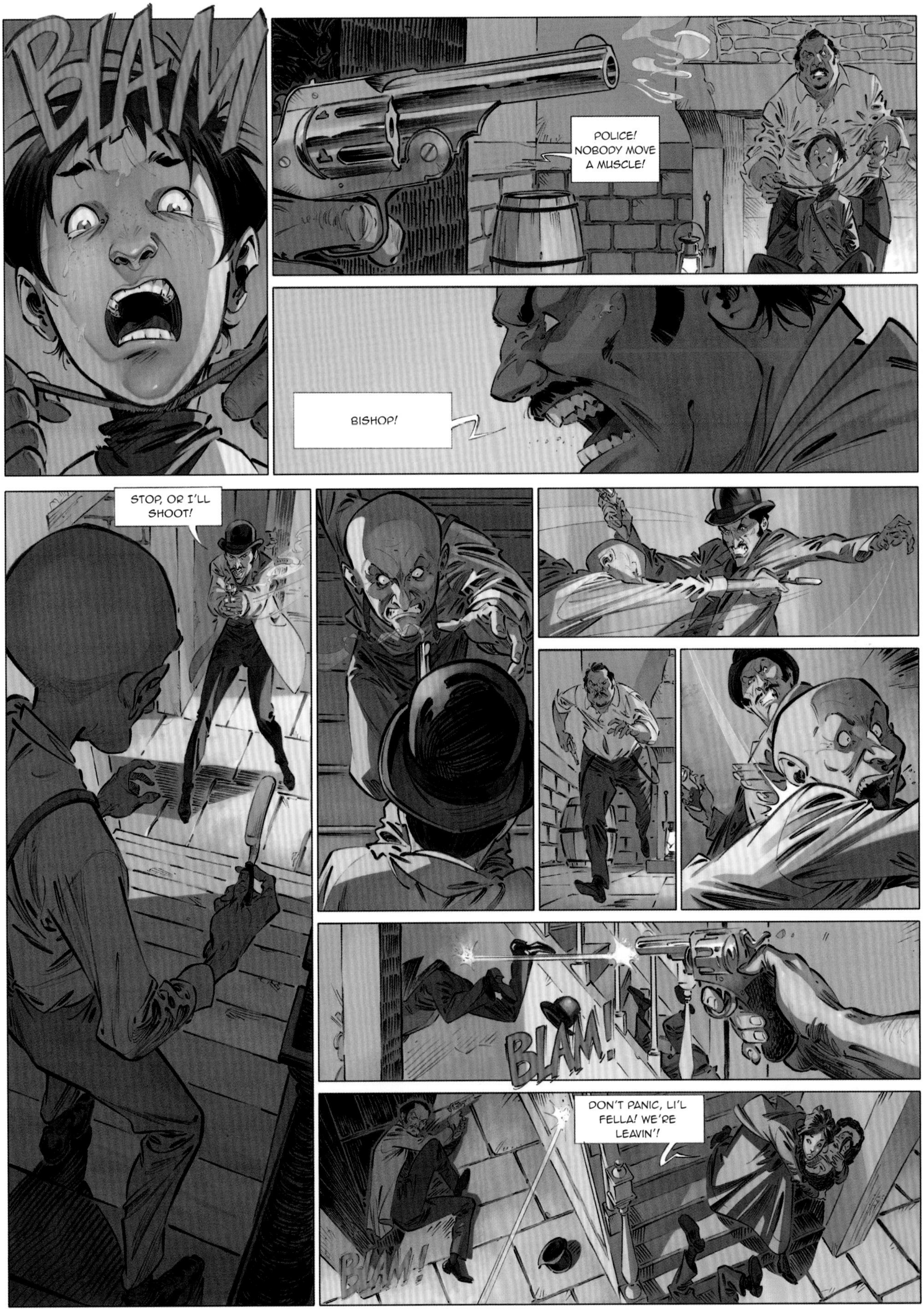
BLAM
POLICE! NOBODY MOVE A MUSCLE!
BISHOP!
STOP, OR I'LL SHOOT!
BLAM!
DON'T PANIC, LI'L FELLA! WE'RE LEAVIN'!
BLAM!

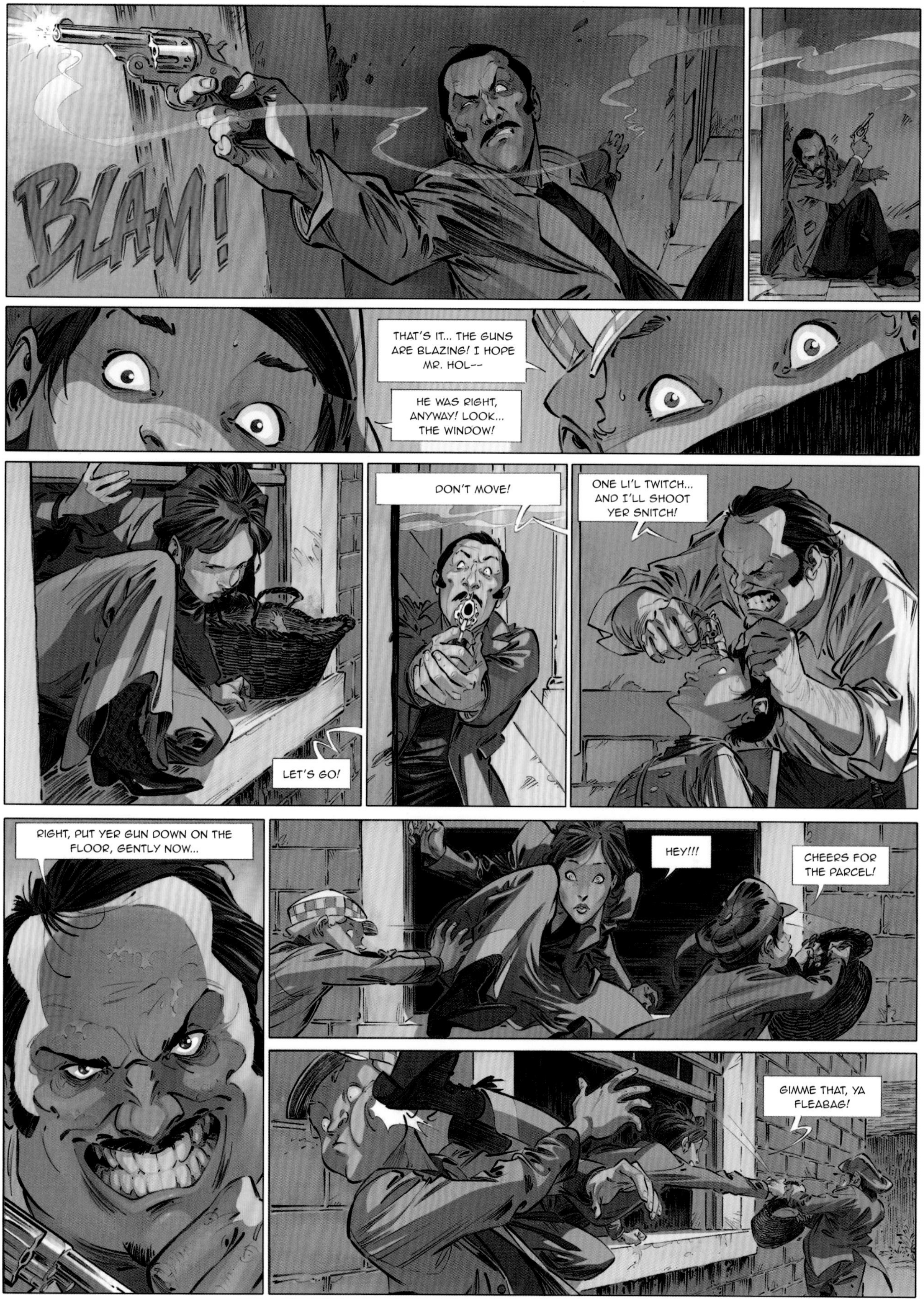
BLAM!
THAT'S IT... THE GUNS ARE BLAZING! I HOPE MR. HOL--
HE WAS RIGHT, ANYWAY! LOOK... THE WINDOW!
LET'S GO!
DON'T MOVE!
ONE LI'L TWITCH... AND I'LL SHOOT YER SNITCH!
RIGHT, PUT YER GUN DOWN ON THE FLOOR, GENTLY NOW...
HEY!!!
CHEERS FOR THE PARCEL!
GIMME THAT, YA FLEABAG!

YEAH, THAT'S RIGHT...

IF YOU WANT A HOSTAGE, TAKE ME INSTEAD OF THE BOY... A SPECIAL BRANCH INSPECTOR'S LIFE IS WORTH MORE THAN--

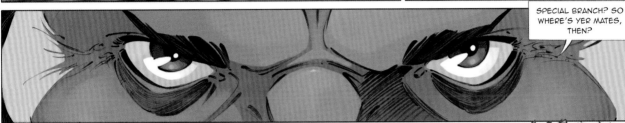
SPECIAL BRANCH? SO WHERE'S YER MATES, THEN?

GET OFF ME, YA TART!

MAOOW

RECKON I AIN'T TWIGGED YET? YOU'RE ONE O' THEM BLEEDIN' PRIVATE COPPERS, LIKE PINKERTON'S IN AMERICA... TREVELYAN THOUGHT HE COULD SWINDLE US, DID HE?

WELL, PASS THIS ON FROM ME...

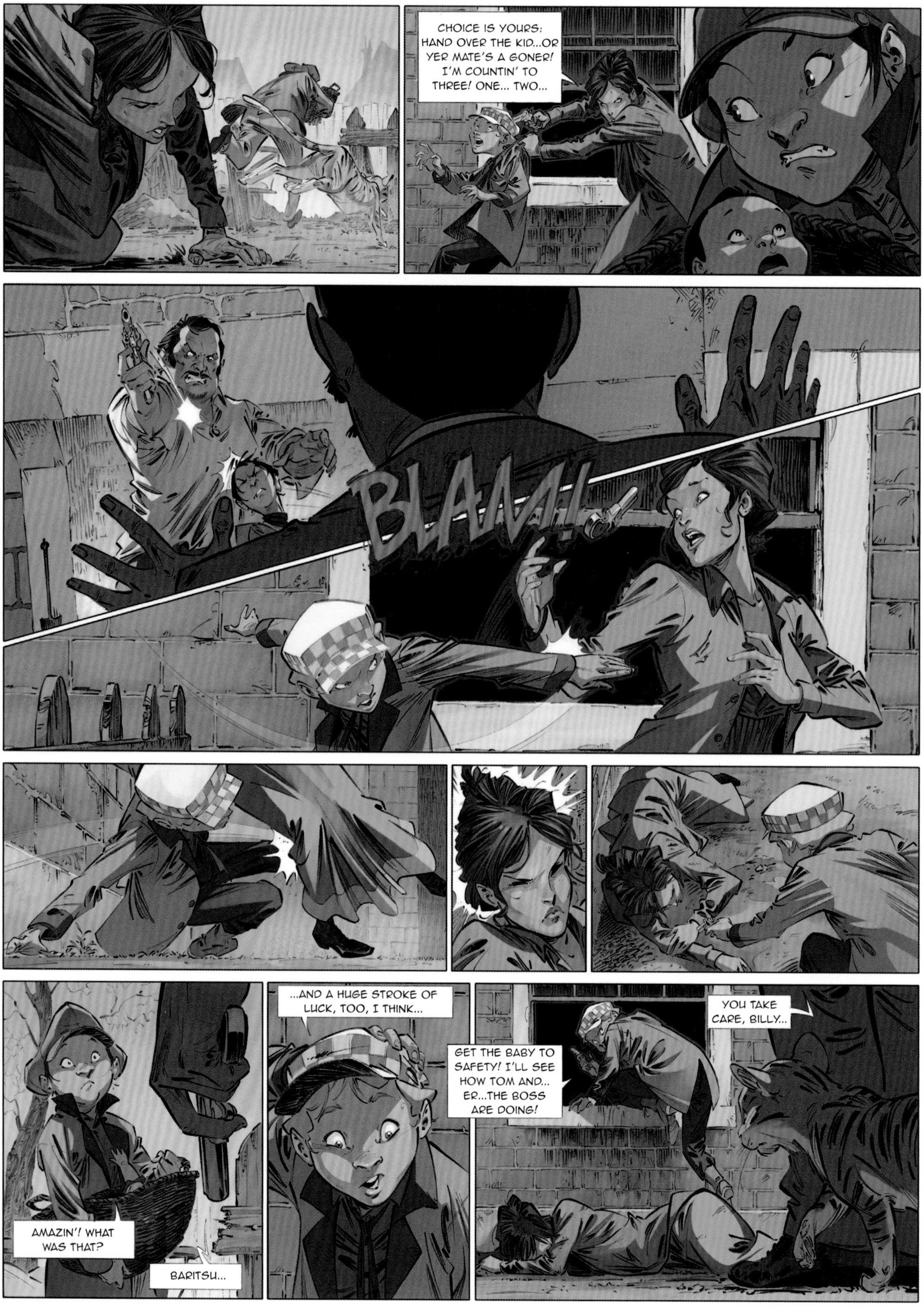
CHOICE IS YOURS: HAND OVER THE KID...OR YER MATE'S A GONER! I'M COUNTIN' TO THREE! ONE... TWO...
BLAM!
...AND A HUGE STROKE OF LUCK, TOO, I THINK...
AMAZIN'! WHAT WAS THAT?
BARITSU...
GET THE BABY TO SAFETY! I'LL SEE HOW TOM AND... ER...THE BOSS ARE DOING!
YOU TAKE CARE, BILLY...

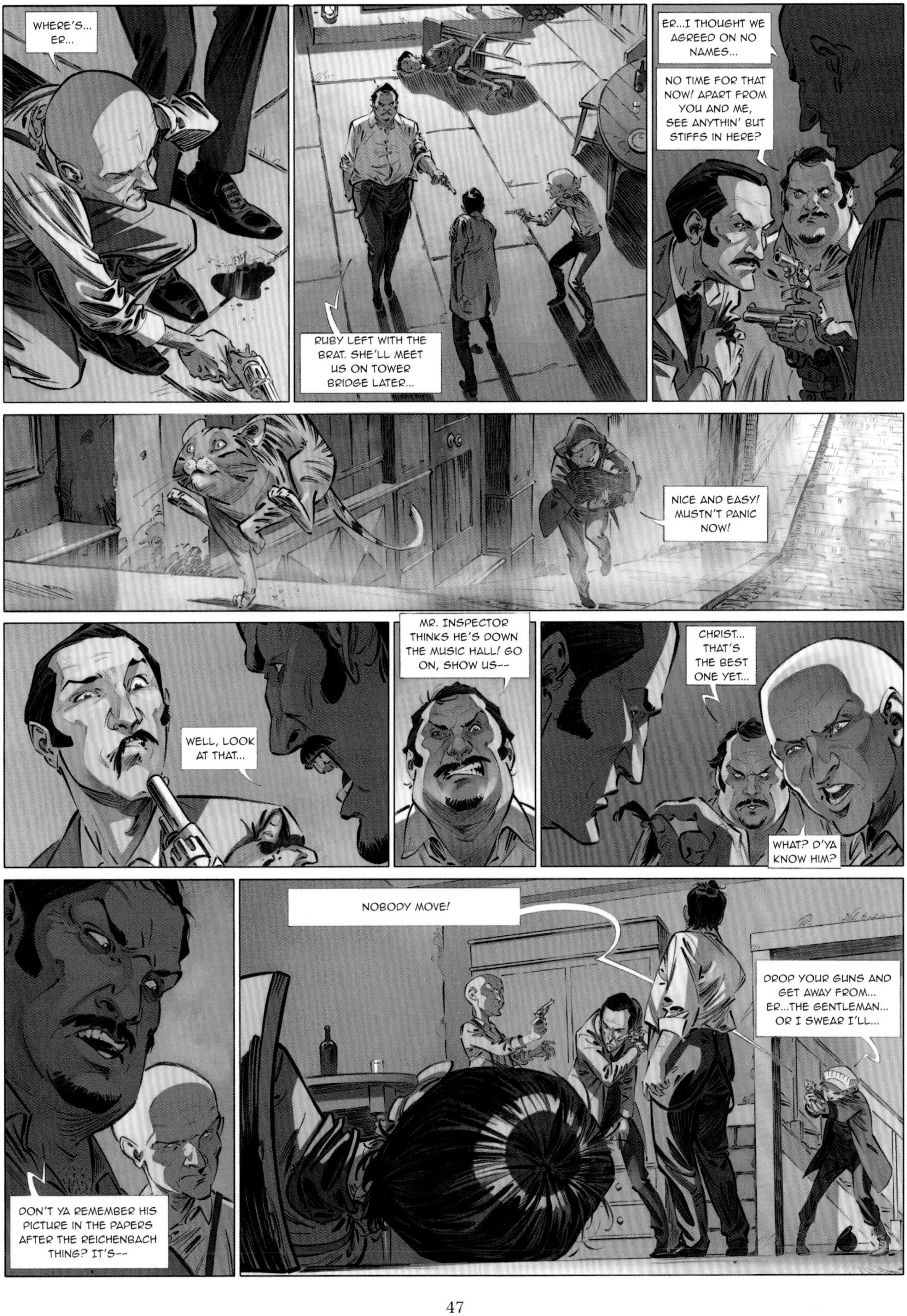
WHERE'S... ER...
RUBY LEFT WITH THE BRAT. SHE'LL MEET US ON TOWER BRIDGE LATER...
ER...I THOUGHT WE AGREED ON NO NAMES...
NO TIME FOR THAT NOW! APART FROM YOU AND ME, SEE ANYTHIN' BUT STIFFS IN HERE?
NICE AND EASY! MUSTN'T PANIC NOW!
WELL, LOOK AT THAT...
MR. INSPECTOR THINKS HE'S DOWN THE MUSIC HALL! GO ON, SHOW US--
CHRIST... THAT'S THE BEST ONE YET...
WHAT? D'YA KNOW HIM?
DON'T YA REMEMBER HIS PICTURE IN THE PAPERS AFTER THE REICHENBACH THING? IT'S--
NOBODY MOVE!
DROP YOUR GUNS AND GET AWAY FROM... ER...THE GENTLEMAN... OR I SWEAR I'LL...

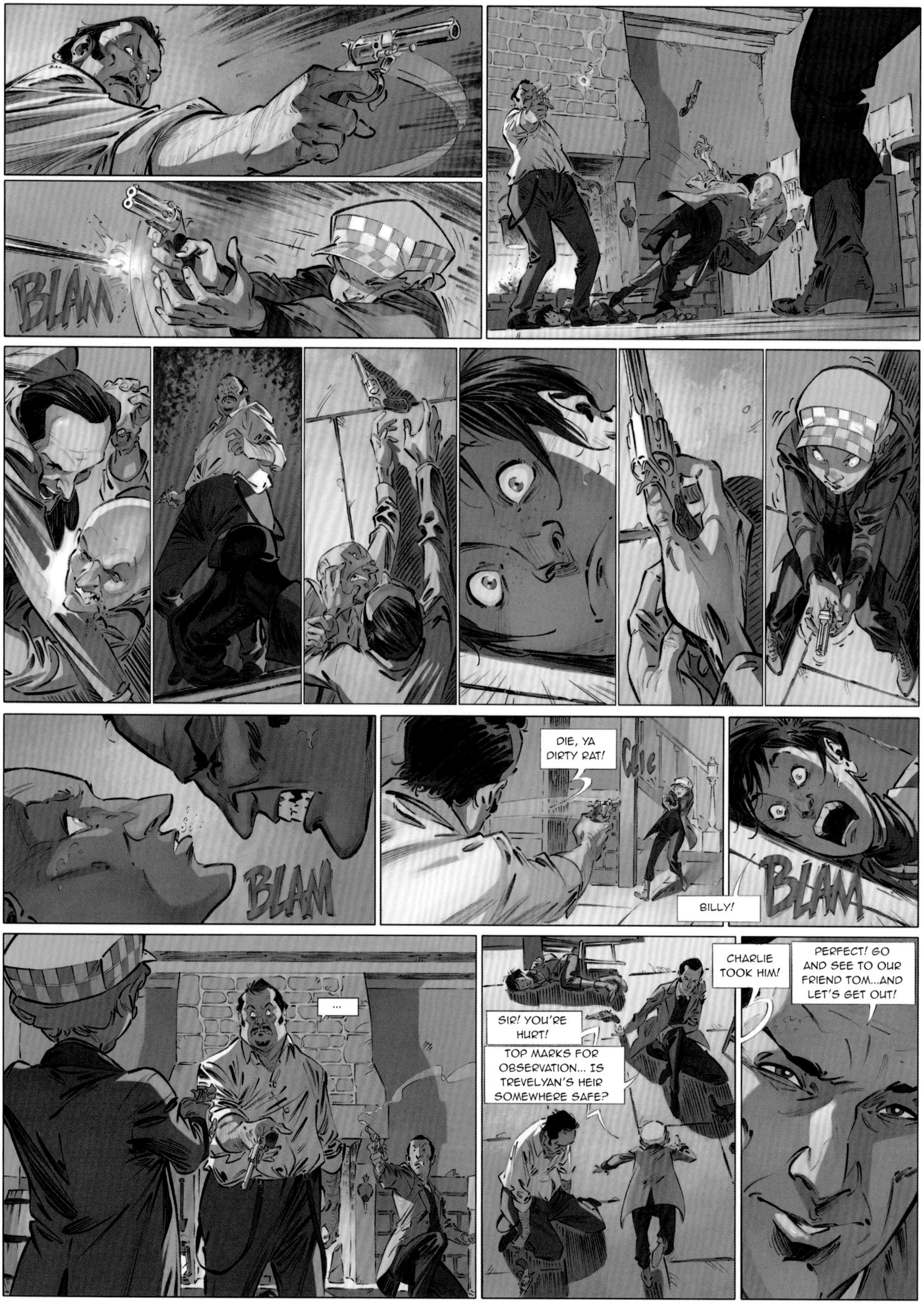
BLAM
BLAM
DIE, YA DIRTY RAT!
BILLY!
BLAM
...
SIR! YOU'RE HURT!
TOP MARKS FOR OBSERVATION... IS TREVELYAN'S HEIR SOMEWHERE SAFE?
CHARLIE TOOK HIM!
PERFECT! GO AND SEE TO OUR FRIEND TOM...AND LET'S GET OUT!

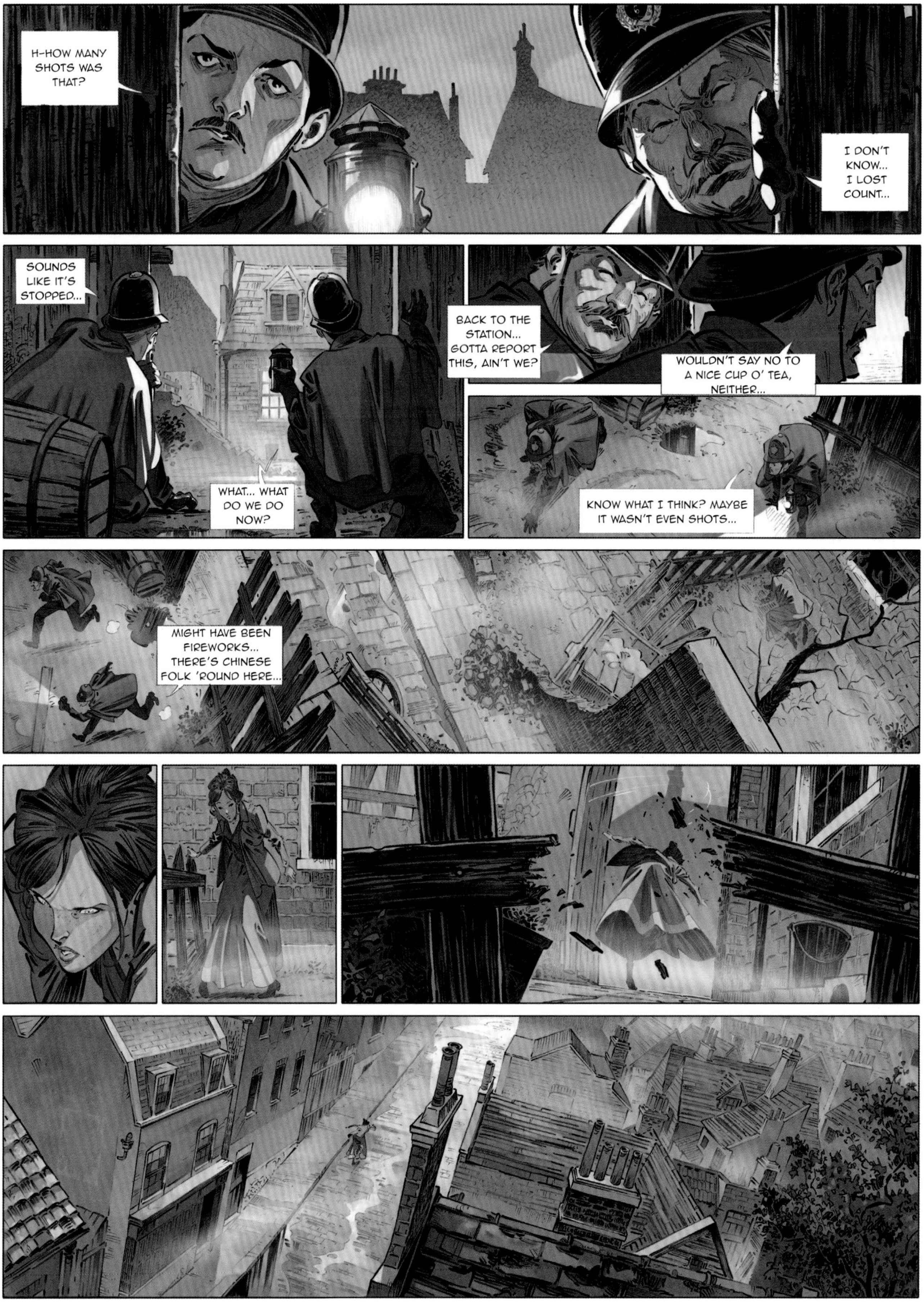
H-HOW MANY SHOTS WAS THAT?
I DON'T KNOW... I LOST COUNT...
SOUNDS LIKE IT'S STOPPED...
WHAT... WHAT DO WE DO NOW?
BACK TO THE STATION... GOTTA REPORT THIS, AIN'T WE?
WOULDN'T SAY NO TO A NICE CUP O' TEA, NEITHER...
KNOW WHAT I THINK? MAYBE IT WASN'T EVEN SHOTS...
MIGHT HAVE BEEN FIREWORKS... THERE'S CHINESE FOLK 'ROUND HERE...

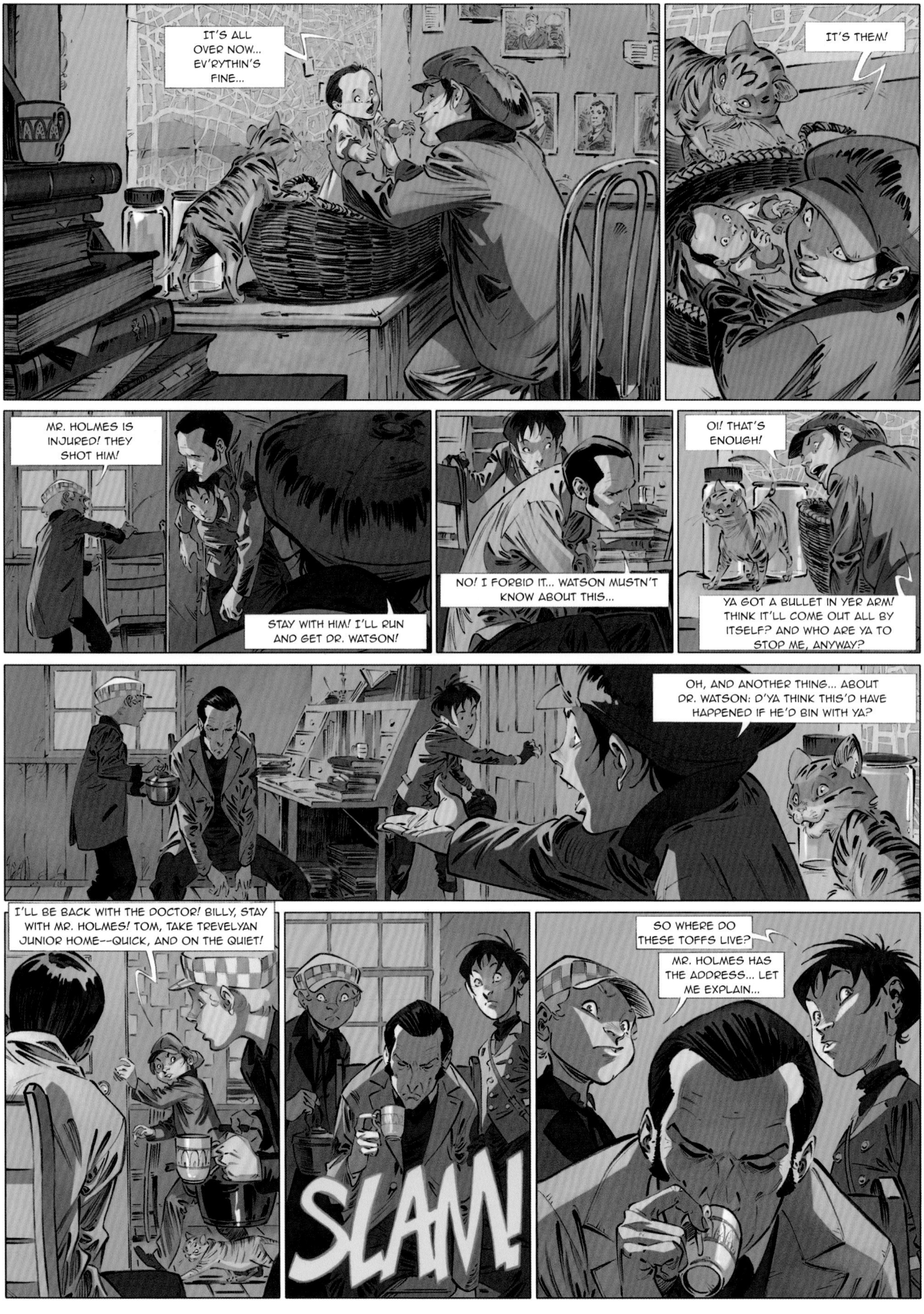
IT'S ALL OVER NOW... EV'RYTHIN'S FINE...
IT'S THEM!
MR. HOLMES IS INJURED! THEY SHOT HIM!
STAY WITH HIM! I'LL RUN AND GET DR. WATSON!
NO! I FORBID IT... WATSON MUSTN'T KNOW ABOUT THIS...
OI! THAT'S ENOUGH!
YA GOT A BULLET IN YER ARM! THINK IT'LL COME OUT ALL BY ITSELF? AND WHO ARE YA TO STOP ME, ANYWAY?
OH, AND ANOTHER THING... ABOUT DR. WATSON: D'YA THINK THIS'D HAVE HAPPENED IF HE'D BIN WITH YA?
I'LL BE BACK WITH THE DOCTOR! BILLY, STAY WITH MR. HOLMES! TOM, TAKE TREVELYAN JUNIOR HOME--QUICK, AND ON THE QUIET!
SLAM!
SO WHERE DO THESE TOFFS LIVE?
MR. HOLMES HAS THE ADDRESS... LET ME EXPLAIN...

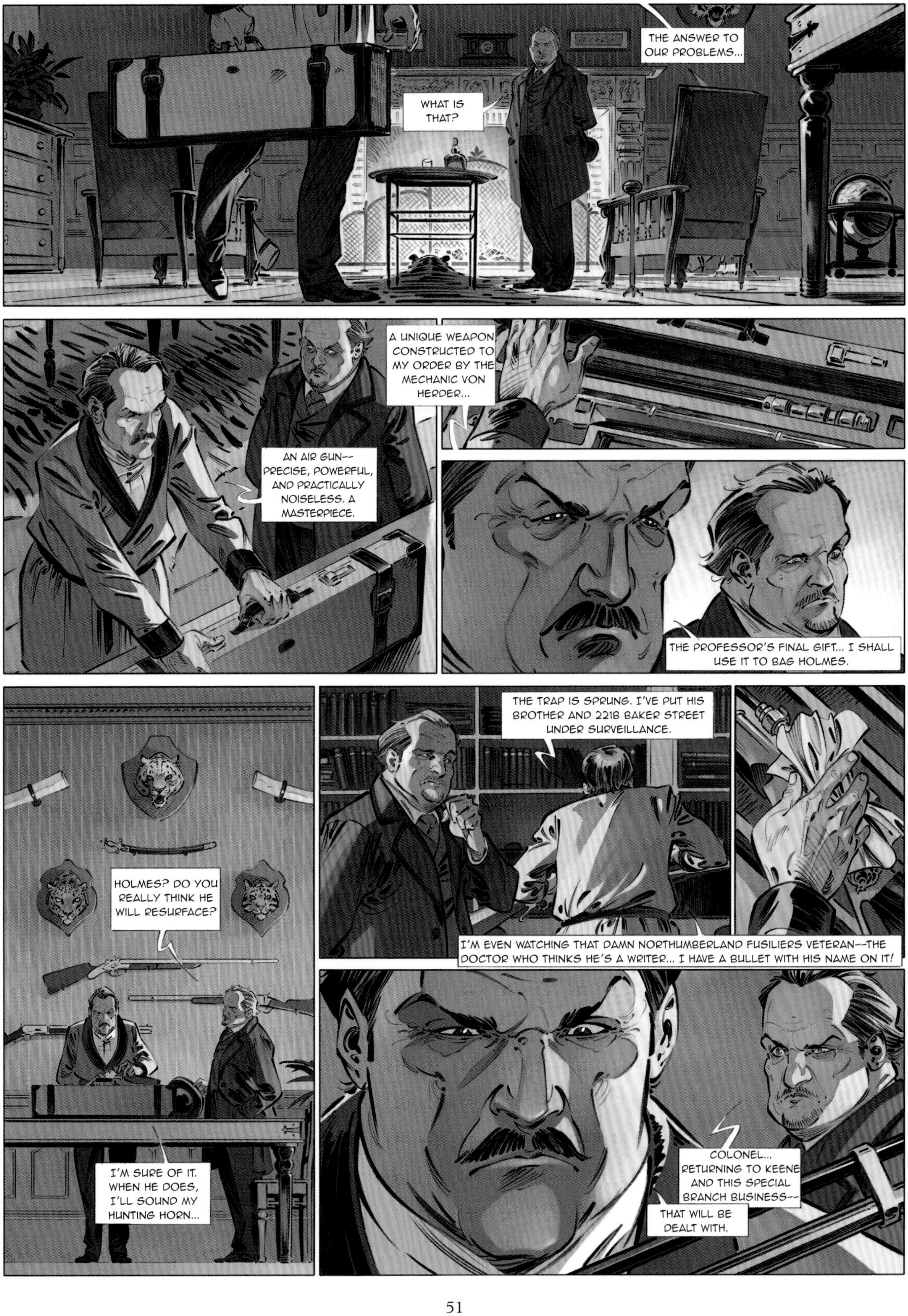
THE ANSWER TO OUR PROBLEMS...
WHAT IS THAT?
A UNIQUE WEAPON CONSTRUCTED TO MY ORDER BY THE MECHANIC VON HERDER...
AN AIR GUN-- PRECISE, POWERFUL, AND PRACTICALLY NOISELESS. A MASTERPIECE.
THE PROFESSOR'S FINAL GIFT... I SHALL USE IT TO BAG HOLMES.
HOLMES? DO YOU REALLY THINK HE WILL RESURFACE?
I'M SURE OF IT. WHEN HE DOES, I'LL SOUND MY HUNTING HORN...
THE TRAP IS SPRUNG. I'VE PUT HIS BROTHER AND 221B BAKER STREET UNDER SURVEILLANCE.
I'M EVEN WATCHING THAT DAMN NORTHUMBERLAND FUSILIERS VETERAN--THE DOCTOR WHO THINKS HE'S A WRITER... I HAVE A BULLET WITH HIS NAME ON IT!
COLONEL... RETURNING TO KEENE AND THIS SPECIAL BRANCH BUSINESS--
THAT WILL BE DEALT WITH.

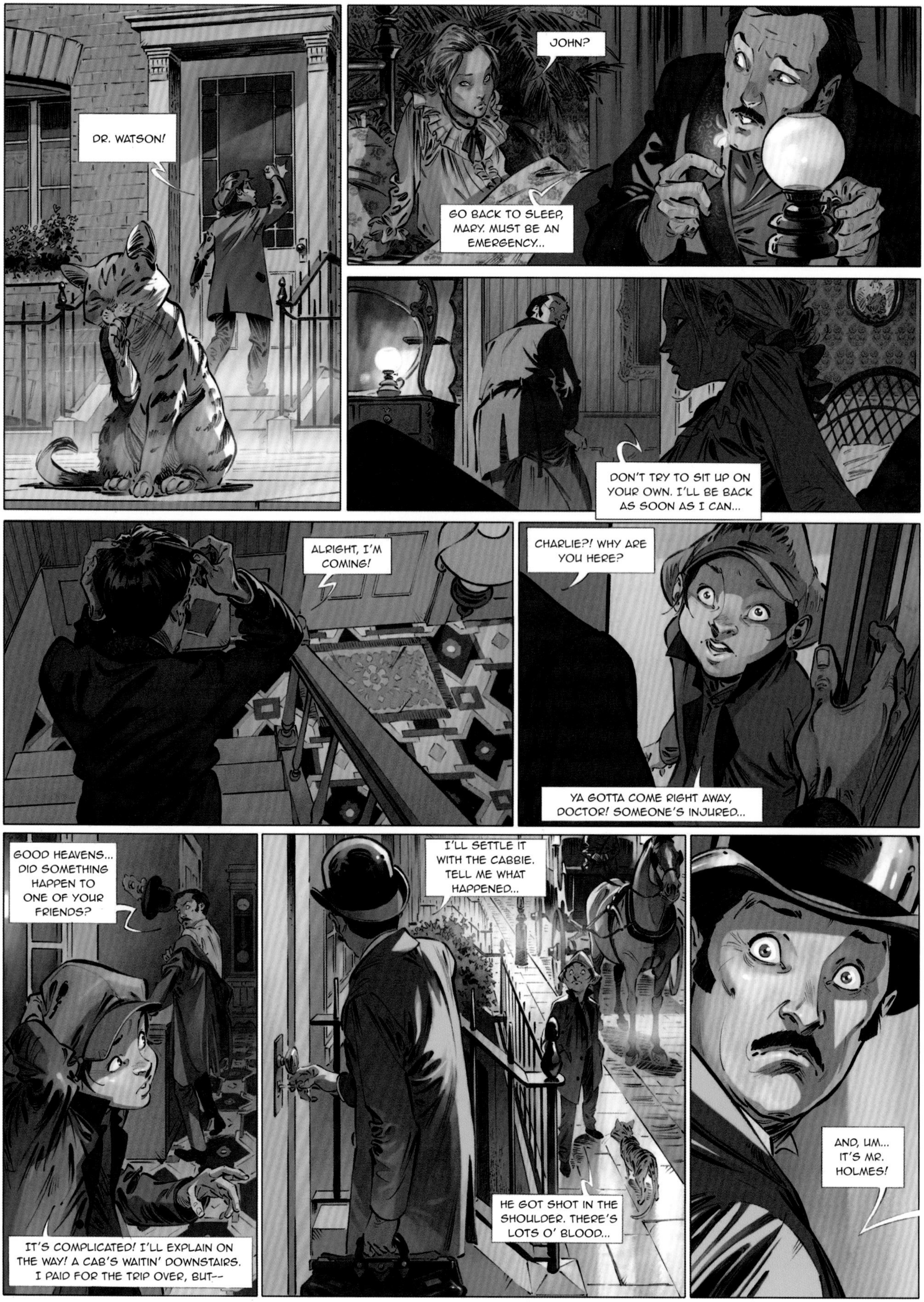
DR. WATSON!
JOHN?
GO BACK TO SLEEP, MARY. MUST BE AN EMERGENCY...
DON'T TRY TO SIT UP ON YOUR OWN. I'LL BE BACK AS SOON AS I CAN...
ALRIGHT, I'M COMING!
CHARLIE?! WHY ARE YOU HERE?
YA GOTTA COME RIGHT AWAY, DOCTOR! SOMEONE'S INJURED...
GOOD HEAVENS... DID SOMETHING HAPPEN TO ONE OF YOUR FRIENDS?
IT'S COMPLICATED! I'LL EXPLAIN ON THE WAY! A CAB'S WAITIN' DOWNSTAIRS. I PAID FOR THE TRIP OVER, BUT--
I'LL SETTLE IT WITH THE CABBIE. TELL ME WHAT HAPPENED...
HE GOT SHOT IN THE SHOULDER. THERE'S LOTS O' BLOOD...
AND, UM... IT'S MR. HOLMES!

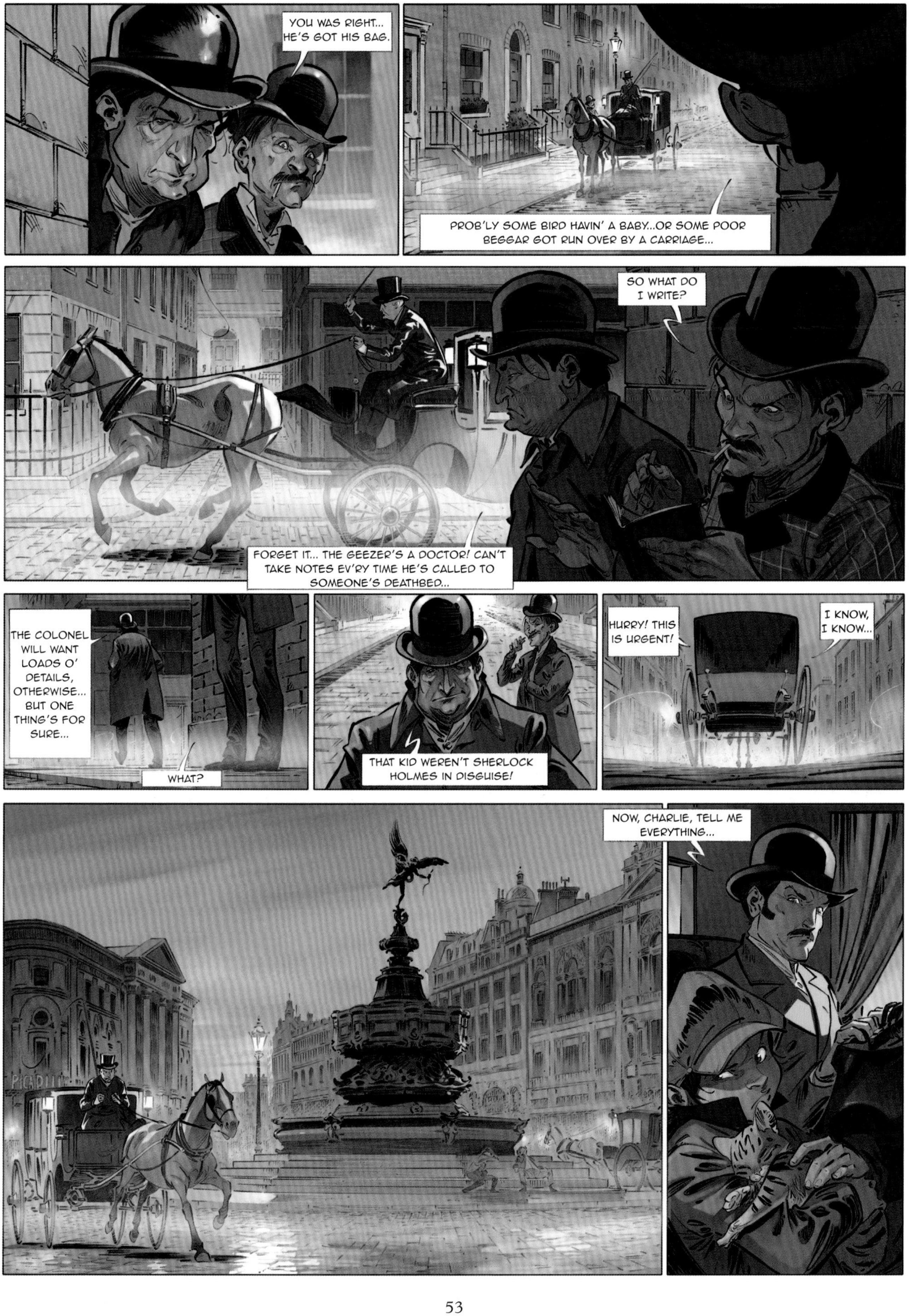

YOU WAS RIGHT... HE'S GOT HIS BAG.
PROB'LY SOME BIRD HAVIN' A BABY...OR SOME POOR BEGGAR GOT RUN OVER BY A CARRIAGE...
SO WHAT DO I WRITE?
FORGET IT... THE GEEZER'S A DOCTOR! CAN'T TAKE NOTES EV'RY TIME HE'S CALLED TO SOMEONE'S DEATHBED...
THE COLONEL WILL WANT LOADS O' DETAILS, OTHERWISE... BUT ONE THING'S FOR SURE...
WHAT?
THAT KID WEREN'T SHERLOCK HOLMES IN DISGUISE!
HURRY! THIS IS URGENT!
I KNOW, I KNOW...
PICADILLY
NOW, CHARLIE, TELL ME EVERYTHING...

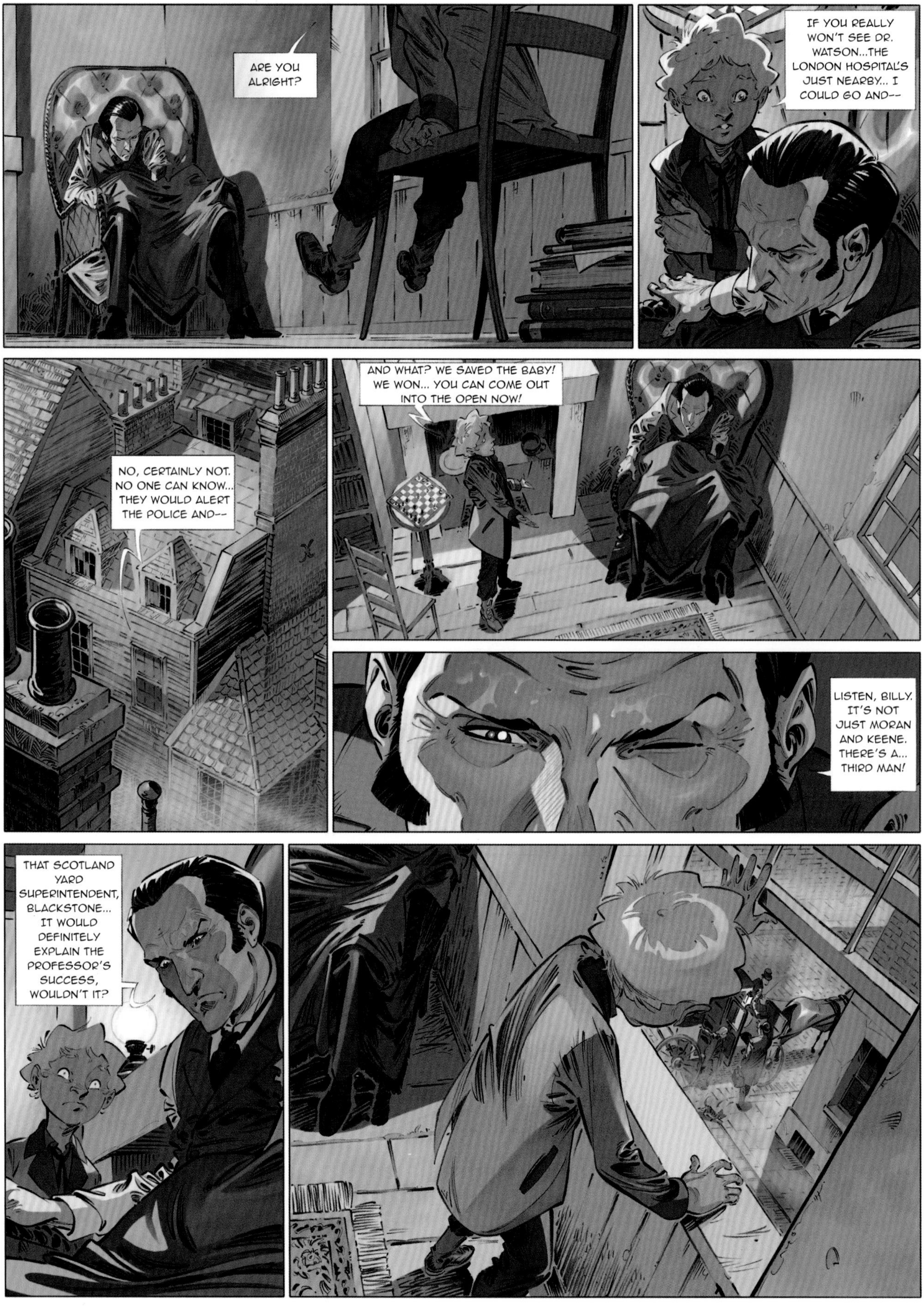

ARE YOU ALRIGHT?
IF YOU REALLY WON'T SEE DR. WATSON...THE LONDON HOSPITAL'S JUST NEARBY... I COULD GO AND--
NO, CERTAINLY NOT. NO ONE CAN KNOW... THEY WOULD ALERT THE POLICE AND--
AND WHAT? WE SAVED THE BABY! WE WON... YOU CAN COME OUT INTO THE OPEN NOW!
LISTEN, BILLY. IT'S NOT JUST MORAN AND KEENE. THERE'S A... THIRD MAN!
THAT SCOTLAND YARD SUPERINTENDENT, BLACKSTONE... IT WOULD DEFINITELY EXPLAIN THE PROFESSOR'S SUCCESS, WOULDN'T IT?

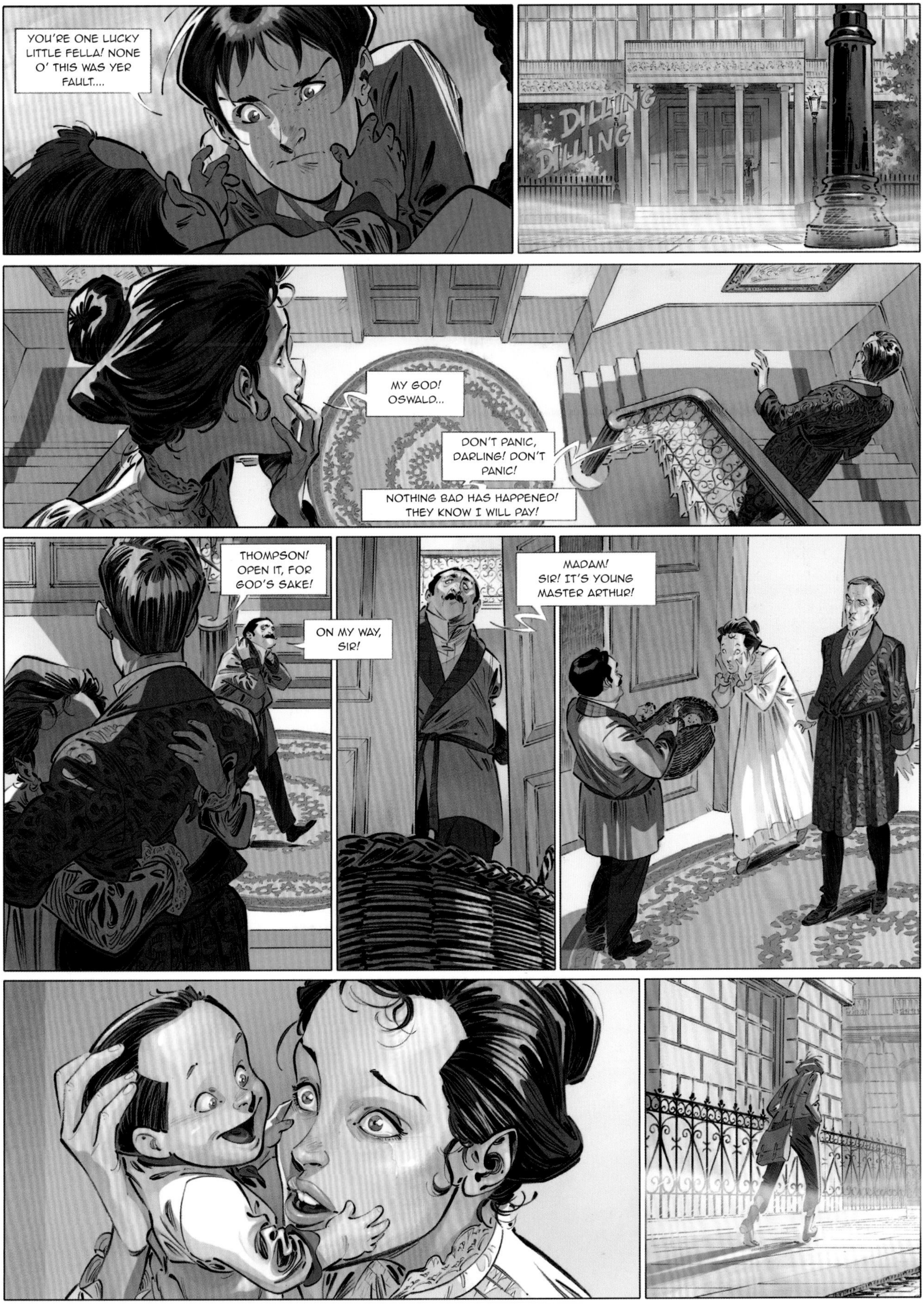
YOU'RE ONE LUCKY LITTLE FELLA! NONE O' THIS WAS YER FAULT....
DILLING DILLING
MY GOD! OSWALD...
DON'T PANIC, DARLING! DON'T PANIC!
NOTHING BAD HAS HAPPENED! THEY KNOW I WILL PAY!
THOMPSON! OPEN IT, FOR GOD'S SAKE!
ON MY WAY, SIR!
MADAM! SIR! IT'S YOUNG MASTER ARTHUR!

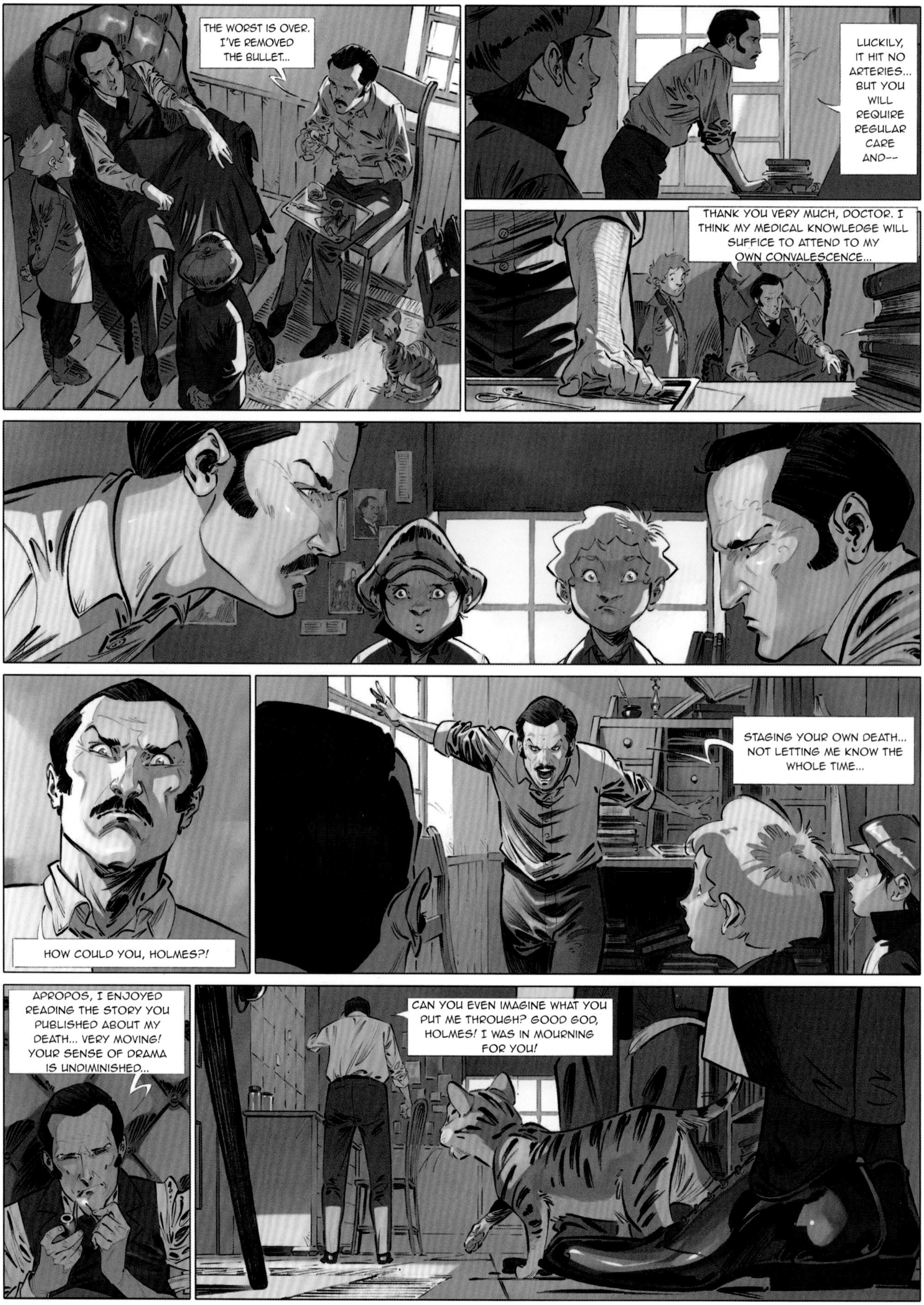
THE WORST IS OVER. I'VE REMOVED THE BULLET...
LUCKILY, IT HIT NO ARTERIES... BUT YOU WILL REQUIRE REGULAR CARE AND--
THANK YOU VERY MUCH, DOCTOR. I THINK MY MEDICAL KNOWLEDGE WILL SUFFICE TO ATTEND TO MY OWN CONVALESCENCE...
HOW COULD YOU, HOLMES?!
STAGING YOUR OWN DEATH... NOT LETTING ME KNOW THE WHOLE TIME...
APROPOS, I ENJOYED READING THE STORY YOU PUBLISHED ABOUT MY DEATH... VERY MOVING! YOUR SENSE OF DRAMA IS UNDIMINISHED...
CAN YOU EVEN IMAGINE WHAT YOU PUT ME THROUGH? GOOD GOD, HOLMES! I WAS IN MOURNING FOR YOU!

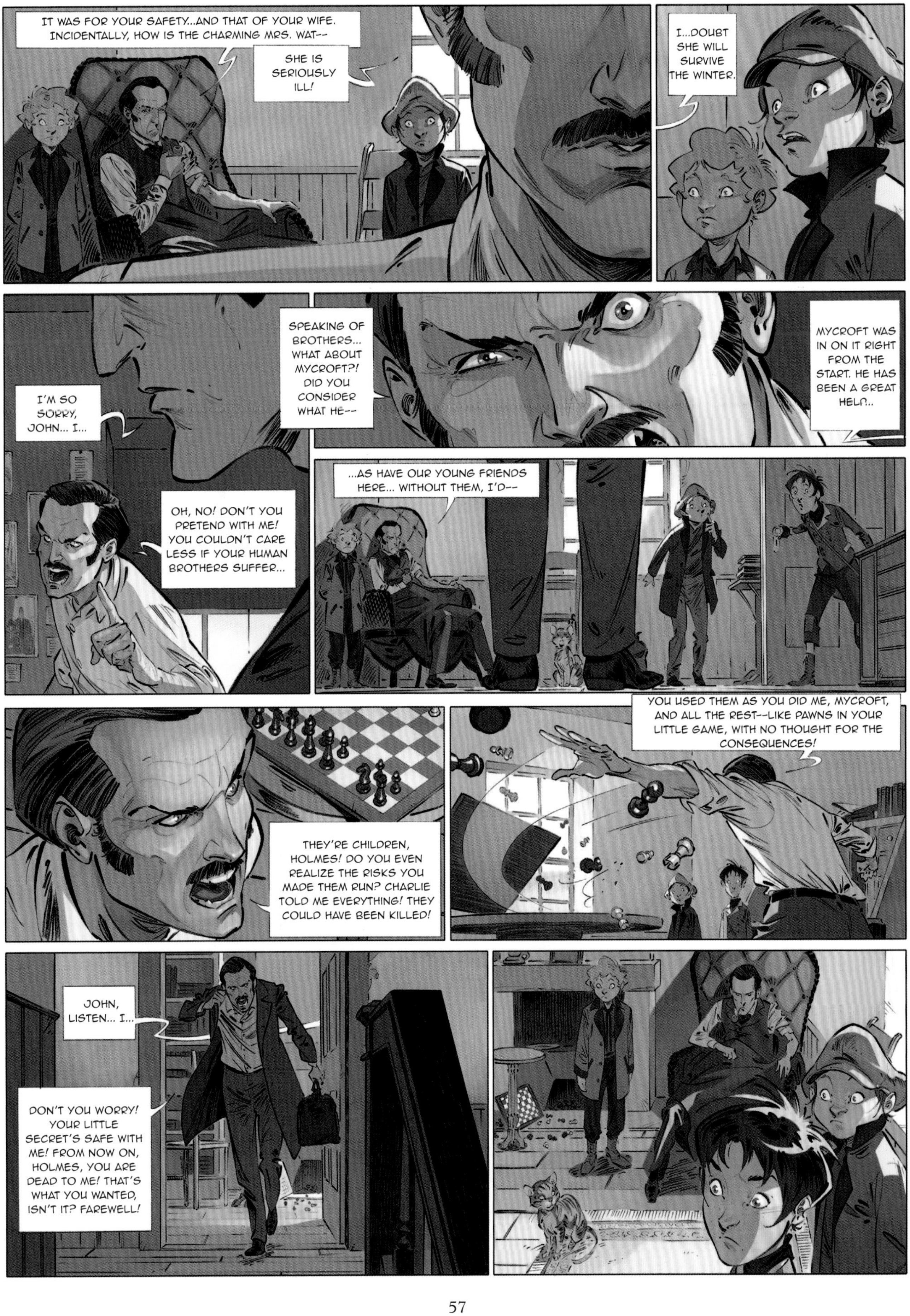

IT WAS FOR YOUR SAFETY...AND THAT OF YOUR WIFE. INCIDENTALLY, HOW IS THE CHARMING MRS. WAT--
SHE IS SERIOUSLY ILL!
I...DOUBT SHE WILL SURVIVE THE WINTER.
I'M SO SORRY, JOHN... I...
SPEAKING OF BROTHERS... WHAT ABOUT MYCROFT?! DID YOU CONSIDER WHAT HE--
MYCROFT WAS IN ON IT RIGHT FROM THE START. HE HAS BEEN A GREAT HELP..
OH, NO! DON'T YOU PRETEND WITH ME! YOU COULDN'T CARE LESS IF YOUR HUMAN BROTHERS SUFFER...
...AS HAVE OUR YOUNG FRIENDS HERE... WITHOUT THEM, I'D--
THEY'RE CHILDREN, HOLMES! DO YOU EVEN REALIZE THE RISKS YOU MADE THEM RUN? CHARLIE TOLD ME EVERYTHING! THEY COULD HAVE BEEN KILLED!
YOU USED THEM AS YOU DID ME, MYCROFT, AND ALL THE REST--LIKE PAWNS IN YOUR LITTLE GAME, WITH NO THOUGHT FOR THE CONSEQUENCES!
JOHN, LISTEN... I...
DON'T YOU WORRY! YOUR LITTLE SECRET'S SAFE WITH ME! FROM NOW ON, HOLMES, YOU ARE DEAD TO ME! THAT'S WHAT YOU WANTED, ISN'T IT? FAREWELL!

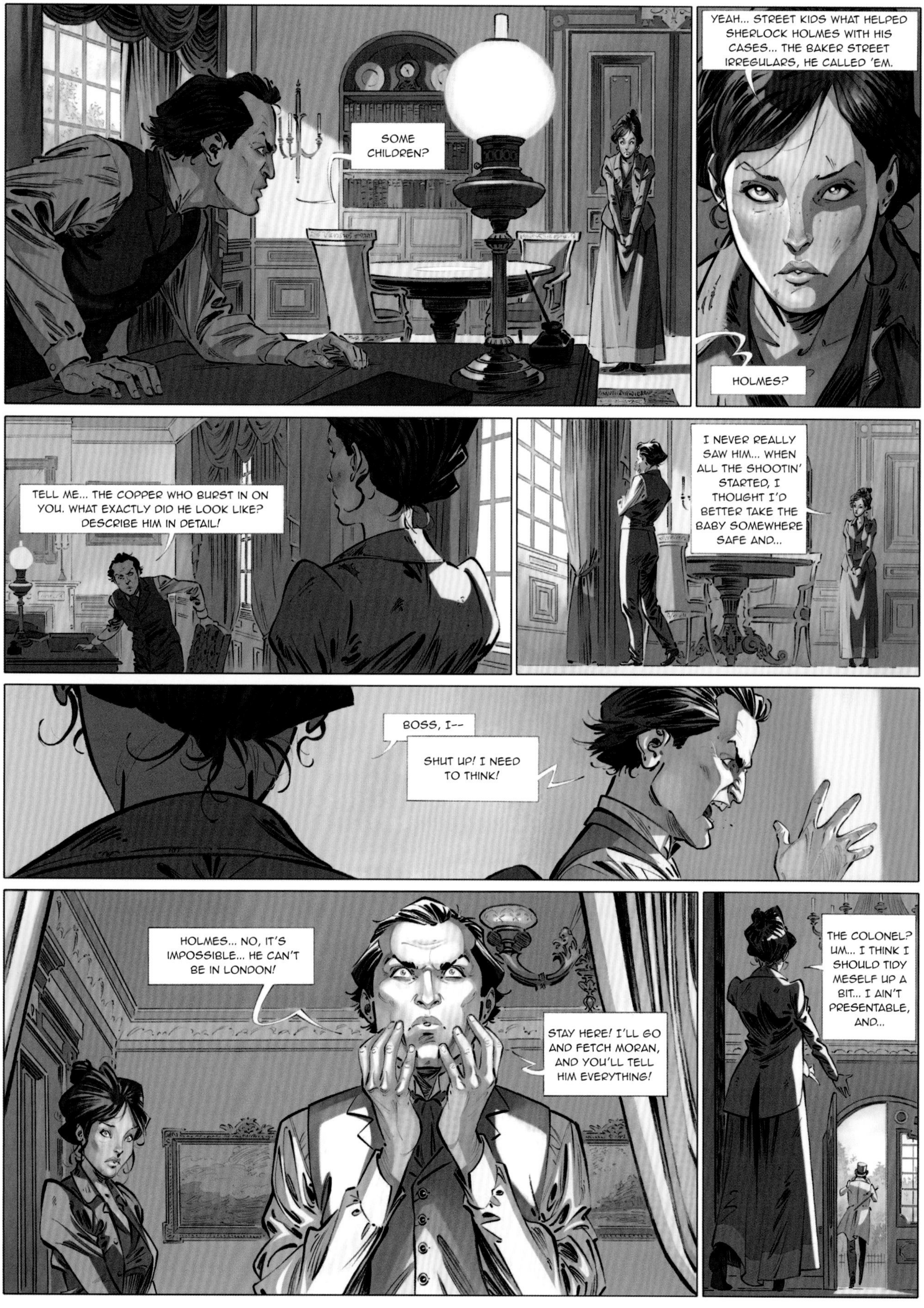
SOME CHILDREN?
YEAH... STREET KIDS WHAT HELPED SHERLOCK HOLMES WITH HIS CASES... THE BAKER STREET IRREGULARS, HE CALLED 'EM.
HOLMES?
TELL ME... THE COPPER WHO BURST IN ON YOU. WHAT EXACTLY DID HE LOOK LIKE? DESCRIBE HIM IN DETAIL!
I NEVER REALLY SAW HIM... WHEN ALL THE SHOOTIN' STARTED, I THOUGHT I'D BETTER TAKE THE BABY SOMEWHERE SAFE AND...
BOSS, I--
SHUT UP! I NEED TO THINK!
HOLMES... NO, IT'S IMPOSSIBLE... HE CAN'T BE IN LONDON!
STAY HERE! I'LL GO AND FETCH MORAN, AND YOU'LL TELL HIM EVERYTHING!
THE COLONEL? UM... I THINK I SHOULD TIDY MESELF UP A BIT... I AIN'T PRESENTABLE, AND...

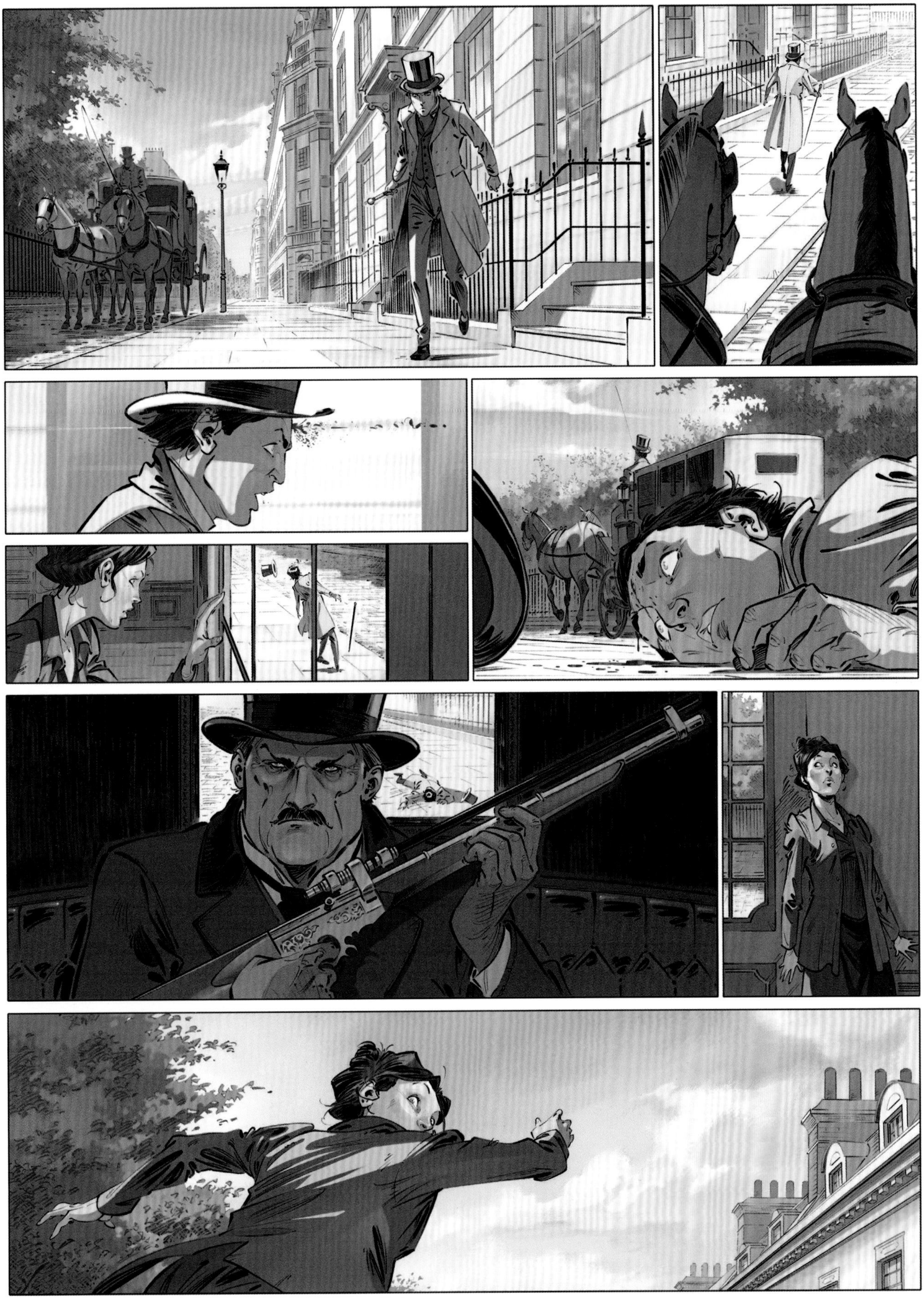

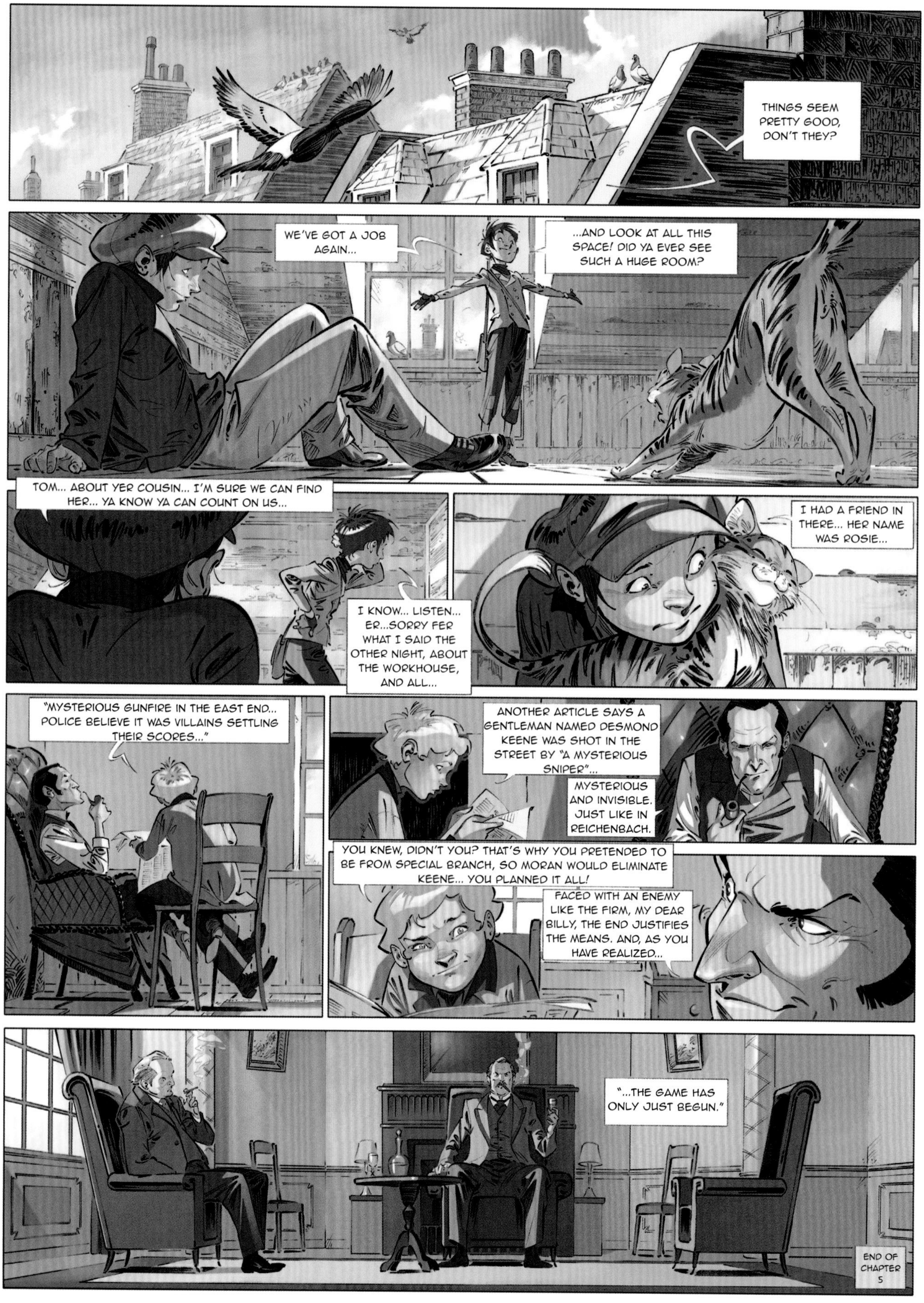
THINGS SEEM PRETTY GOOD, DON'T THEY?
WE'VE GOT A JOB AGAIN...
...AND LOOK AT ALL THIS SPACE! DID YA EVER SEE SUCH A HUGE ROOM?
TOM... ABOUT YER COUSIN... I'M SURE WE CAN FIND HER... YA KNOW YA CAN COUNT ON US...
I KNOW... LISTEN... ER...SORRY FER WHAT I SAID THE OTHER NIGHT, ABOUT THE WORKHOUSE, AND ALL...
I HAD A FRIEND IN THERE... HER NAME WAS ROSIE...
"MYSTERIOUS GUNFIRE IN THE EAST END... POLICE BELIEVE IT WAS VILLAINS SETTLING THEIR SCORES..."
ANOTHER ARTICLE SAYS A GENTLEMAN NAMED DESMOND KEENE WAS SHOT IN THE STREET BY "A MYSTERIOUS SNIPER"...
MYSTERIOUS AND INVISIBLE. JUST LIKE IN REICHENBACH.
YOU KNEW, DIDN'T YOU? THAT'S WHY YOU PRETENDED TO BE FROM SPECIAL BRANCH, SO MORAN WOULD ELIMINATE KEENE... YOU PLANNED IT ALL!
FACED WITH AN ENEMY LIKE THE FIRM, MY DEAR BILLY, THE END JUSTIFIES THE MEANS. AND, AS YOU HAVE REALIZED...
"...THE GAME HAS ONLY JUST BEGUN."
END OF CHAPTER 5

The Man from the Yard

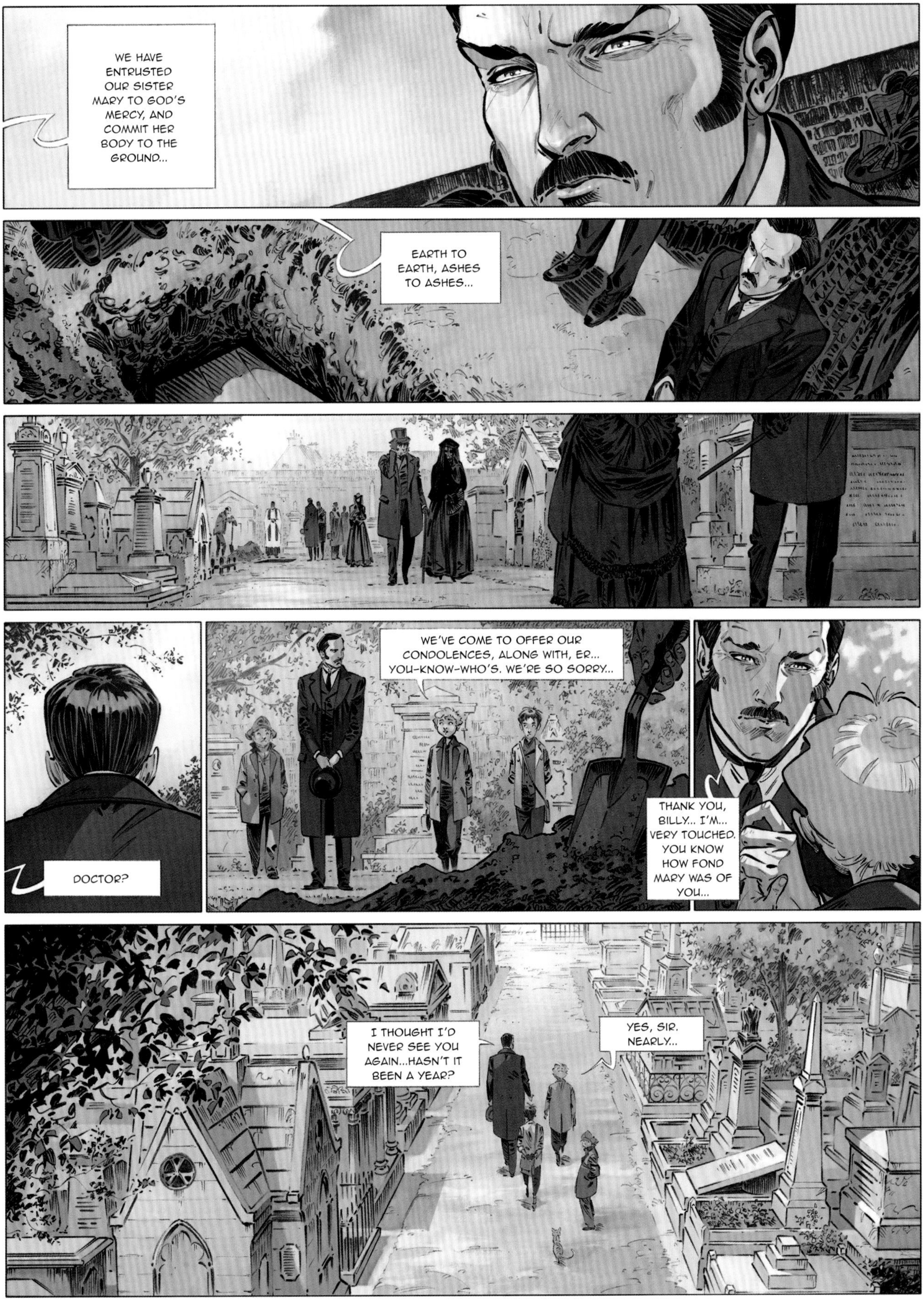
WE HAVE ENTRUSTED OUR SISTER MARY TO GOD'S MERCY, AND COMMIT HER BODY TO THE GROUND...
EARTH TO EARTH, ASHES TO ASHES...
DOCTOR?
WE'VE COME TO OFFER OUR CONDOLENCES, ALONG WITH, ER... YOU-KNOW-WHO'S. WE'RE SO SORRY...
THANK YOU, BILLY... I'M... VERY TOUCHED. YOU KNOW HOW FOND MARY WAS OF YOU...
I THOUGHT I'D NEVER SEE YOU AGAIN...HASN'T IT BEEN A YEAR?
YES, SIR. NEARLY...

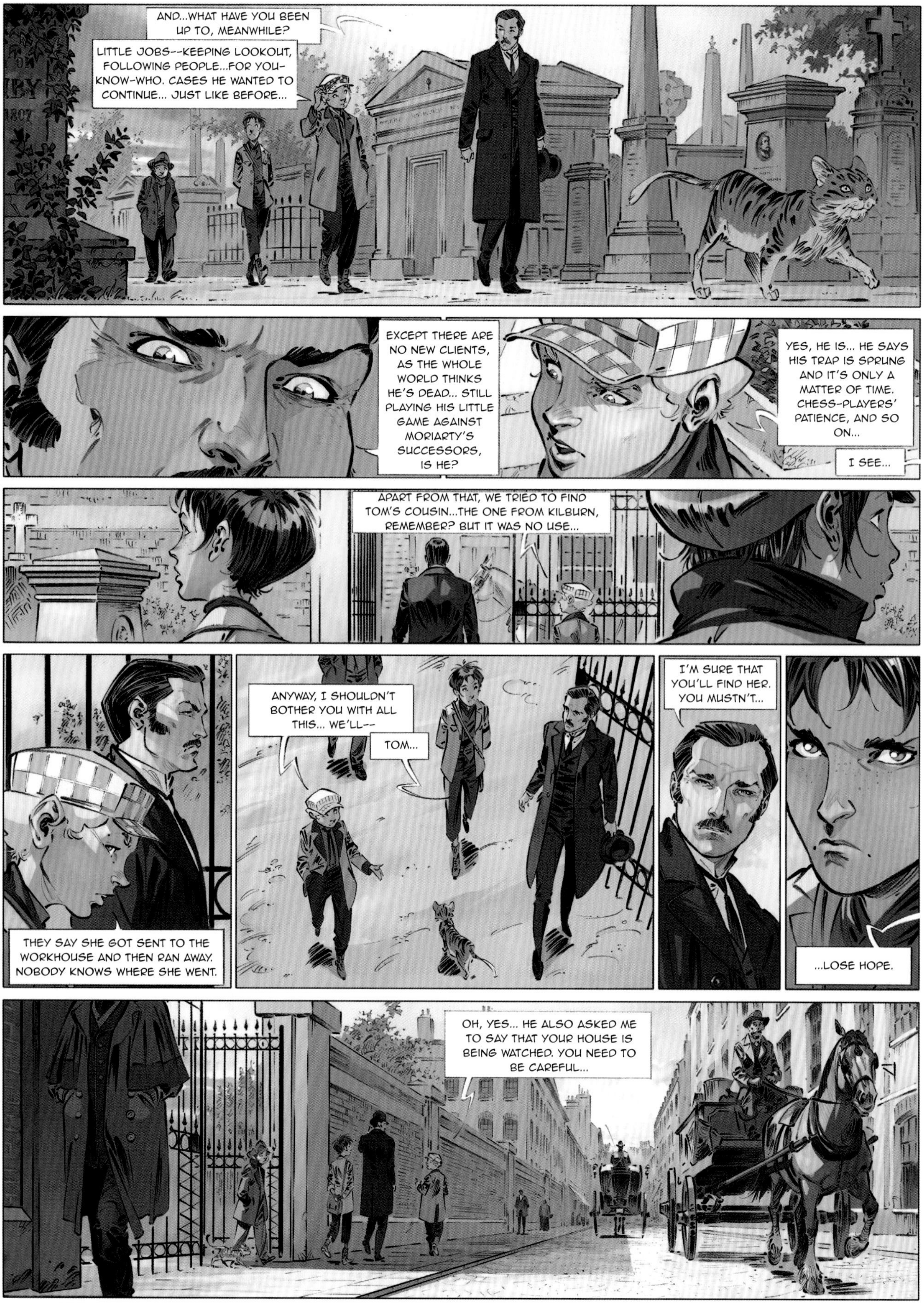
AND...WHAT HAVE YOU BEEN UP TO, MEANWHILE?
LITTLE JOBS--KEEPING LOOKOUT, FOLLOWING PEOPLE...FOR YOU-KNOW-WHO. CASES HE WANTED TO CONTINUE... JUST LIKE BEFORE...
EXCEPT THERE ARE NO NEW CLIENTS, AS THE WHOLE WORLD THINKS HE'S DEAD... STILL PLAYING HIS LITTLE GAME AGAINST MORIARTY'S SUCCESSORS, IS HE?
YES, HE IS... HE SAYS HIS TRAP IS SPRUNG AND IT'S ONLY A MATTER OF TIME. CHESS-PLAYERS' PATIENCE, AND SO ON...
I SEE...
APART FROM THAT, WE TRIED TO FIND TOM'S COUSIN...THE ONE FROM KILBURN, REMEMBER? BUT IT WAS NO USE...
THEY SAY SHE GOT SENT TO THE WORKHOUSE AND THEN RAN AWAY. NOBODY KNOWS WHERE SHE WENT.
ANYWAY, I SHOULDN'T BOTHER YOU WITH ALL THIS... WE'LL--
TOM...
I'M SURE THAT YOU'LL FIND HER. YOU MUSTN'T...
...LOSE HOPE.
OH, YES... HE ALSO ASKED ME TO SAY THAT YOUR HOUSE IS BEING WATCHED. YOU NEED TO BE CAREFUL...

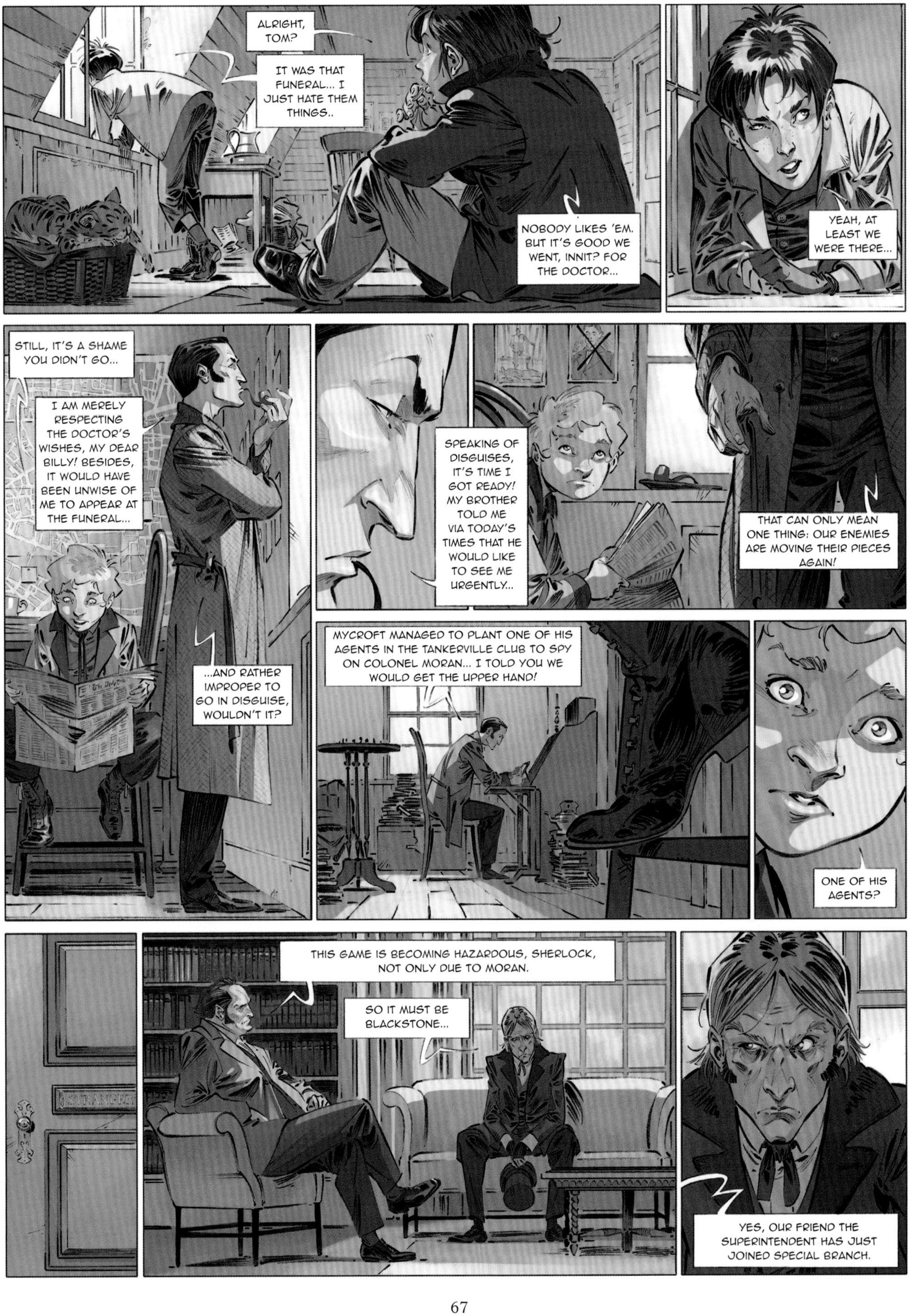
ALRIGHT, TOM?
IT WAS THAT FUNERAL... I JUST HATE THEM THINGS..
NOBODY LIKES 'EM. BUT IT'S GOOD WE WENT, INNIT? FOR THE DOCTOR...
YEAH, AT LEAST WE WERE THERE...
STILL, IT'S A SHAME YOU DIDN'T GO...
I AM MERELY RESPECTING THE DOCTOR'S WISHES, MY DEAR BILLY! BESIDES, IT WOULD HAVE BEEN UNWISE OF ME TO APPEAR AT THE FUNERAL...
...AND RATHER IMPROPER TO GO IN DISGUISE, WOULDN'T IT?
SPEAKING OF DISGUISES, IT'S TIME I GOT READY! MY BROTHER TOLD ME VIA TODAY'S TIMES THAT HE WOULD LIKE TO SEE ME URGENTLY...
THAT CAN ONLY MEAN ONE THING: OUR ENEMIES ARE MOVING THEIR PIECES AGAIN!
MYCROFT MANAGED TO PLANT ONE OF HIS AGENTS IN THE TANKERVILLE CLUB TO SPY ON COLONEL MORAN... I TOLD YOU WE WOULD GET THE UPPER HAND!
ONE OF HIS AGENTS?
STRANGER
THIS GAME IS BECOMING HAZARDOUS, SHERLOCK, NOT ONLY DUE TO MORAN.
SO IT MUST BE BLACKSTONE...
YES, OUR FRIEND THE SUPERINTENDENT HAS JUST JOINED SPECIAL BRANCH.

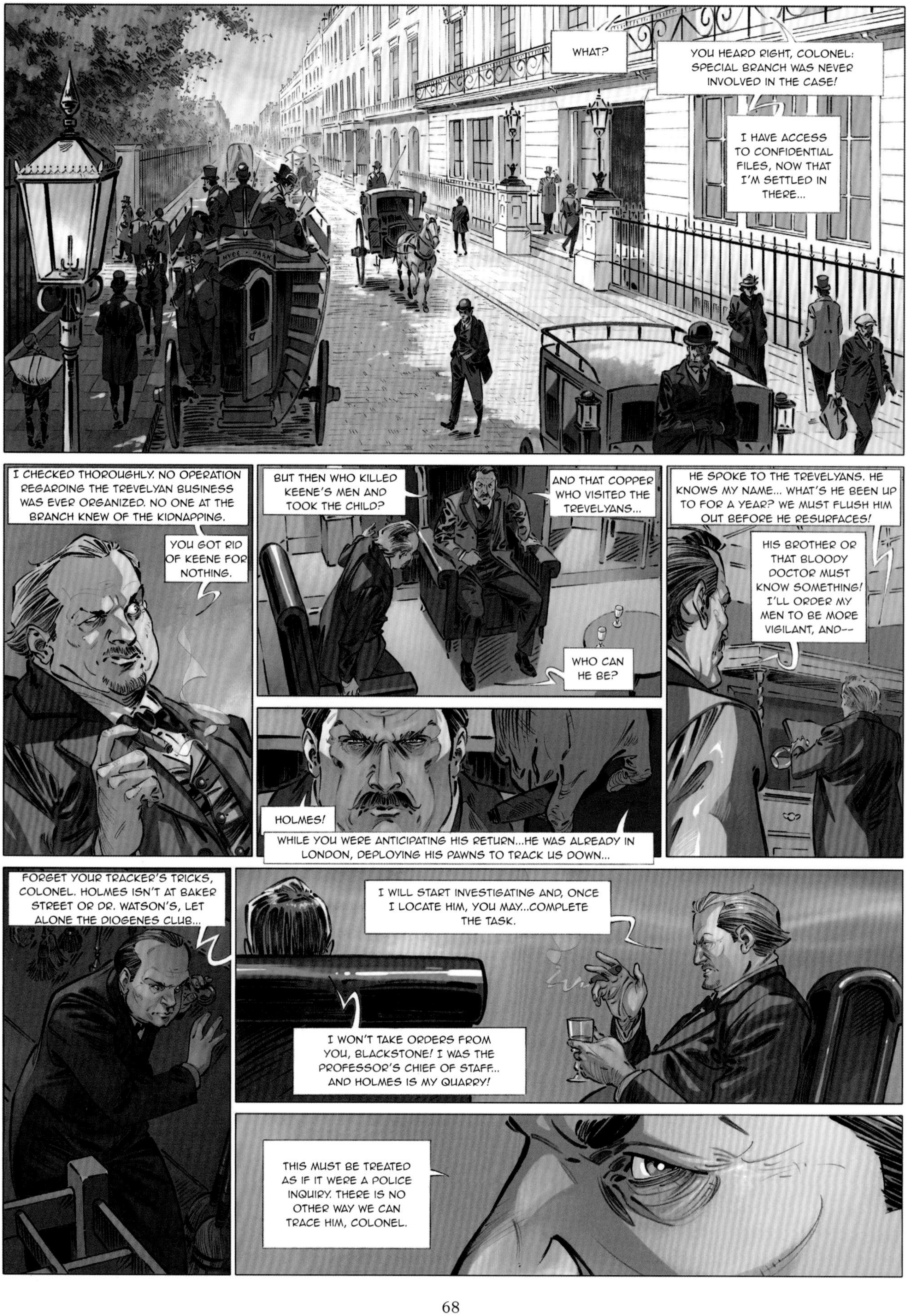
WHAT?
YOU HEARD RIGHT, COLONEL: SPECIAL BRANCH WAS NEVER INVOLVED IN THE CASE!
I HAVE ACCESS TO CONFIDENTIAL FILES, NOW THAT I'M SETTLED IN THERE...
I CHECKED THOROUGHLY. NO OPERATION REGARDING THE TREVELYAN BUSINESS WAS EVER ORGANIZED. NO ONE AT THE BRANCH KNEW OF THE KIDNAPPING.
YOU GOT RID OF KEENE FOR NOTHING.
BUT THEN WHO KILLED KEENE'S MEN AND TOOK THE CHILD?
AND THAT COPPER WHO VISITED THE TREVELYANS...
WHO CAN HE BE?
HOLMES!
WHILE YOU WERE ANTICIPATING HIS RETURN...HE WAS ALREADY IN LONDON, DEPLOYING HIS PAWNS TO TRACK US DOWN...
HE SPOKE TO THE TREVELYANS. HE KNOWS MY NAME... WHAT'S HE BEEN UP TO FOR A YEAR? WE MUST FLUSH HIM OUT BEFORE HE RESURFACES!
HIS BROTHER OR THAT BLOODY DOCTOR MUST KNOW SOMETHING! I'LL ORDER MY MEN TO BE MORE VIGILANT, AND--
FORGET YOUR TRACKER'S TRICKS, COLONEL. HOLMES ISN'T AT BAKER STREET OR DR. WATSON'S, LET ALONE THE DIOGENES CLUB...
I WILL START INVESTIGATING AND, ONCE I LOCATE HIM, YOU MAY...COMPLETE THE TASK.
I WON'T TAKE ORDERS FROM YOU, BLACKSTONE! I WAS THE PROFESSOR'S CHIEF OF STAFF... AND HOLMES IS MY QUARRY!
THIS MUST BE TREATED AS IF IT WERE A POLICE INQUIRY. THERE IS NO OTHER WAY WE CAN TRACE HIM, COLONEL.

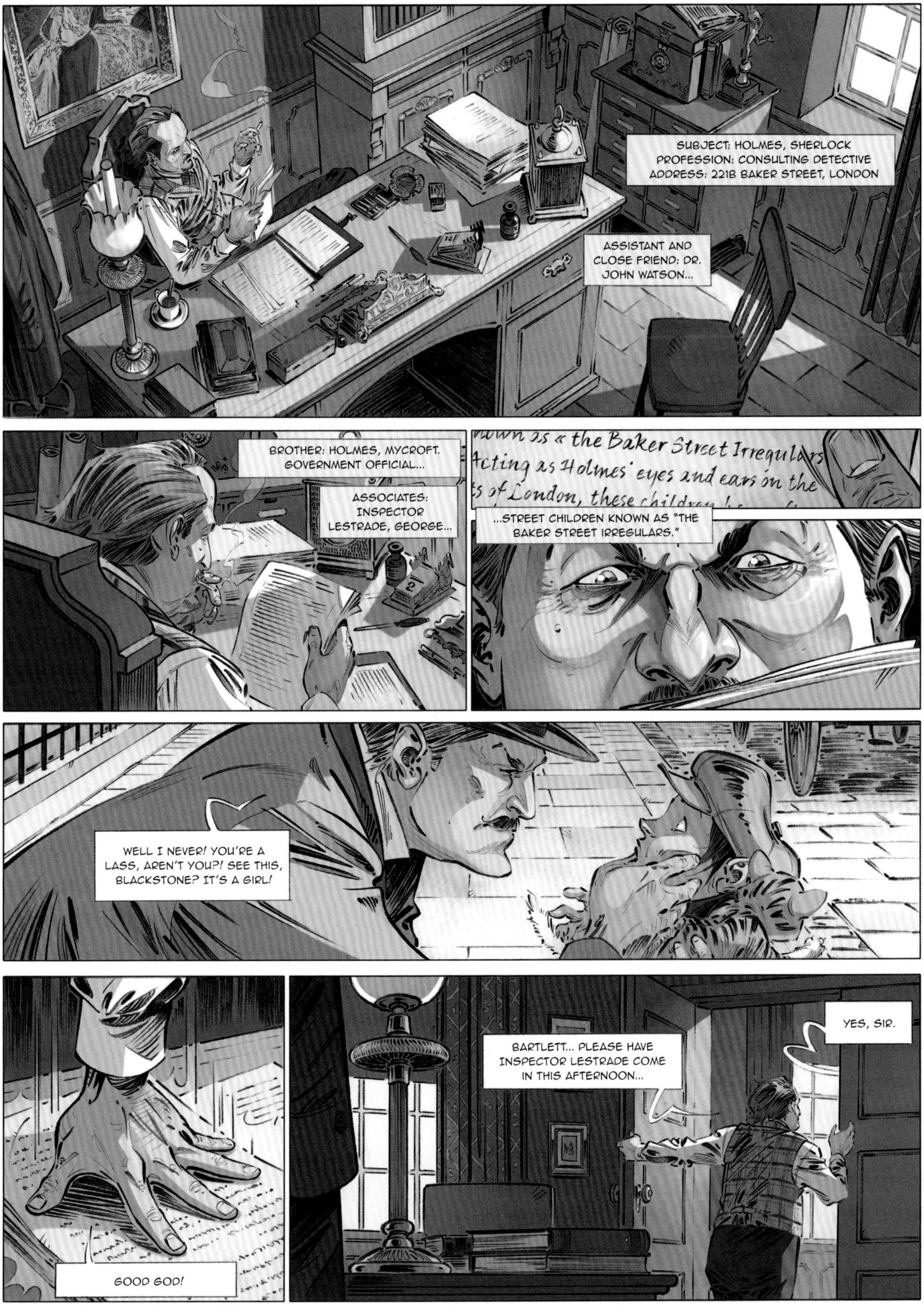
SUBJECT: HOLMES, SHERLOCK
PROFESSION: CONSULTING DETECTIVE
ADDRESS: 221B BAKER STREET, LONDON
ASSISTANT AND CLOSE FRIEND: DR. JOHN WATSON...
BROTHER: HOLMES, MYCROFT. GOVERNMENT OFFICIAL...
ASSOCIATES: INSPECTOR LESTRADE, GEORGE...
« the Baker Street Irregul
Acting as Holmes' eyes and ears on the
of London, these children
...STREET CHILDREN KNOWN AS "THE BAKER STREET IRREGULARS."
WELL I NEVER! YOU'RE A LASS, AREN'T YOU?! SEE THIS, BLACKSTONE? IT'S A GIRL!
GOOD GOD!
BARTLETT... PLEASE HAVE INSPECTOR LESTRADE COME IN THIS AFTERNOON...
YES, SIR.

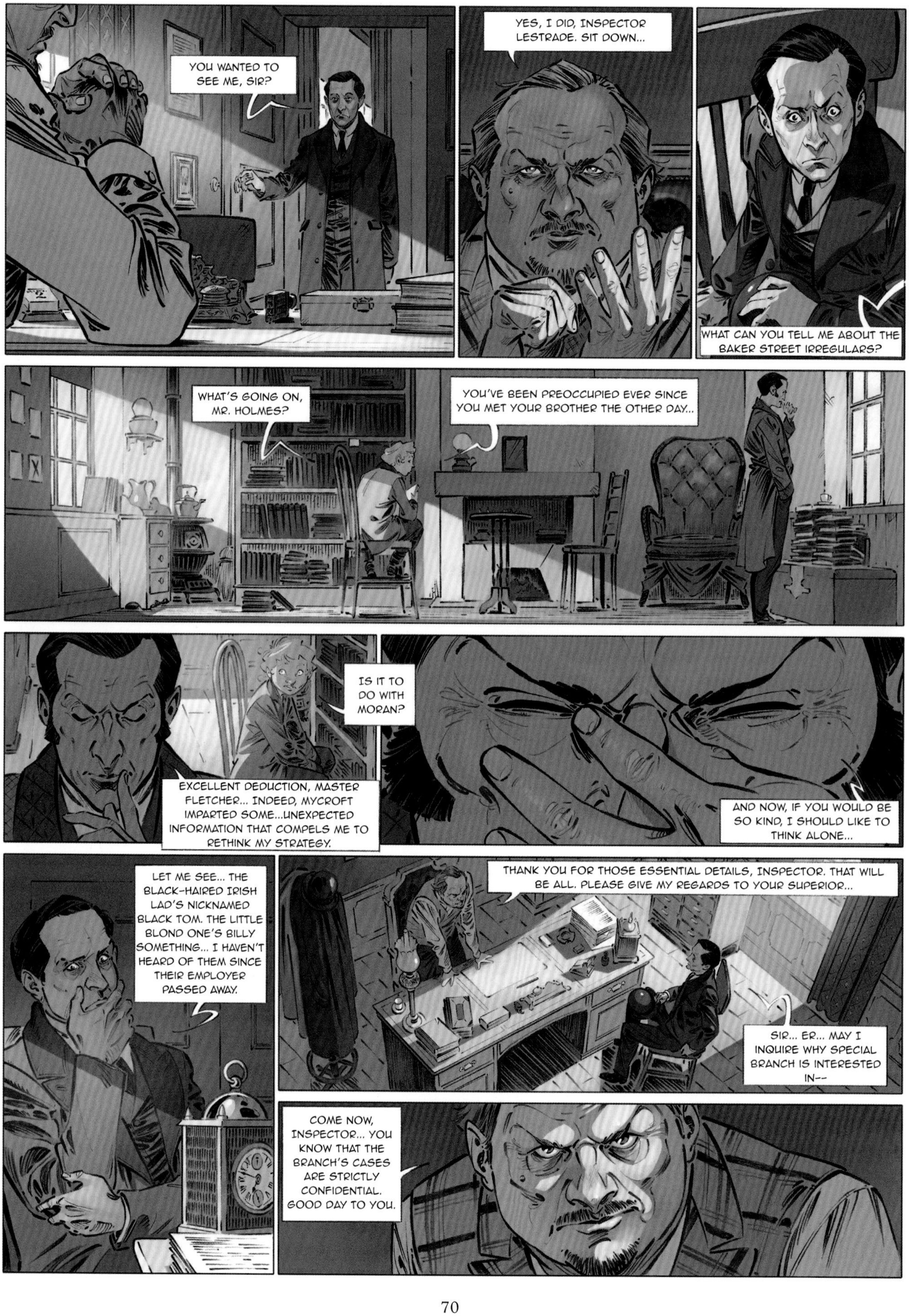
YOU WANTED TO SEE ME, SIR?
YES, I DID, INSPECTOR LESTRADE. SIT DOWN...
WHAT CAN YOU TELL ME ABOUT THE BAKER STREET IRREGULARS?
WHAT'S GOING ON, MR. HOLMES?
YOU'VE BEEN PREOCCUPIED EVER SINCE YOU MET YOUR BROTHER THE OTHER DAY...
IS IT TO DO WITH MORAN?
EXCELLENT DEDUCTION, MASTER FLETCHER... INDEED, MYCROFT IMPARTED SOME...UNEXPECTED INFORMATION THAT COMPELS ME TO RETHINK MY STRATEGY.
AND NOW, IF YOU WOULD BE SO KIND, I SHOULD LIKE TO THINK ALONE...
LET ME SEE... THE BLACK-HAIRED IRISH LAD'S NICKNAMED BLACK TOM. THE LITTLE BLOND ONE'S BILLY SOMETHING... I HAVEN'T HEARD OF THEM SINCE THEIR EMPLOYER PASSED AWAY.
THANK YOU FOR THOSE ESSENTIAL DETAILS, INSPECTOR. THAT WILL BE ALL. PLEASE GIVE MY REGARDS TO YOUR SUPERIOR...
SIR... ER... MAY I INQUIRE WHY SPECIAL BRANCH IS INTERESTED IN--
COME NOW, INSPECTOR... YOU KNOW THAT THE BRANCH'S CASES ARE STRICTLY CONFIDENTIAL. GOOD DAY TO YOU.

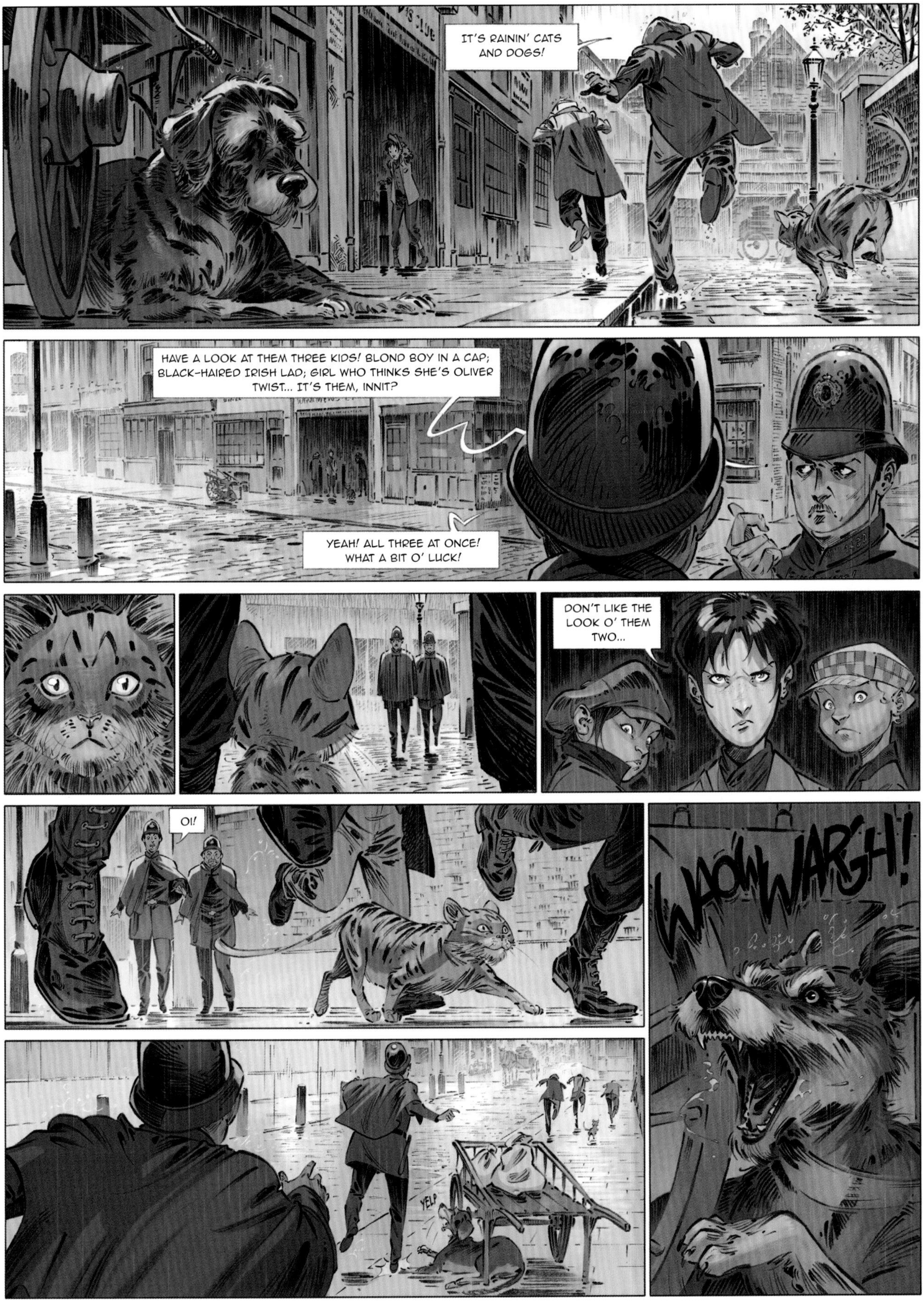
IT'S RAININ' CATS AND DOGS!
HAVE A LOOK AT THEM THREE KIDS! BLOND BOY IN A CAP; BLACK-HAIRED IRISH LAD; GIRL WHO THINKS SHE'S OLIVER TWIST... IT'S THEM, INNIT?
YEAH! ALL THREE AT ONCE! WHAT A BIT O' LUCK!
DON'T LIKE THE LOOK O' THEM TWO...
OI!
WAOWWARGH!
YELP

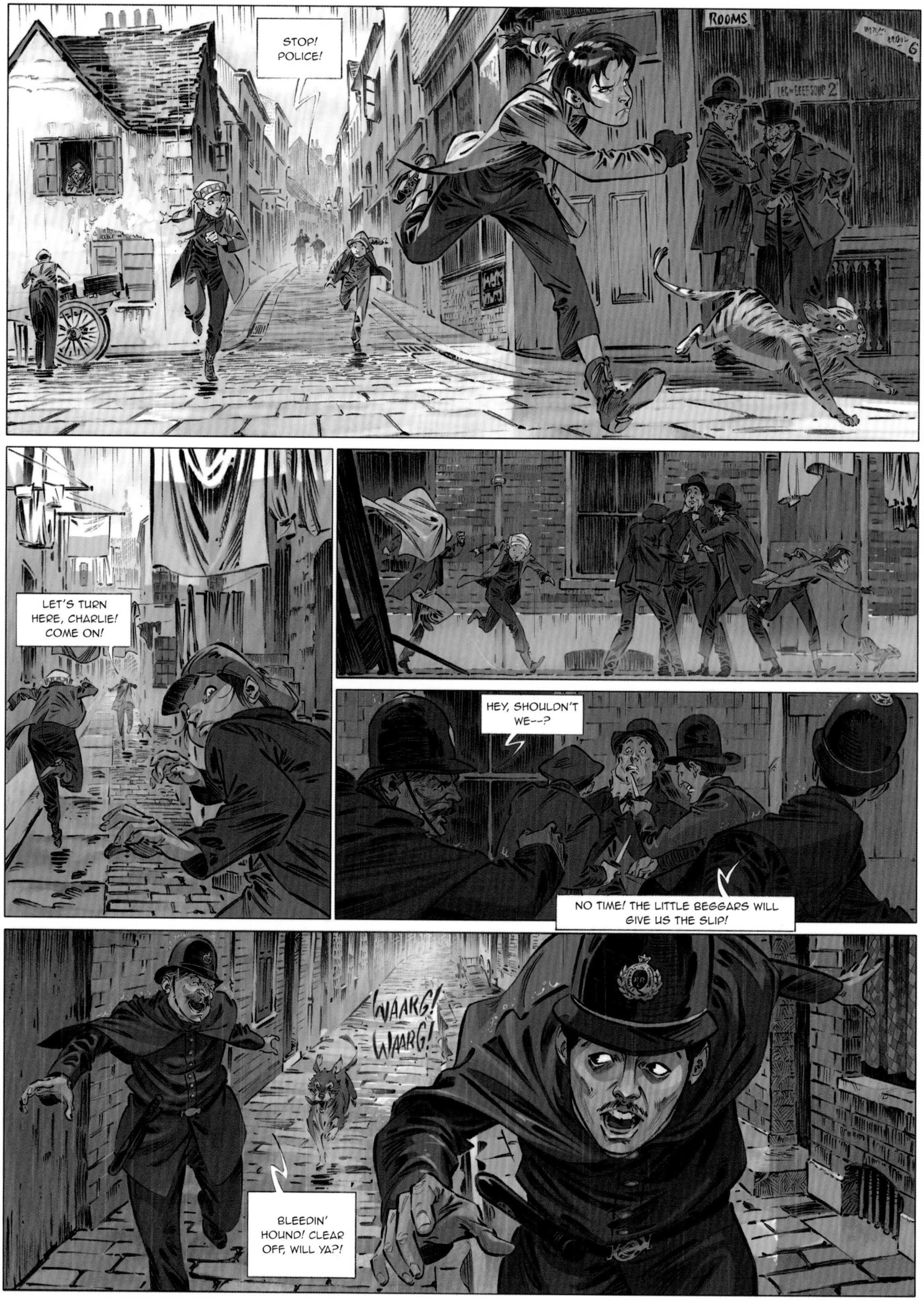
STOP! POLICE!
ROOMS
LET'S TURN HERE, CHARLIE! COME ON!
HEY, SHOULDN'T WE--?
NO TIME! THE LITTLE BEGGARS WILL GIVE US THE SLIP!
WAARG! WAARG!
BLEEDIN' HOUND! CLEAR OFF, WILL YA?!

BLOODY MONGREL! WE WERE THIS CLOSE TO NABBIN' THEM!

YELP!

DON'T WORRY... THEY CAN'T RUN FOREVER!

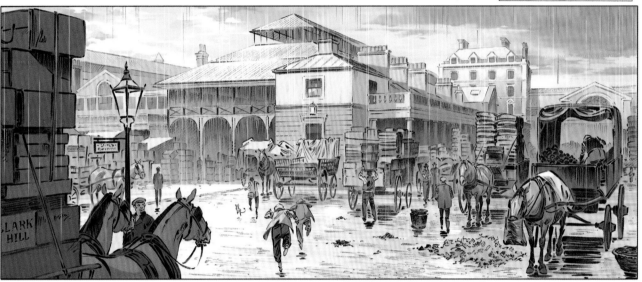

RIGHT, WE'VE LOST THAT PAIR O' CHUMPS...

WHAT DID THEM LOONIES WANT WITH US? WE AIN'T DONE NOTHIN', FOR ONCE...

I SHOULD TELL YOU SOMETHING... MAYBE IT'S NOTHING, BUT...

YEAH, IT'S WEIRD... DID YA SEE HOW THEY STARED AT US BEFORE THEY RAN? IT WAS LIKE THEY RECOGNIZED US...

REMEMBER BLACKSTONE, THE BLOKE FROM THE FIRM WITH MORAN OUTSIDE THE TANKERVILLE?

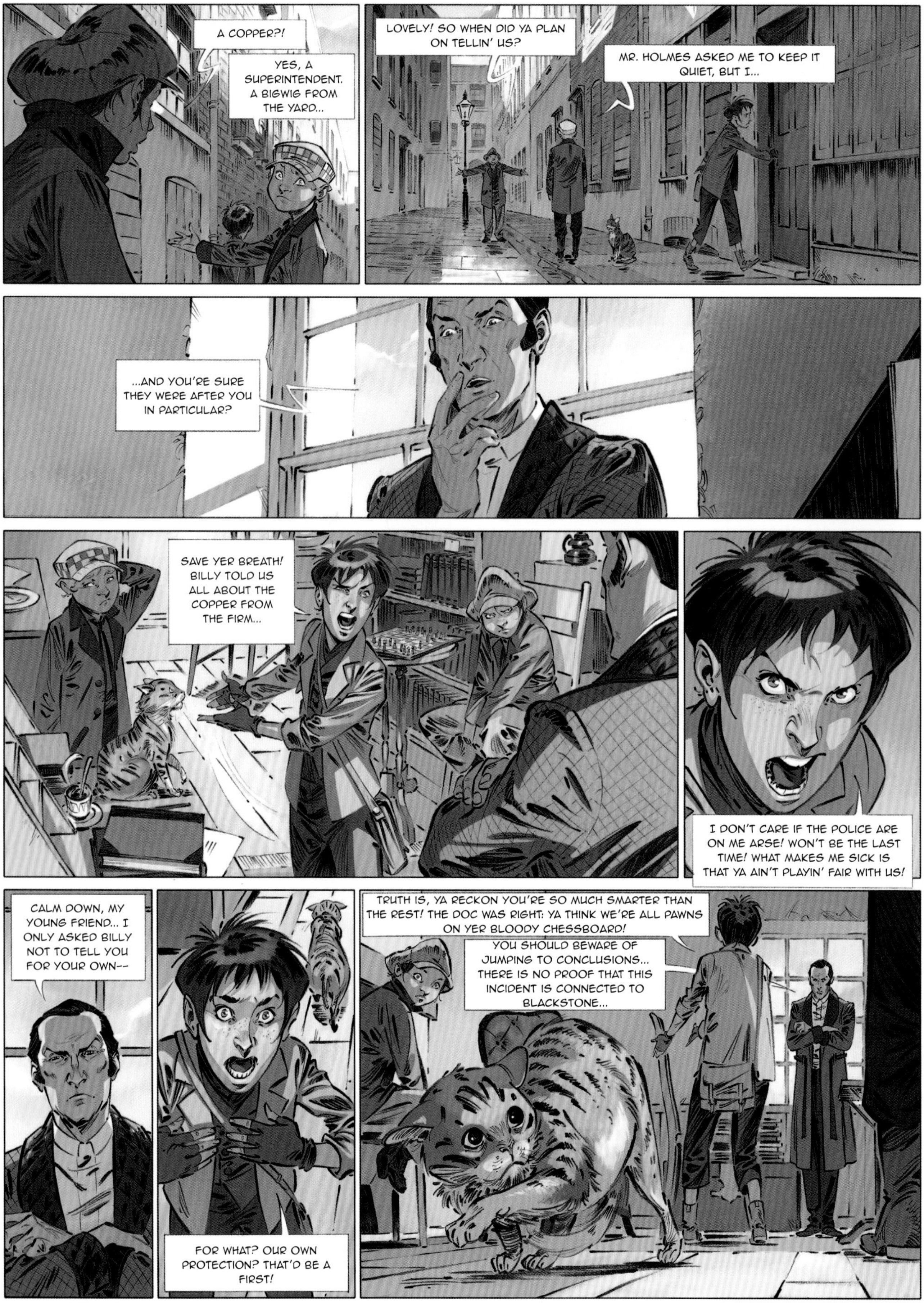
A COPPER?!
YES, A SUPERINTENDENT. A BIGWIG FROM THE YARD...
LOVELY! SO WHEN DID YA PLAN ON TELLIN' US?
MR. HOLMES ASKED ME TO KEEP IT QUIET, BUT I...
...AND YOU'RE SURE THEY WERE AFTER YOU IN PARTICULAR?
SAVE YER BREATH! BILLY TOLD US ALL ABOUT THE COPPER FROM THE FIRM...
I DON'T CARE IF THE POLICE ARE ON ME ARSE! WON'T BE THE LAST TIME! WHAT MAKES ME SICK IS THAT YA AIN'T PLAYIN' FAIR WITH US!
CALM DOWN, MY YOUNG FRIEND... I ONLY ASKED BILLY NOT TO TELL YOU FOR YOUR OWN--
FOR WHAT? OUR OWN PROTECTION? THAT'D BE A FIRST!
TRUTH IS, YA RECKON YOU'RE SO MUCH SMARTER THAN THE REST! THE DOC WAS RIGHT: YA THINK WE'RE ALL PAWNS ON YER BLOODY CHESSBOARD!
YOU SHOULD BEWARE OF JUMPING TO CONCLUSIONS... THERE IS NO PROOF THAT THIS INCIDENT IS CONNECTED TO BLACKSTONE...

INSPECTOR BRADDOCK, SIR... ABOUT YOUR MEMORANDUM...ON THOSE THREE BRATS... I KNOW ONE OF THEM.

THE IRISH KID, "BLACK TOM"... REAL NAME'S TOMMY O'ROURKE, A MASTER BURGLAR.

I NICKED HIM WHEN I WAS WORKING IN KILBURN, BUT THE BASTARD SLIPPED THROUGH MY FINGERS.

WHAT EXACTLY IS THIS "MATTER OF NATIONAL CONCERN"?

THAT'S TOP SECRET, INSPECTOR... SUFFICE TO SAY THAT THIS IRISH BOY AND HIS FRIENDS COULD HELP LEAD US TO A DEADLY UNDERGROUND ORGANIZATION...

DOCTOR WATSON...

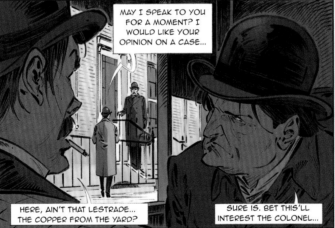

MAY I SPEAK TO YOU FOR A MOMENT? I WOULD LIKE YOUR OPINION ON A CASE...

HERE, AIN'T THAT LESTRADE... THE COPPER FROM THE YARD?

SURE IS. BET THIS'LL INTEREST THE COLONEL...

THE ENTIRE METROPOLITAN POLICE ARE AFTER THEM... ORDERS FROM SPECIAL BRANCH!

AND YOU REALLY THINK THESE KIDS CAN LEAD US TO HOLMES?

AND LESTRADE? HE HADN'T SEEN WATSON FOR OVER A YEAR, THEN SUDDENLY--

OF COURSE! THEY'VE BEEN HIS EYES AND EARS SINCE HE GOT BACK TO LONDON... BUT NOW WE'VE IDENTIFIED THEM, THE GAME CHANGES.

I REPEAT: EVERYTHING IS UNDER CONTROL! HAVE PATIENCE, COLONEL... YOU'LL SOON HAVE HOLMES IN YOUR SIGHTS. UNTIL THEN, NO RECKLESS MANEUVERS!

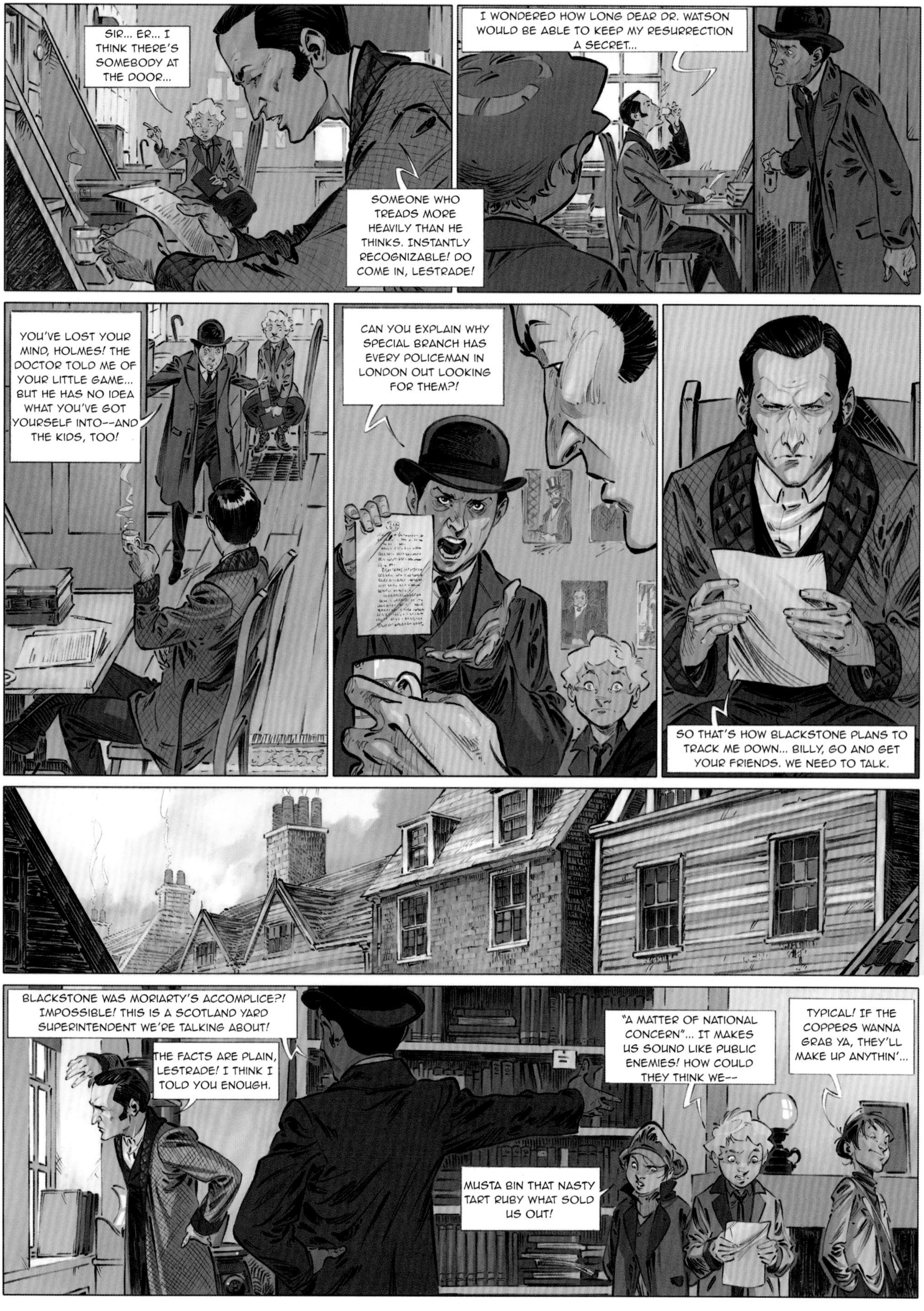
SIR... ER... I THINK THERE'S SOMEBODY AT THE DOOR...
SOMEONE WHO TREADS MORE HEAVILY THAN HE THINKS. INSTANTLY RECOGNIZABLE! DO COME IN, LESTRADE!
I WONDERED HOW LONG DEAR DR. WATSON WOULD BE ABLE TO KEEP MY RESURRECTION A SECRET...
YOU'VE LOST YOUR MIND, HOLMES! THE DOCTOR TOLD ME OF YOUR LITTLE GAME... BUT HE HAS NO IDEA WHAT YOU'VE GOT YOURSELF INTO--AND THE KIDS, TOO!
CAN YOU EXPLAIN WHY SPECIAL BRANCH HAS EVERY POLICEMAN IN LONDON OUT LOOKING FOR THEM?!
SO THAT'S HOW BLACKSTONE PLANS TO TRACK ME DOWN... BILLY, GO AND GET YOUR FRIENDS. WE NEED TO TALK.
BLACKSTONE WAS MORIARTY'S ACCOMPLICE?! IMPOSSIBLE! THIS IS A SCOTLAND YARD SUPERINTENDENT WE'RE TALKING ABOUT!
THE FACTS ARE PLAIN, LESTRADE! I THINK I TOLD YOU ENOUGH.
"A MATTER OF NATIONAL CONCERN"... IT MAKES US SOUND LIKE PUBLIC ENEMIES! HOW COULD THEY THINK WE--
TYPICAL! IF THE COPPERS WANNA GRAB YA, THEY'LL MAKE UP ANYTHIN'...
MUSTA BIN THAT NASTY TART RUBY WHAT SOLD US OUT!

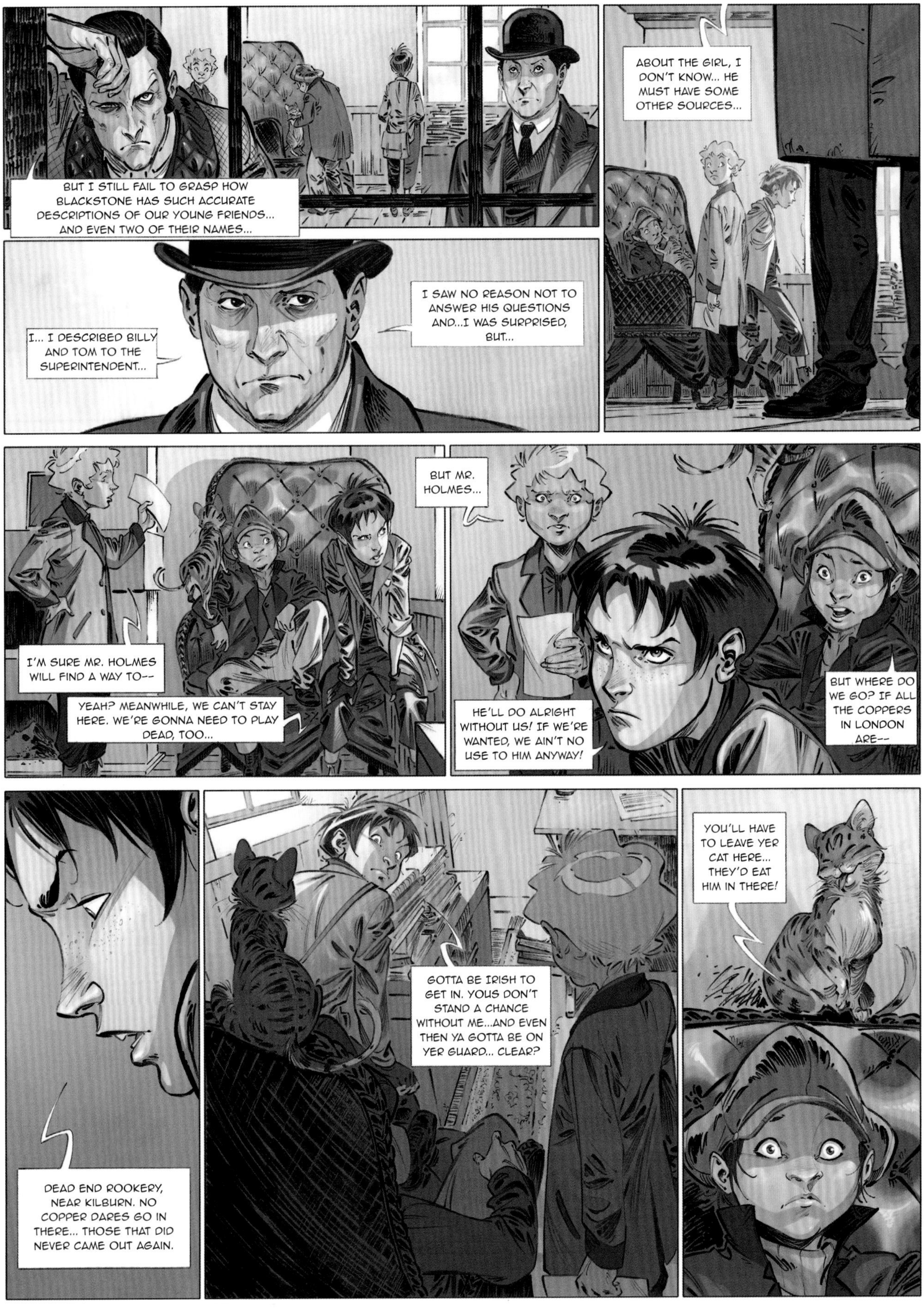
BUT I STILL FAIL TO GRASP HOW BLACKSTONE HAS SUCH ACCURATE DESCRIPTIONS OF OUR YOUNG FRIENDS... AND EVEN TWO OF THEIR NAMES...
I... I DESCRIBED BILLY AND TOM TO THE SUPERINTENDENT...
I SAW NO REASON NOT TO ANSWER HIS QUESTIONS AND...I WAS SURPRISED, BUT...
ABOUT THE GIRL, I DON'T KNOW... HE MUST HAVE SOME OTHER SOURCES...
I'M SURE MR. HOLMES WILL FIND A WAY TO--
YEAH? MEANWHILE, WE CAN'T STAY HERE. WE'RE GONNA NEED TO PLAY DEAD, TOO...
BUT MR. HOLMES...
HE'LL DO ALRIGHT WITHOUT US! IF WE'RE WANTED, WE AIN'T NO USE TO HIM ANYWAY!
BUT WHERE DO WE GO? IF ALL THE COPPERS IN LONDON ARE--
DEAD END ROOKERY, NEAR KILBURN. NO COPPER DARES GO IN THERE... THOSE THAT DID NEVER CAME OUT AGAIN.
GOTTA BE IRISH TO GET IN. YOUS DON'T STAND A CHANCE WITHOUT ME...AND EVEN THEN YA GOTTA BE ON YER GUARD... CLEAR?
YOU'LL HAVE TO LEAVE YER CAT HERE... THEY'D EAT HIM IN THERE!

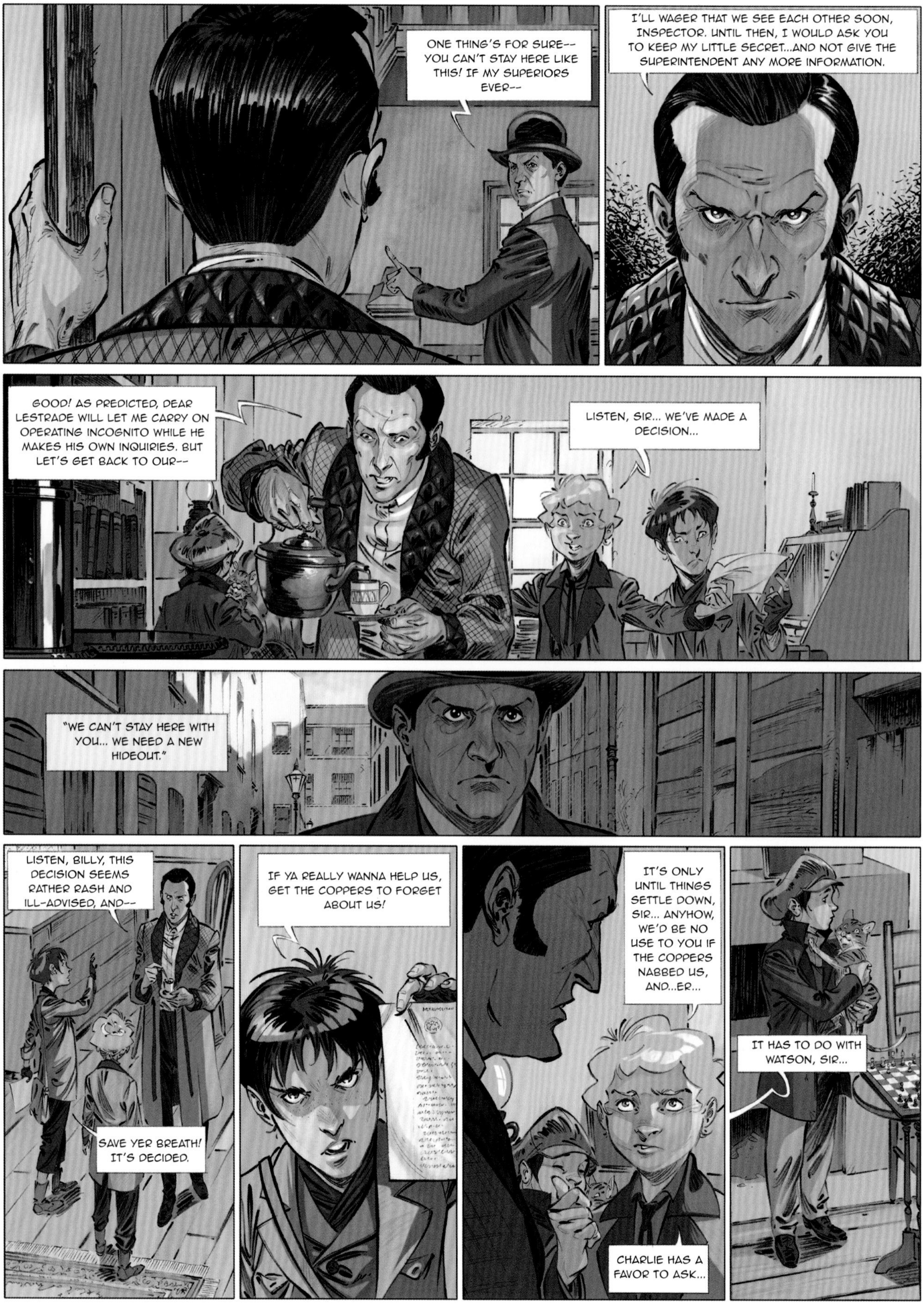
ONE THING'S FOR SURE-- YOU CAN'T STAY HERE LIKE THIS! IF MY SUPERIORS EVER--
I'LL WAGER THAT WE SEE EACH OTHER SOON, INSPECTOR. UNTIL THEN, I WOULD ASK YOU TO KEEP MY LITTLE SECRET...AND NOT GIVE THE SUPERINTENDENT ANY MORE INFORMATION.
GOOD! AS PREDICTED, DEAR LESTRADE WILL LET ME CARRY ON OPERATING INCOGNITO WHILE HE MAKES HIS OWN INQUIRIES. BUT LET'S GET BACK TO OUR--
LISTEN, SIR... WE'VE MADE A DECISION...
"WE CAN'T STAY HERE WITH YOU... WE NEED A NEW HIDEOUT."
LISTEN, BILLY, THIS DECISION SEEMS RATHER RASH AND ILL-ADVISED, AND--
SAVE YER BREATH! IT'S DECIDED.
IF YA REALLY WANNA HELP US, GET THE COPPERS TO FORGET ABOUT US!
IT'S ONLY UNTIL THINGS SETTLE DOWN, SIR... ANYHOW, WE'D BE NO USE TO YOU IF THE COPPERS NABBED US, AND...ER...
CHARLIE HAS A FAVOR TO ASK...
IT HAS TO DO WITH WATSON, SIR...

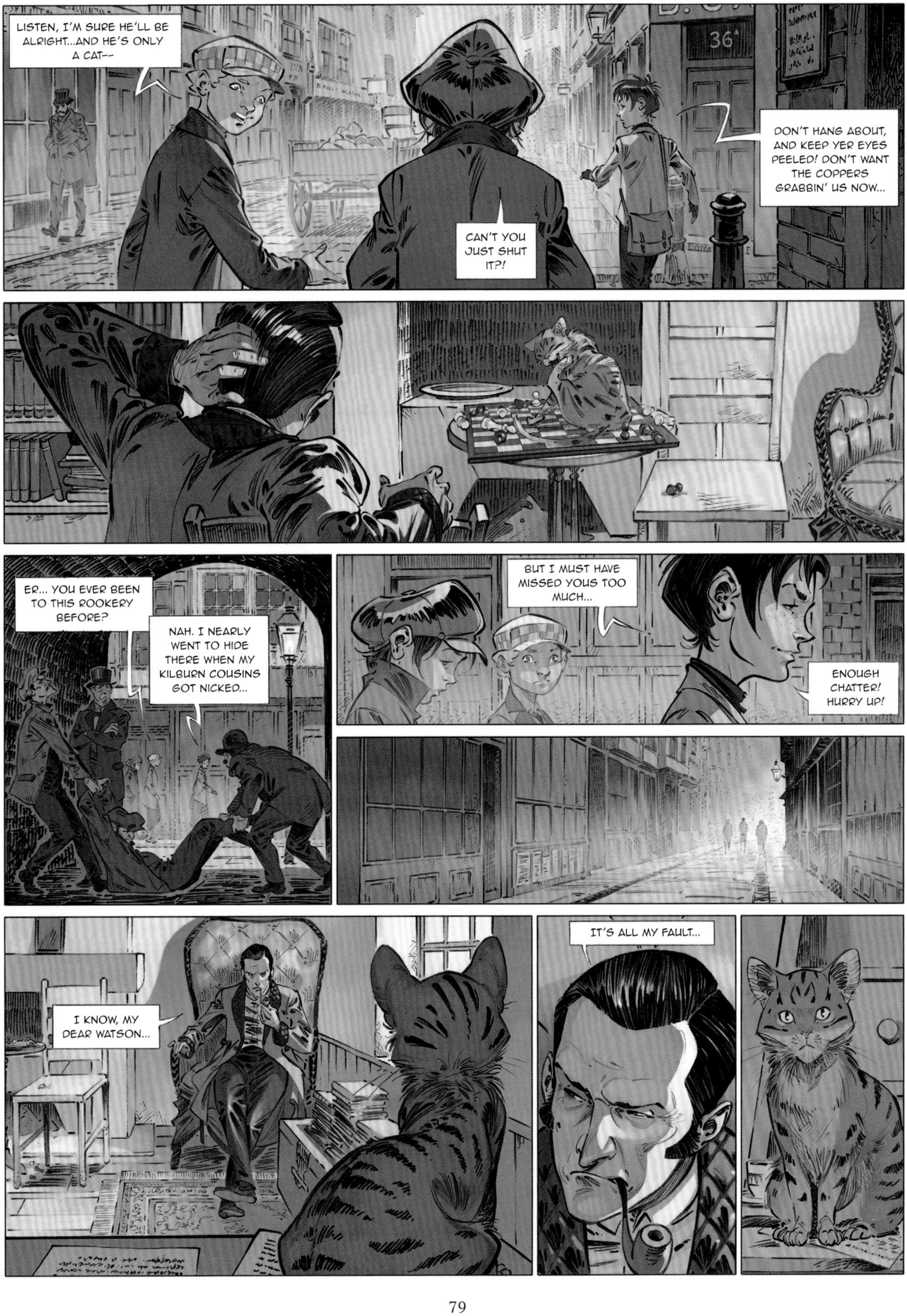
LISTEN, I'M SURE HE'LL BE ALRIGHT...AND HE'S ONLY A CAT--
DON'T HANG ABOUT, AND KEEP YER EYES PEELED! DON'T WANT THE COPPERS GRABBIN' US NOW...
CAN'T YOU JUST SHUT IT?!
ER... YOU EVER BEEN TO THIS ROOKERY BEFORE?
NAH. I NEARLY WENT TO HIDE THERE WHEN MY KILBURN COUSINS GOT NICKED...
BUT I MUST HAVE MISSED YOUS TOO MUCH...
ENOUGH CHATTER! HURRY UP!
I KNOW, MY DEAR WATSON...
IT'S ALL MY FAULT...

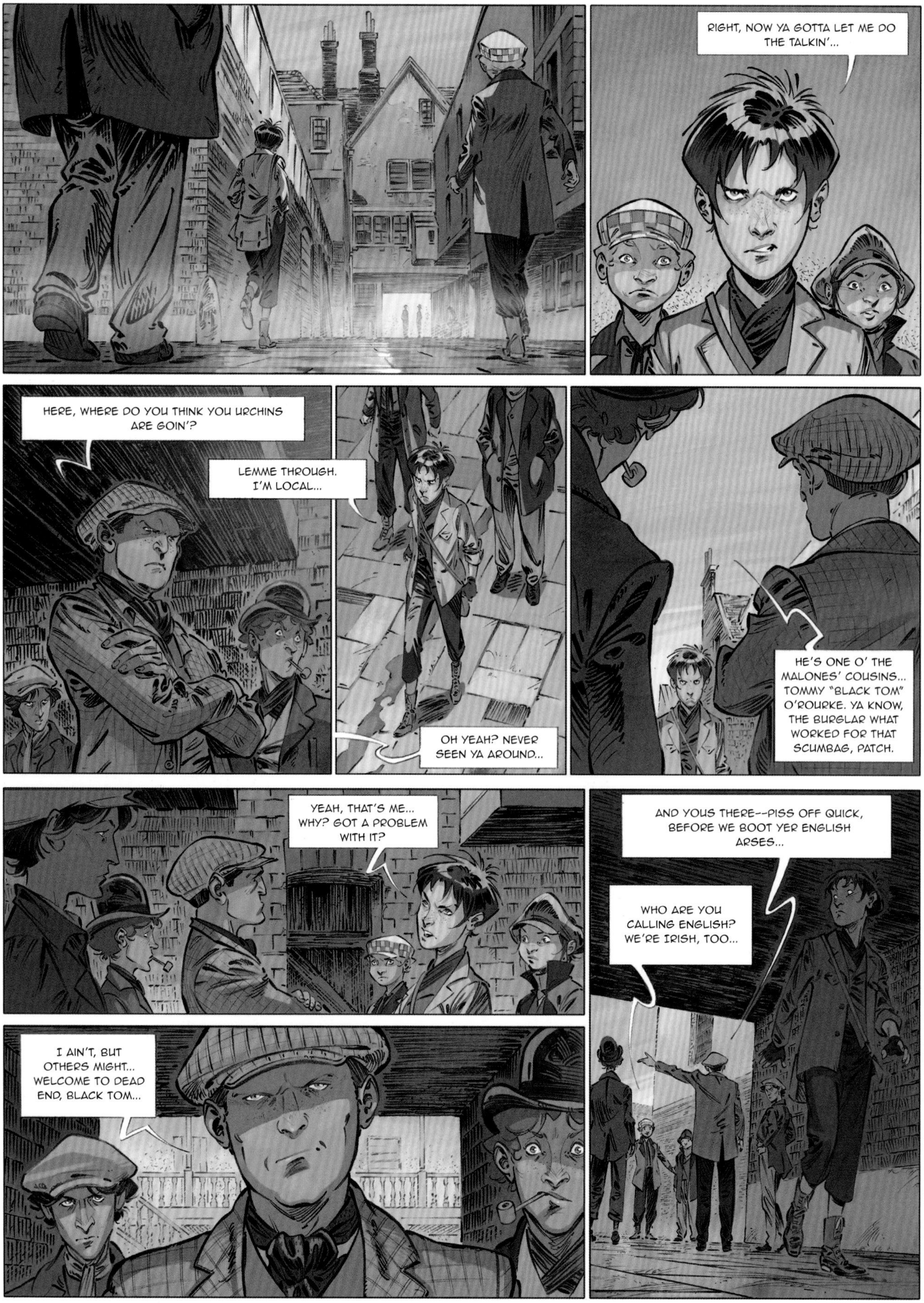
RIGHT, NOW YA GOTTA LET ME DO THE TALKIN'...
HERE, WHERE DO YOU THINK YOU URCHINS ARE GOIN'?
LEMME THROUGH. I'M LOCAL...
OH YEAH? NEVER SEEN YA AROUND...
HE'S ONE O' THE MALONES' COUSINS... TOMMY "BLACK TOM" O'ROURKE. YA KNOW, THE BURGLAR WHAT WORKED FOR THAT SCUMBAG, PATCH.
YEAH, THAT'S ME... WHY? GOT A PROBLEM WITH IT?
I AIN'T, BUT OTHERS MIGHT... WELCOME TO DEAD END, BLACK TOM...
AND YOUS THERE--PISS OFF QUICK, BEFORE WE BOOT YER ENGLISH ARSES...
WHO ARE YOU CALLING ENGLISH? WE'RE IRISH, TOO...

YEAH, RIGHT! AND MY DA'S THE ARCHBISHOP O' CANTERBURY!

HUH! D'YA WANT US TO SING YA SONGS FROM THE OL' COUNTRY, WHILE WE'RE AT IT?

THEY'RE WITH ME, RIGHT? I'M UP TO HERE WITH YER DOORMAN ROUTINE... GET YER MATES OUTTA THE WAY!

WHY DON'T YA SHUT YER BIG TRAP?!

TOM?!

KITTY?

TOM! WHAT ARE YOU DOIN' HERE?

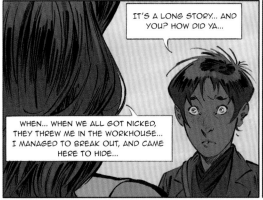

IT'S A LONG STORY... AND YOU? HOW DID YA...

WHEN... WHEN WE ALL GOT NICKED, THEY THREW ME IN THE WORKHOUSE... I MANAGED TO BREAK OUT, AND CAME HERE TO HIDE...

I HAD NOWHERE TO GO...

HEAR THAT, CHARLIE? SHE DID A BUNK, JUST LIKE YOU...

CHARLIE...AND BILLY, IS IT? TOM TOLD ME SO MUCH ABOUT YOUS...

HELLO... WE HEARD A LOT ABOUT YOU, TOO...

I DIDN'T THINK I'D SEE YA AGAIN...

IT'S A HUGE STROKE OF LUCK!

BUT NOT FOR EV'RYONE, BY THE LOOKS OF IT...

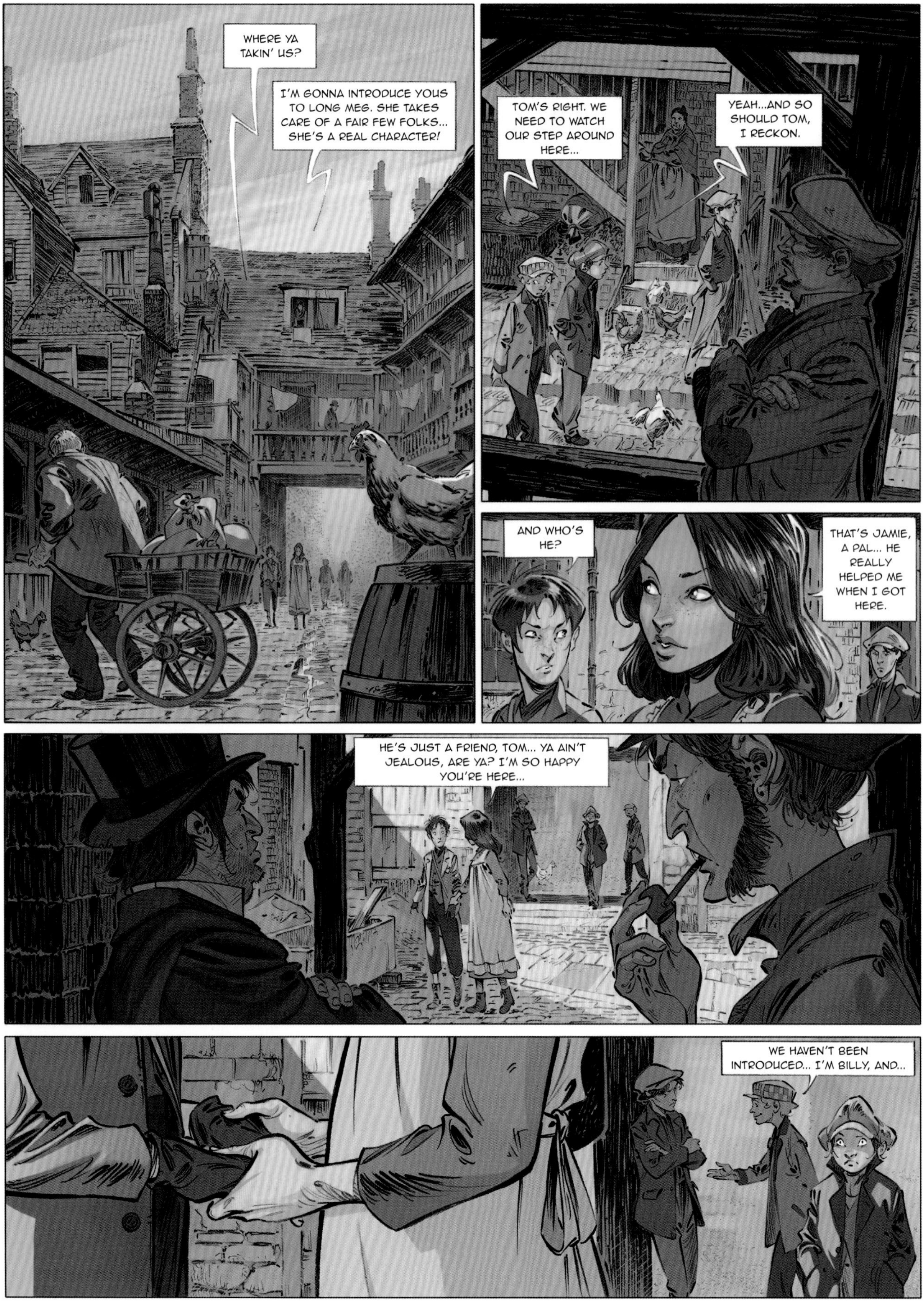
WHERE YA TAKIN' US?
I'M GONNA INTRODUCE YOUS TO LONG MEG. SHE TAKES CARE OF A FAIR FEW FOLKS... SHE'S A REAL CHARACTER!
TOM'S RIGHT. WE NEED TO WATCH OUR STEP AROUND HERE...
YEAH...AND SO SHOULD TOM, I RECKON.
AND WHO'S HE?
THAT'S JAMIE, A PAL... HE REALLY HELPED ME WHEN I GOT HERE.
HE'S JUST A FRIEND, TOM... YA AIN'T JEALOUS, ARE YA? I'M SO HAPPY YOU'RE HERE...
WE HAVEN'T BEEN INTRODUCED... I'M BILLY, AND...

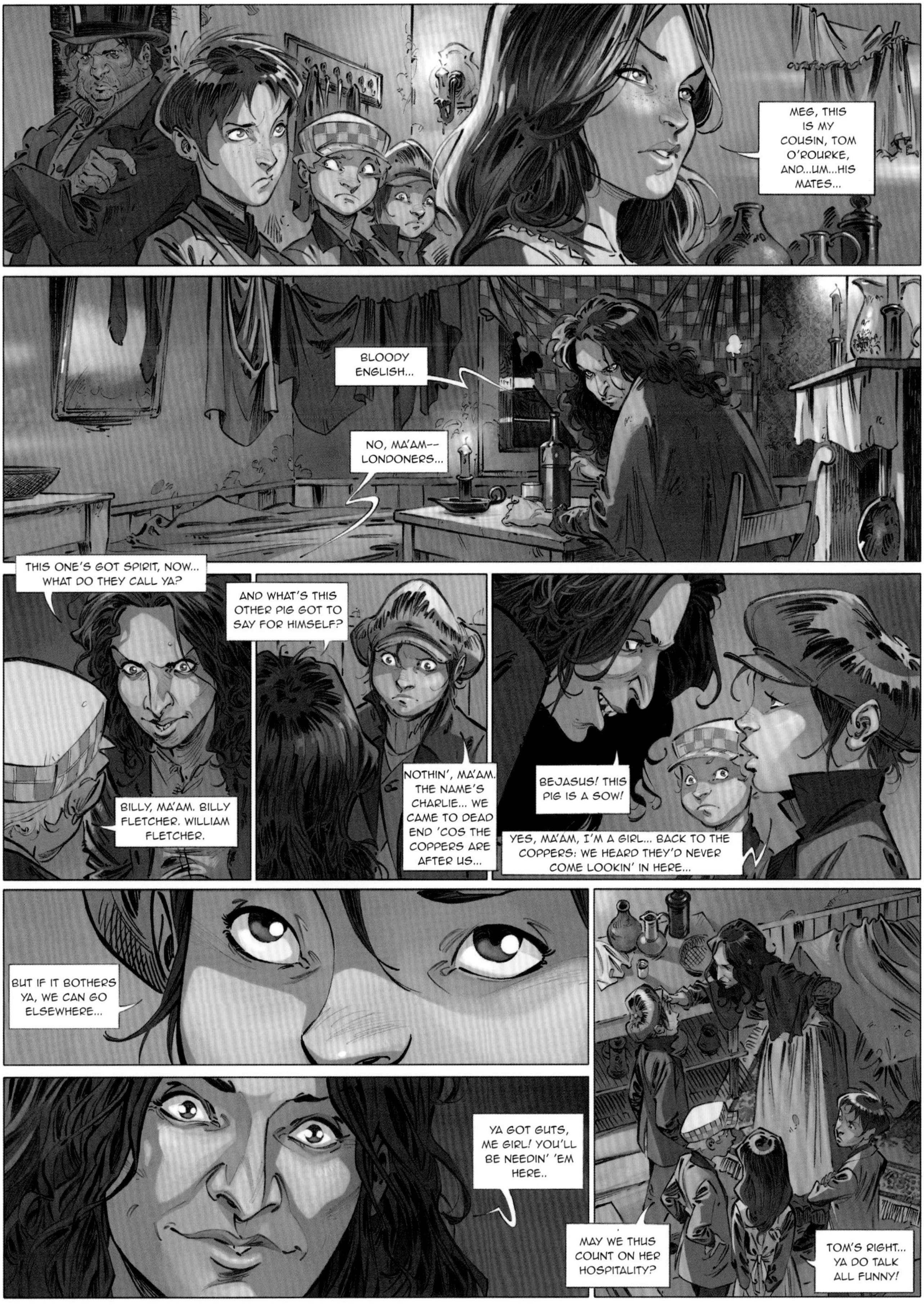
MEG, THIS IS MY COUSIN, TOM O'ROURKE, AND...UM...HIS MATES...
BLOODY ENGLISH...
NO, MA'AM-- LONDONERS...
THIS ONE'S GOT SPIRIT, NOW... WHAT DO THEY CALL YA?
BILLY, MA'AM. BILLY FLETCHER. WILLIAM FLETCHER.
AND WHAT'S THIS OTHER PIG GOT TO SAY FOR HIMSELF?
NOTHIN', MA'AM. THE NAME'S CHARLIE... WE CAME TO DEAD END 'COS THE COPPERS ARE AFTER US...
BEJASUS! THIS PIG IS A SOW!
YES, MA'AM, I'M A GIRL... BACK TO THE COPPERS: WE HEARD THEY'D NEVER COME LOOKIN' IN HERE...
BUT IF IT BOTHERS YA, WE CAN GO ELSEWHERE...
YA GOT GUTS, ME GIRL! YOU'LL BE NEEDIN' 'EM HERE..
MAY WE THUS COUNT ON HER HOSPITALITY?
TOM'S RIGHT... YA DO TALK ALL FUNNY!

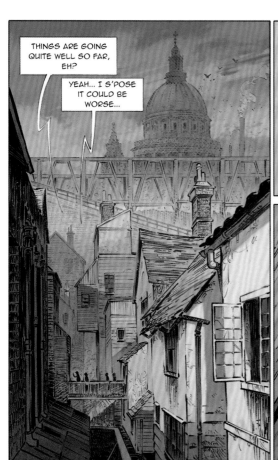

THINGS ARE GOING QUITE WELL SO FAR, EH?

YEAH... I S'POSE IT COULD BE WORSE...

FOR TOM, THINGS ARE LOOKING--

CAREFUL, ME LAD!

BILLY! LOOK OUT!

WHACK

ALRIGHT, BILLY?!

HUH? ER...YEAH... I THINK...

BOY'S MORE SHAKEN THAN HURT. DIDN'T THEY TELL YA TO WATCH YER STEP HERE?

GOOD THING YA AIN'T AS TALL AS A COPPER...

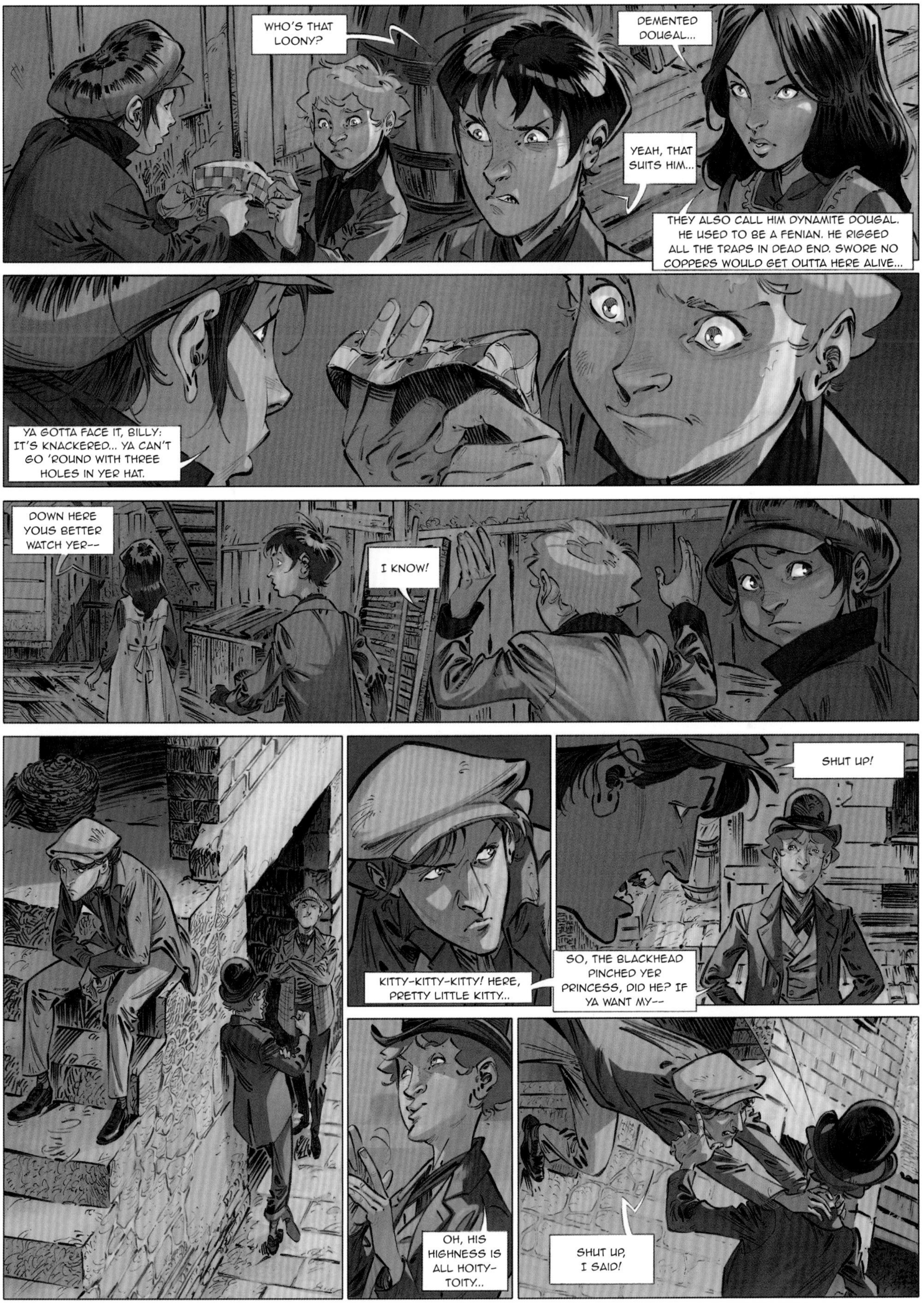
WHO'S THAT LOONY?
DEMENTED DOUGAL...
YEAH, THAT SUITS HIM...
THEY ALSO CALL HIM DYNAMITE DOUGAL. HE USED TO BE A FENIAN. HE RIGGED ALL THE TRAPS IN DEAD END. SWORE NO COPPERS WOULD GET OUTTA HERE ALIVE...
YA GOTTA FACE IT, BILLY: IT'S KNACKERED... YA CAN'T GO 'ROUND WITH THREE HOLES IN YER HAT.
DOWN HERE YOUS BETTER WATCH YER--
I KNOW!
KITTY-KITTY-KITTY! HERE, PRETTY LITTLE KITTY...
SHUT UP!
SO, THE BLACKHEAD PINCHED YER PRINCESS, DID HE? IF YA WANT MY--
OH, HIS HIGHNESS IS ALL HOITY-TOITY...
SHUT UP, I SAID!

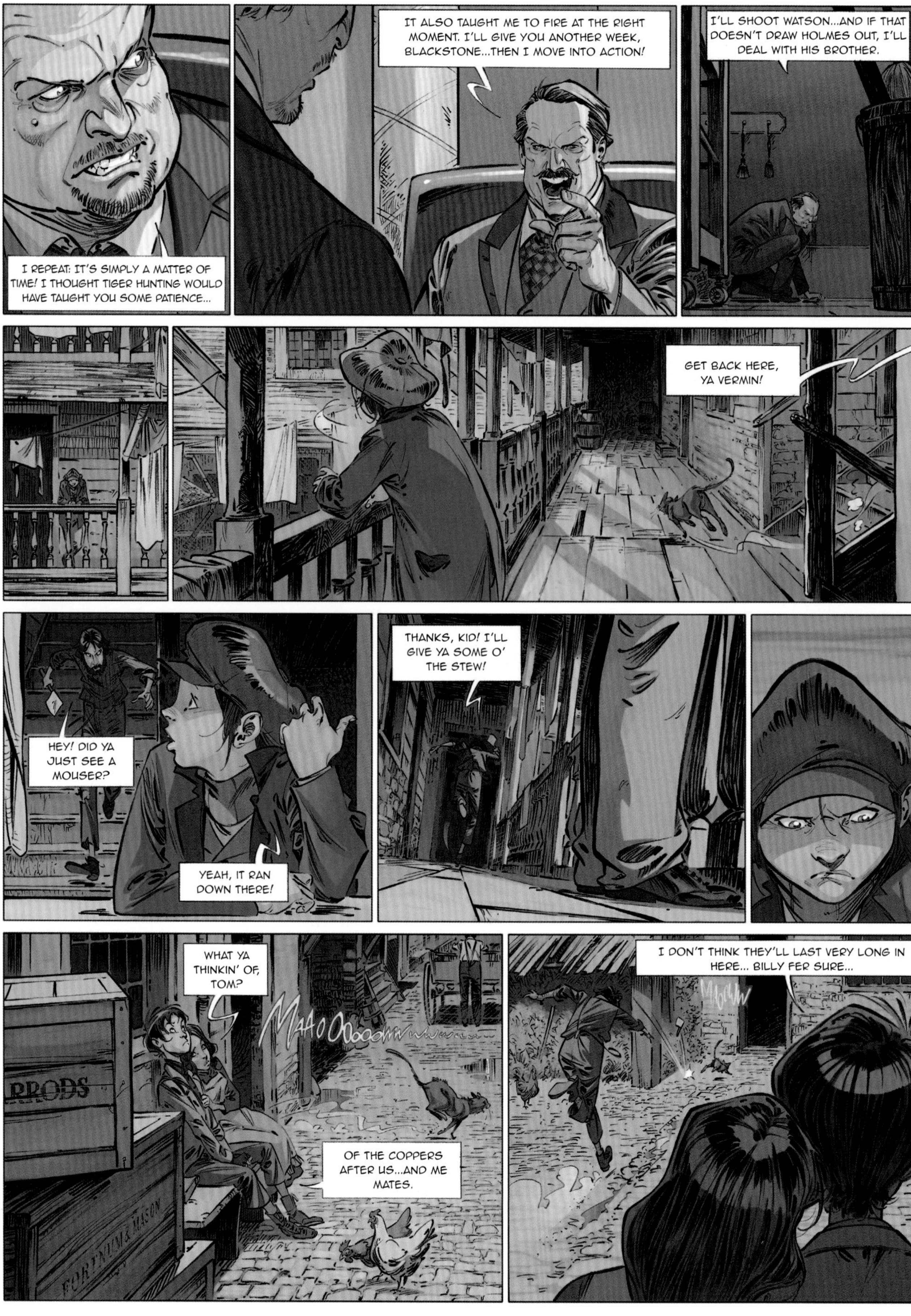
I REPEAT: IT'S SIMPLY A MATTER OF TIME! I THOUGHT TIGER HUNTING WOULD HAVE TAUGHT YOU SOME PATIENCE...
IT ALSO TAUGHT ME TO FIRE AT THE RIGHT MOMENT. I'LL GIVE YOU ANOTHER WEEK, BLACKSTONE...THEN I MOVE INTO ACTION!
I'LL SHOOT WATSON...AND IF THAT DOESN'T DRAW HOLMES OUT, I'LL DEAL WITH HIS BROTHER.
GET BACK HERE, YA VERMIN!
HEY! DID YA JUST SEE A MOUSER?
YEAH, IT RAN DOWN THERE!
THANKS, KID! I'LL GIVE YA SOME O' THE STEW!
WHAT YA THINKIN' OF, TOM?
OF THE COPPERS AFTER US...AND ME MATES.
I DON'T THINK THEY'LL LAST VERY LONG IN HERE... BILLY FER SURE...

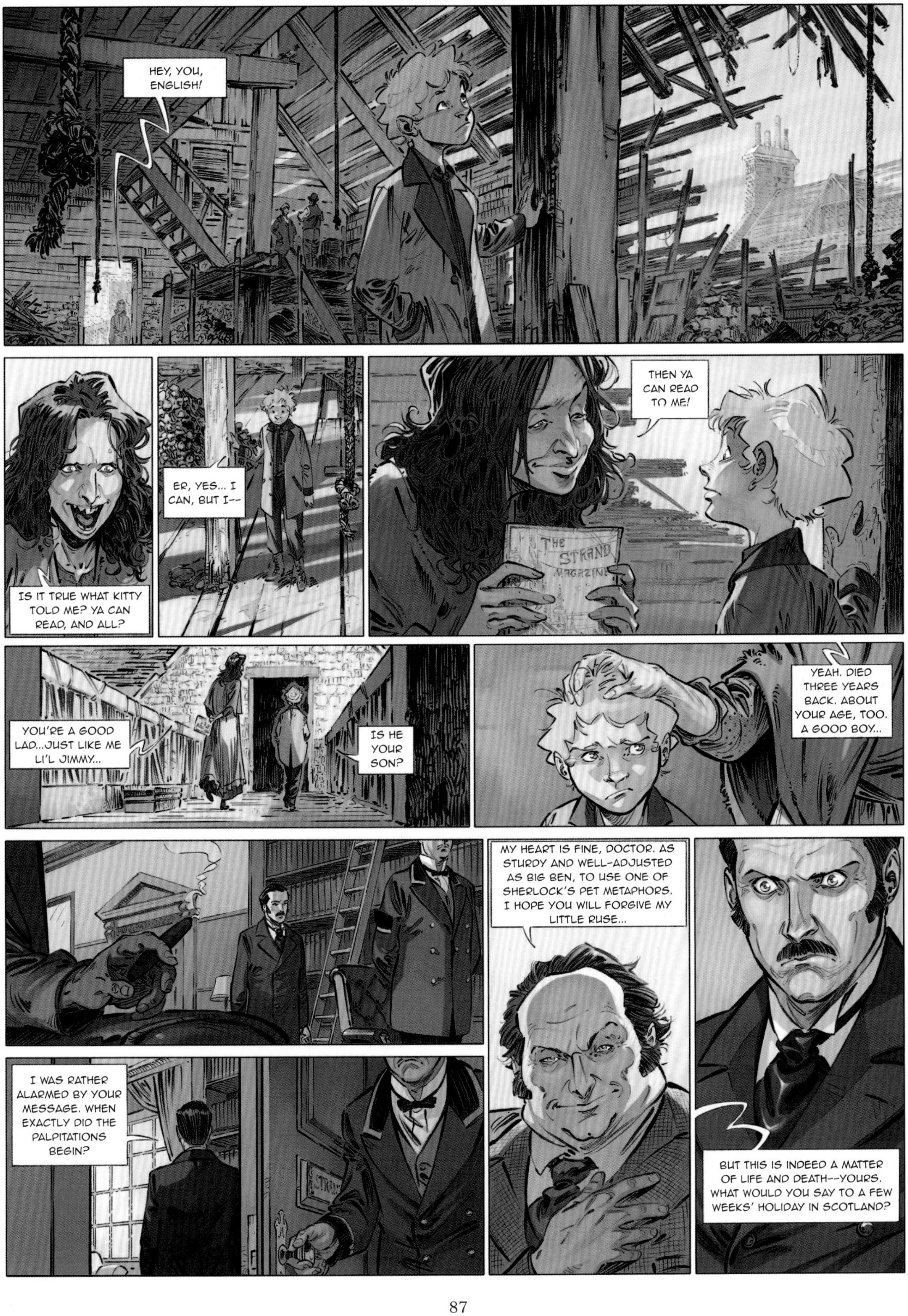
HEY, YOU, ENGLISH!
IS IT TRUE WHAT KITTY TOLD ME? YA CAN READ, AND ALL?
ER, YES... I CAN, BUT I--
THEN YA CAN READ TO ME!
THE STRAND MAGAZINE
YOU'RE A GOOD LAD...JUST LIKE ME LI'L JIMMY...
IS HE YOUR SON?
YEAH. DIED THREE YEARS BACK. ABOUT YOUR AGE, TOO. A GOOD BOY...
I WAS RATHER ALARMED BY YOUR MESSAGE. WHEN EXACTLY DID THE PALPITATIONS BEGIN?
MY HEART IS FINE, DOCTOR. AS STURDY AND WELL-ADJUSTED AS BIG BEN, TO USE ONE OF SHERLOCK'S PET METAPHORS. I HOPE YOU WILL FORGIVE MY LITTLE RUSE...
BUT THIS IS INDEED A MATTER OF LIFE AND DEATH--YOURS. WHAT WOULD YOU SAY TO A FEW WEEKS' HOLIDAY IN SCOTLAND?

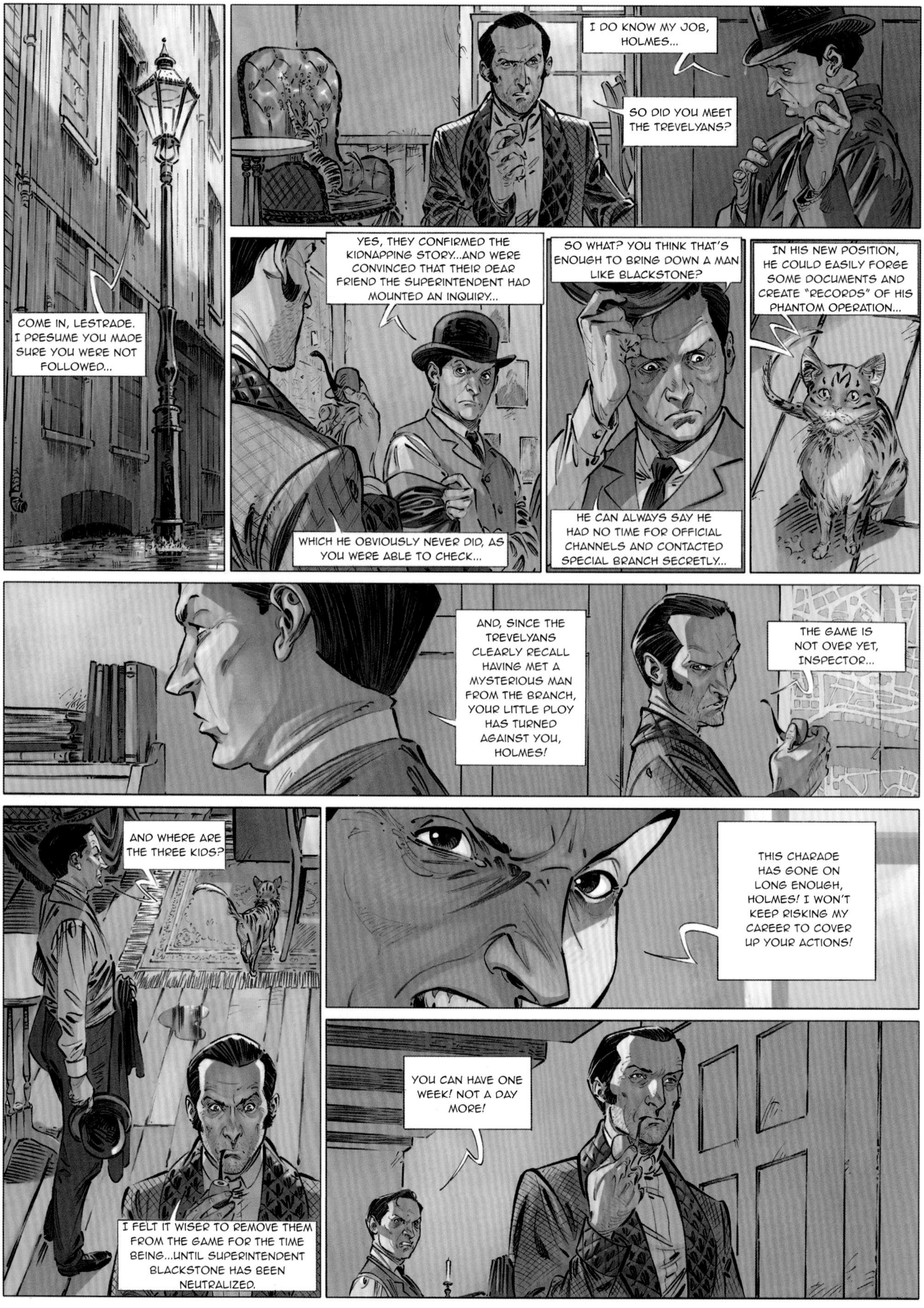
COME IN, LESTRADE. I PRESUME YOU MADE SURE YOU WERE NOT FOLLOWED...
I DO KNOW MY JOB, HOLMES...
SO DID YOU MEET THE TREVELYANS?
YES, THEY CONFIRMED THE KIDNAPPING STORY...AND WERE CONVINCED THAT THEIR DEAR FRIEND THE SUPERINTENDENT HAD MOUNTED AN INQUIRY...
WHICH HE OBVIOUSLY NEVER DID, AS YOU WERE ABLE TO CHECK...
SO WHAT? YOU THINK THAT'S ENOUGH TO BRING DOWN A MAN LIKE BLACKSTONE?
HE CAN ALWAYS SAY HE HAD NO TIME FOR OFFICIAL CHANNELS AND CONTACTED SPECIAL BRANCH SECRETLY...
IN HIS NEW POSITION, HE COULD EASILY FORGE SOME DOCUMENTS AND CREATE "RECORDS" OF HIS PHANTOM OPERATION...
AND, SINCE THE TREVELYANS CLEARLY RECALL HAVING MET A MYSTERIOUS MAN FROM THE BRANCH, YOUR LITTLE PLOY HAS TURNED AGAINST YOU, HOLMES!
THE GAME IS NOT OVER YET, INSPECTOR...
AND WHERE ARE THE THREE KIDS?
I FELT IT WISER TO REMOVE THEM FROM THE GAME FOR THE TIME BEING...UNTIL SUPERINTENDENT BLACKSTONE HAS BEEN NEUTRALIZED.
THIS CHARADE HAS GONE ON LONG ENOUGH, HOLMES! I WON'T KEEP RISKING MY CAREER TO COVER UP YOUR ACTIONS!
YOU CAN HAVE ONE WEEK! NOT A DAY MORE!

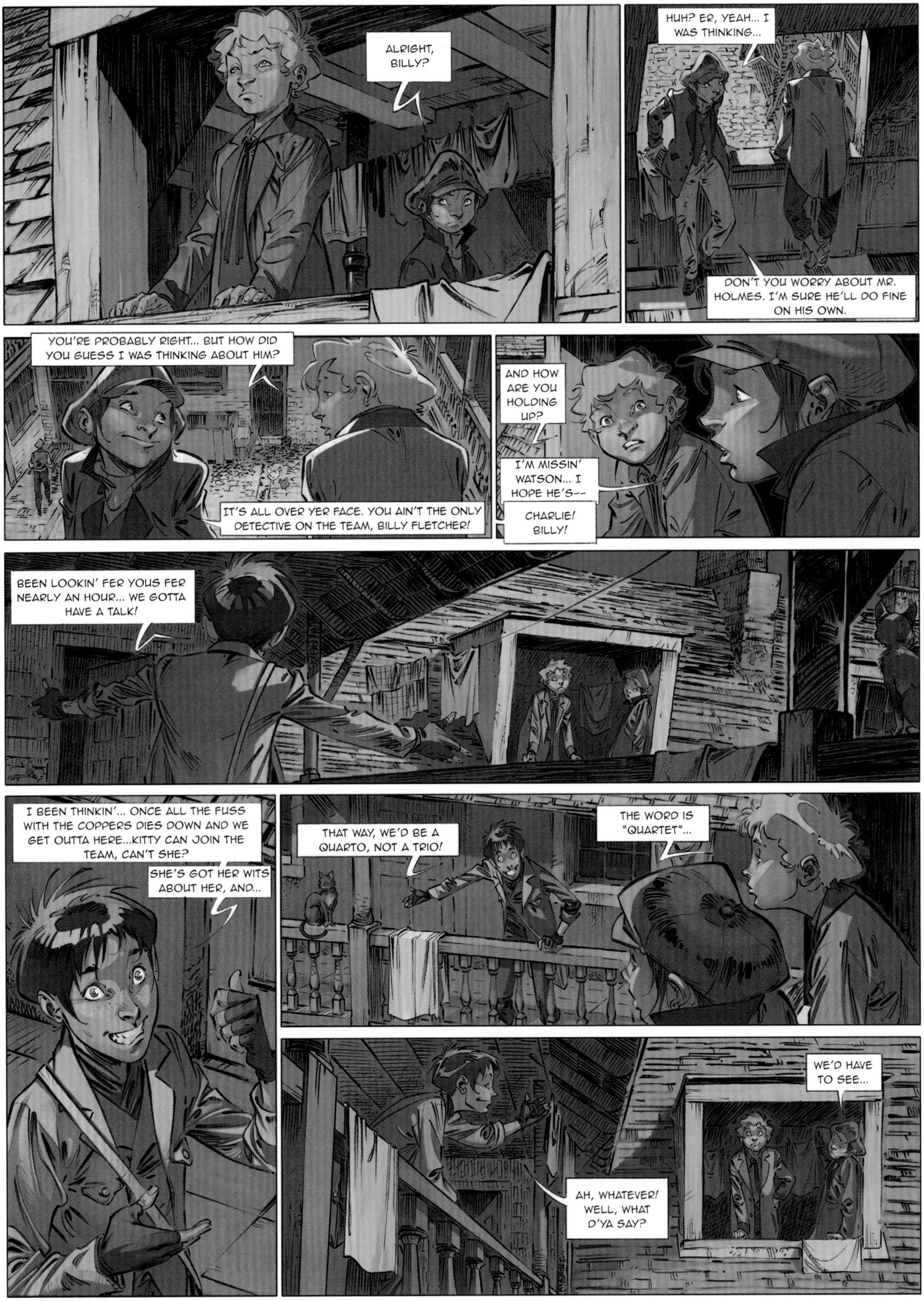
ALRIGHT, BILLY?
HUH? ER, YEAH... I WAS THINKING...
DON'T YOU WORRY ABOUT MR. HOLMES. I'M SURE HE'LL DO FINE ON HIS OWN.
YOU'RE PROBABLY RIGHT... BUT HOW DID YOU GUESS I WAS THINKING ABOUT HIM?
IT'S ALL OVER YER FACE. YOU AIN'T THE ONLY DETECTIVE ON THE TEAM, BILLY FLETCHER!
AND HOW ARE YOU HOLDING UP?
I'M MISSIN' WATSON... I HOPE HE'S--
CHARLIE! BILLY!
BEEN LOOKIN' FER YOUS FER NEARLY AN HOUR... WE GOTTA HAVE A TALK!
I BEEN THINKIN'... ONCE ALL THE FUSS WITH THE COPPERS DIES DOWN AND WE GET OUTTA HERE...KITTY CAN JOIN THE TEAM, CAN'T SHE?
SHE'S GOT HER WITS ABOUT HER, AND...
THAT WAY, WE'D BE A QUARTO, NOT A TRIO!
THE WORD IS "QUARTET"...
WE'D HAVE TO SEE...
AH, WHATEVER! WELL, WHAT D'YA SAY?

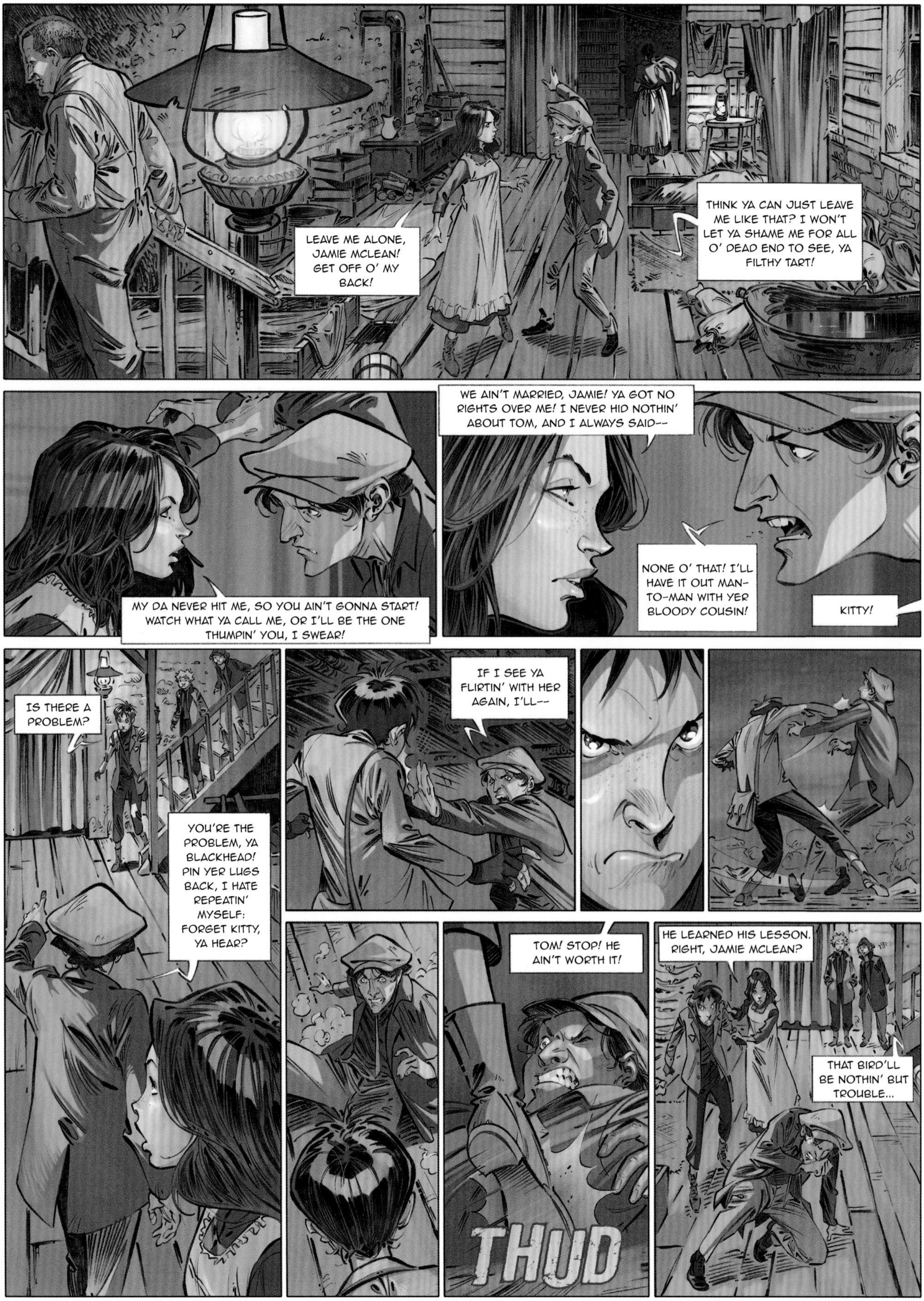
LEAVE ME ALONE, JAMIE MCLEAN! GET OFF O' MY BACK!
THINK YA CAN JUST LEAVE ME LIKE THAT? I WON'T LET YA SHAME ME FOR ALL O' DEAD END TO SEE, YA FILTHY TART!
MY DA NEVER HIT ME, SO YOU AIN'T GONNA START! WATCH WHAT YA CALL ME, OR I'LL BE THE ONE THUMPIN' YOU, I SWEAR!
WE AIN'T MARRIED, JAMIE! YA GOT NO RIGHTS OVER ME! I NEVER HID NOTHIN' ABOUT TOM, AND I ALWAYS SAID--
NONE O' THAT! I'LL HAVE IT OUT MAN-TO-MAN WITH YER BLOODY COUSIN!
KITTY!
IS THERE A PROBLEM?
YOU'RE THE PROBLEM, YA BLACKHEAD! PIN YER LUGS BACK, I HATE REPEATIN' MYSELF: FORGET KITTY, YA HEAR?
IF I SEE YA FLIRTIN' WITH HER AGAIN, I'LL--
TOM! STOP! HE AIN'T WORTH IT!
THUD
HE LEARNED HIS LESSON. RIGHT, JAMIE MCLEAN?
THAT BIRD'LL BE NOTHIN' BUT TROUBLE...

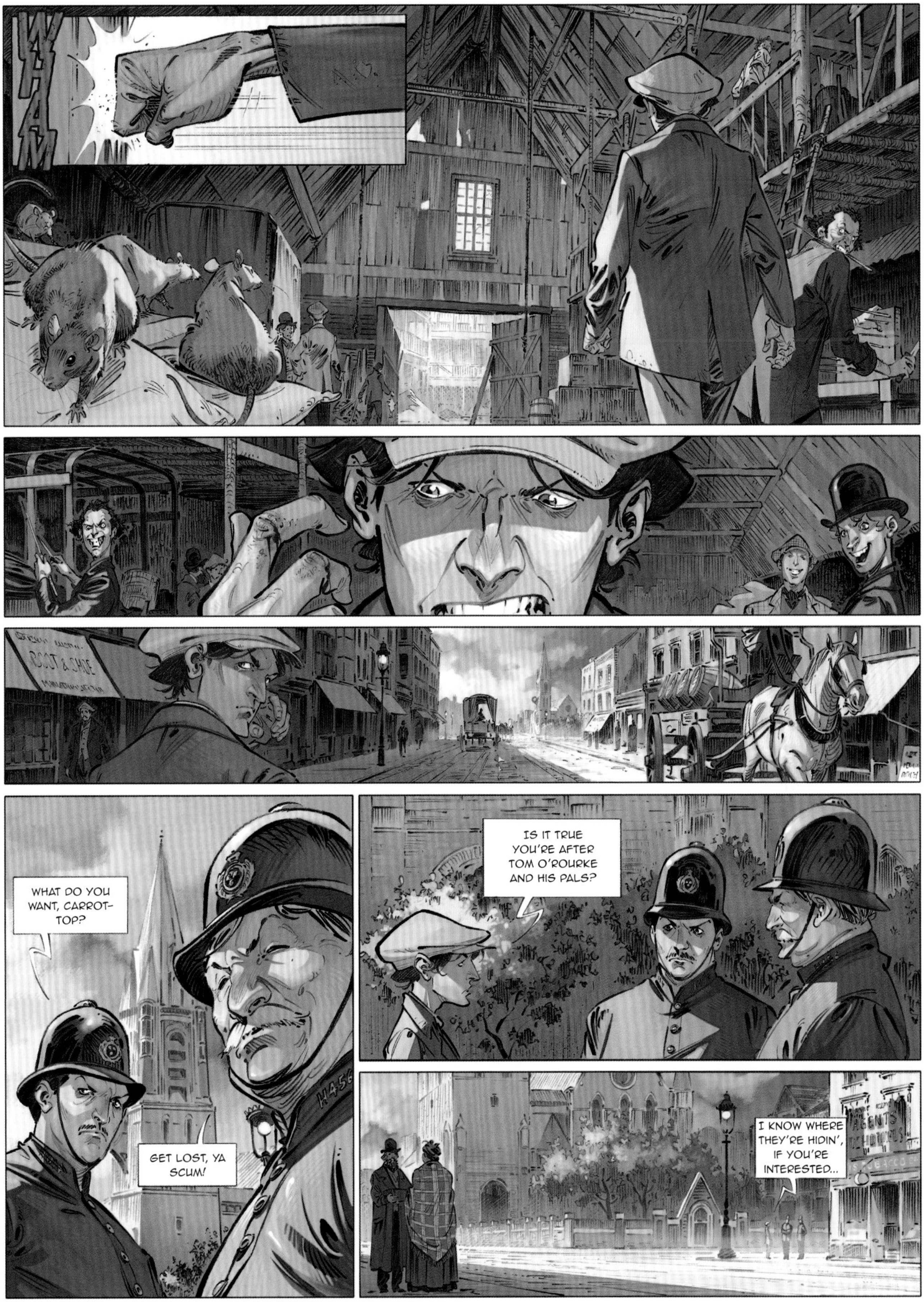
WHAM
WHAT DO YOU WANT, CARROT-TOP?
GET LOST, YA SCUM!
IS IT TRUE YOU'RE AFTER TOM O'ROURKE AND HIS PALS?
I KNOW WHERE THEY'RE HIDIN', IF YOU'RE INTERESTED...

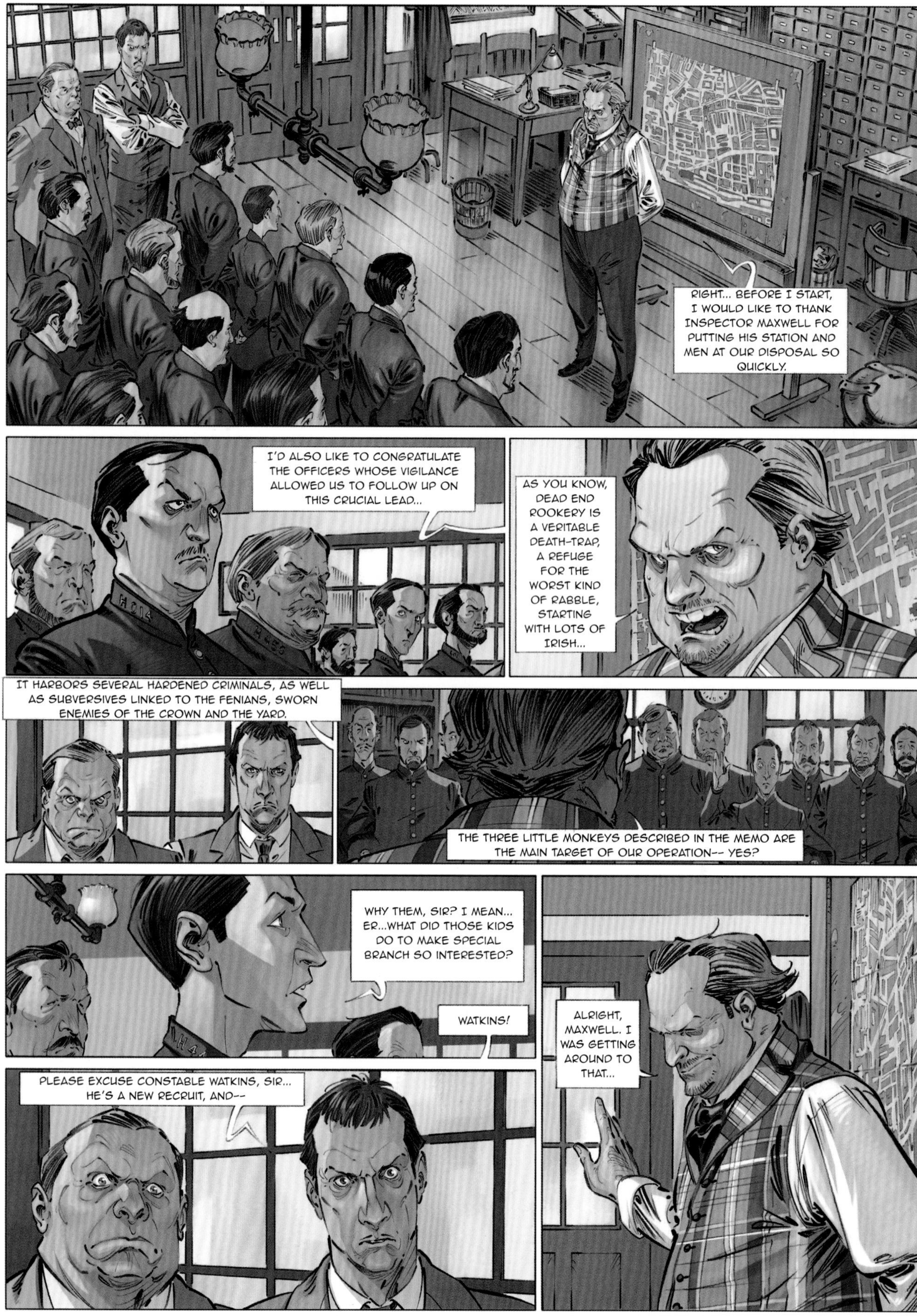
RIGHT... BEFORE I START, I WOULD LIKE TO THANK INSPECTOR MAXWELL FOR PUTTING HIS STATION AND MEN AT OUR DISPOSAL SO QUICKLY.
I'D ALSO LIKE TO CONGRATULATE THE OFFICERS WHOSE VIGILANCE ALLOWED US TO FOLLOW UP ON THIS CRUCIAL LEAD...
AS YOU KNOW, DEAD END ROOKERY IS A VERITABLE DEATH-TRAP, A REFUGE FOR THE WORST KIND OF RABBLE, STARTING WITH LOTS OF IRISH...
IT HARBORS SEVERAL HARDENED CRIMINALS, AS WELL AS SUBVERSIVES LINKED TO THE FENIANS, SWORN ENEMIES OF THE CROWN AND THE YARD.
THE THREE LITTLE MONKEYS DESCRIBED IN THE MEMO ARE THE MAIN TARGET OF OUR OPERATION-- YES?
WHY THEM, SIR? I MEAN... ER...WHAT DID THOSE KIDS DO TO MAKE SPECIAL BRANCH SO INTERESTED?
WATKINS!
PLEASE EXCUSE CONSTABLE WATKINS, SIR... HE'S A NEW RECRUIT, AND--
ALRIGHT, MAXWELL. I WAS GETTING AROUND TO THAT...

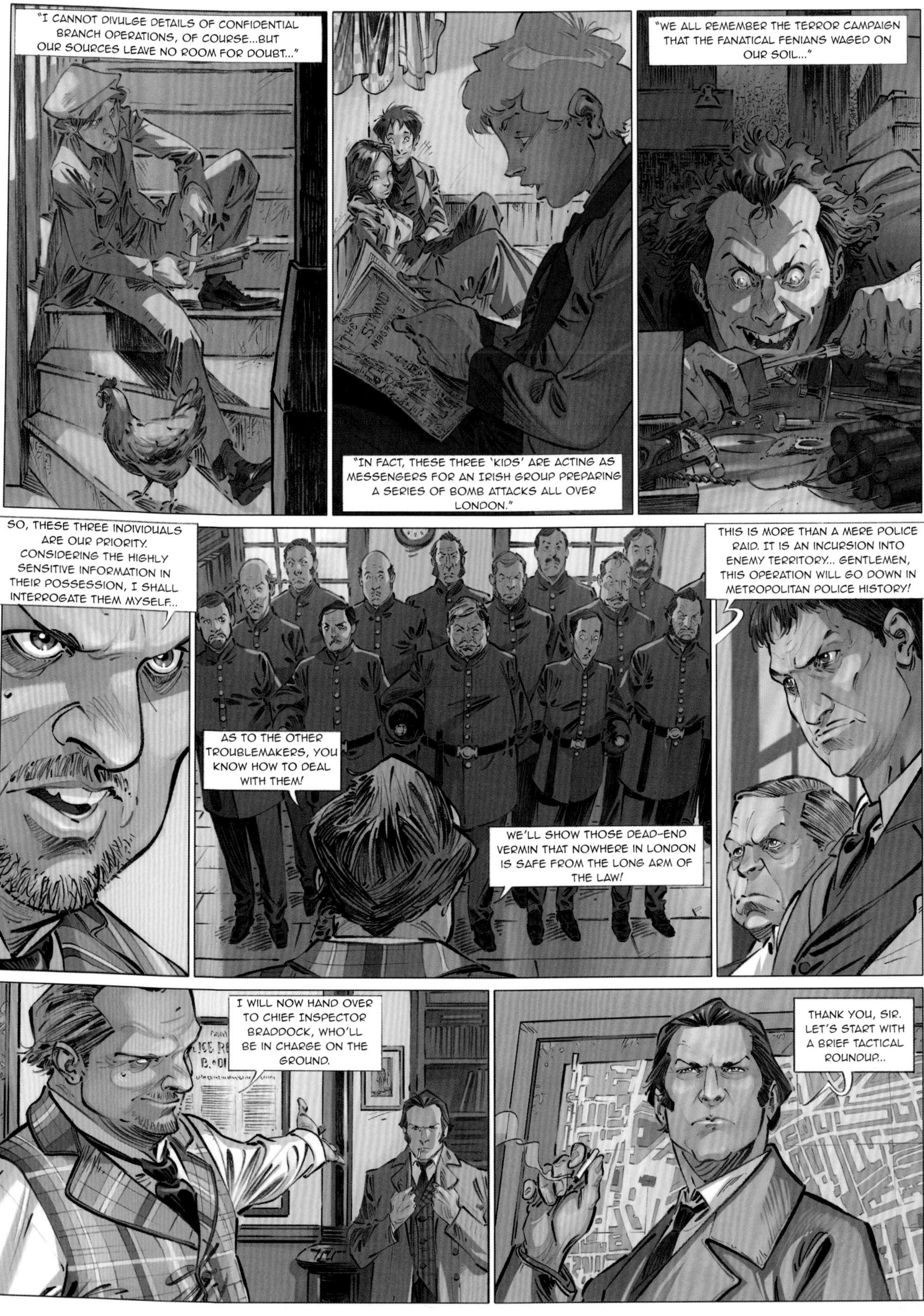
"I CANNOT DIVULGE DETAILS OF CONFIDENTIAL BRANCH OPERATIONS, OF COURSE...BUT OUR SOURCES LEAVE NO ROOM FOR DOUBT..."
"IN FACT, THESE THREE 'KIDS' ARE ACTING AS MESSENGERS FOR AN IRISH GROUP PREPARING A SERIES OF BOMB ATTACKS ALL OVER LONDON."
"WE ALL REMEMBER THE TERROR CAMPAIGN THAT THE FANATICAL FENIANS WAGED ON OUR SOIL..."
SO, THESE THREE INDIVIDUALS ARE OUR PRIORITY. CONSIDERING THE HIGHLY SENSITIVE INFORMATION IN THEIR POSSESSION, I SHALL INTERROGATE THEM MYSELF...
AS TO THE OTHER TROUBLEMAKERS, YOU KNOW HOW TO DEAL WITH THEM!
WE'LL SHOW THOSE DEAD-END VERMIN THAT NOWHERE IN LONDON IS SAFE FROM THE LONG ARM OF THE LAW!
THIS IS MORE THAN A MERE POLICE RAID. IT IS AN INCURSION INTO ENEMY TERRITORY... GENTLEMEN, THIS OPERATION WILL GO DOWN IN METROPOLITAN POLICE HISTORY!
I WILL NOW HAND OVER TO CHIEF INSPECTOR BRADDOCK, WHO'LL BE IN CHARGE ON THE GROUND.
THANK YOU, SIR. LET'S START WITH A BRIEF TACTICAL ROUNDUP...

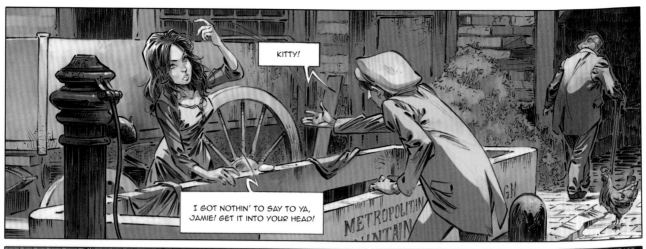

KITTY!

I GOT NOTHIN' TO SAY TO YA, JAMIE! GET IT INTO YOUR HEAD!

COME WITH ME! WE GOTTA HIDE! THE COPPERS ARE GONNA RAID US...

COPPERS? WHAT ARE YA SAYIN'? THEY...

JAMIE... DON'T TELL ME YOU'VE GONE AND--

IF I WAS HIM, I'D NEVER LET SOME BIRD START--

LORD JESUS!

THE PIGS!

RIGHT! LET'S CLEAN UP THIS RAT HOLE!

COPPERS! THERE'S A WHOLE ARMY OF 'EM!

COME WITH ME, I TELL YA!

GET OFF, YA FILTHY SQUEALER!

THE COPPERS! IT'S THE COPPERS!

LET 'EM COME!

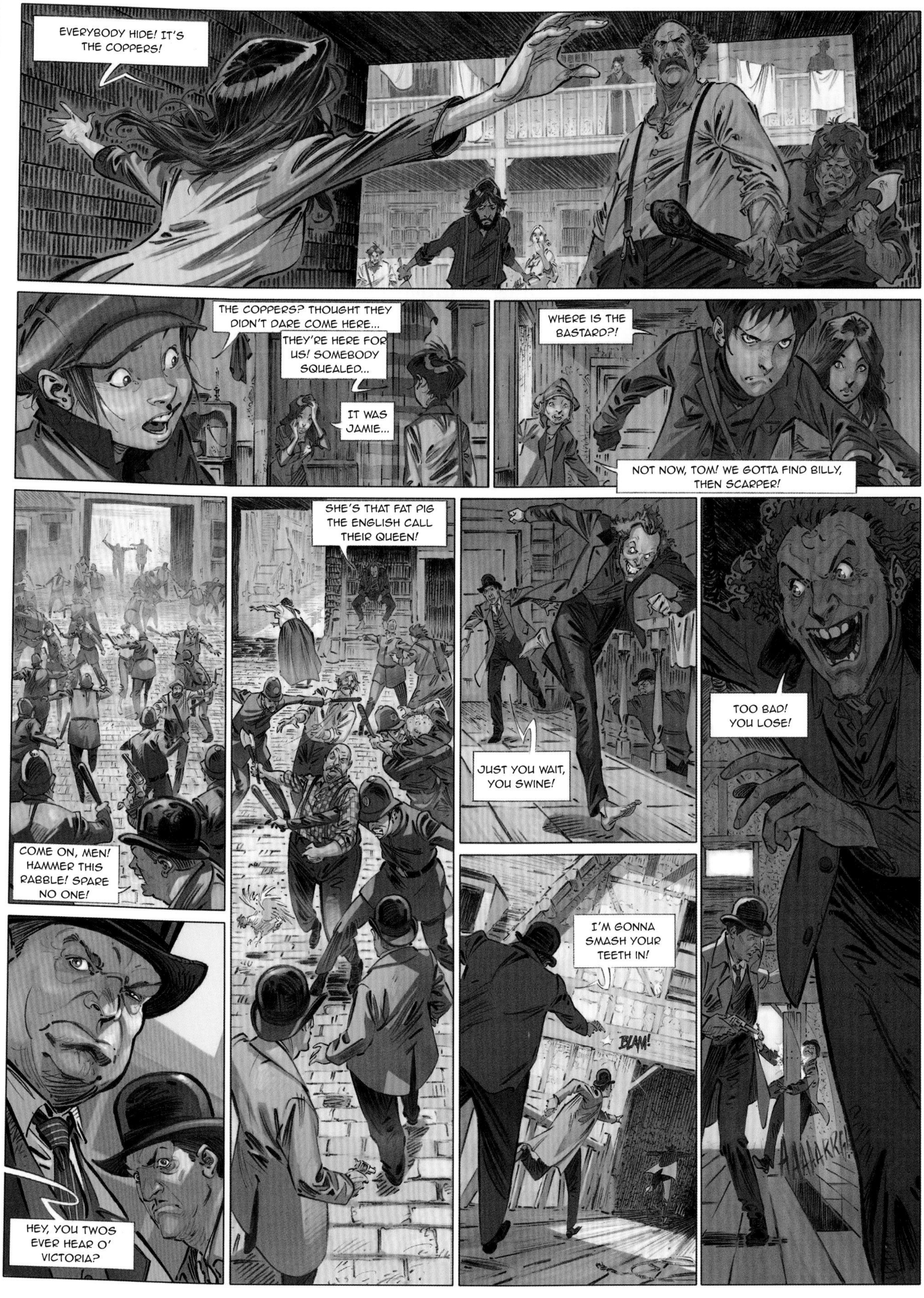
EVERYBODY HIDE! IT'S THE COPPERS!
THE COPPERS? THOUGHT THEY DIDN'T DARE COME HERE...
THEY'RE HERE FOR US! SOMEBODY SQUEALED...
IT WAS JAMIE...
WHERE IS THE BASTARD?!
NOT NOW, TOM! WE GOTTA FIND BILLY, THEN SCARPER!
COME ON, MEN! HAMMER THIS RABBLE! SPARE NO ONE!
HEY, YOU TWOS EVER HEAR O' VICTORIA?
SHE'S THAT FAT PIG THE ENGLISH CALL THEIR QUEEN!
JUST YOU WAIT, YOU SWINE!
TOO BAD! YOU LOSE!
I'M GONNA SMASH YOUR TEETH IN!
BLAM!
AAAAAKK!

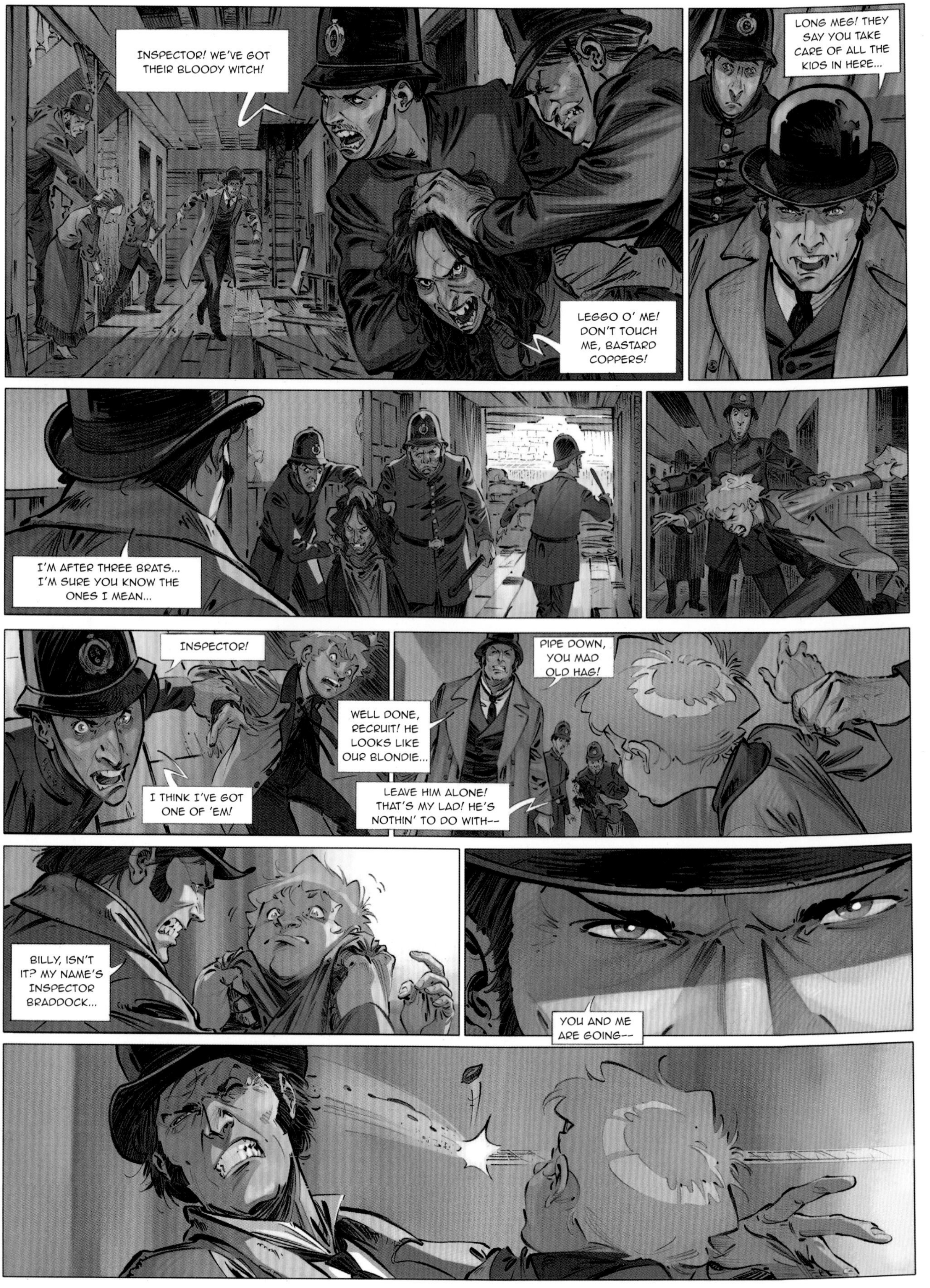
INSPECTOR! WE'VE GOT THEIR BLOODY WITCH!
LEGGO O' ME! DON'T TOUCH ME, BASTARD COPPERS!
LONG MEG! THEY SAY YOU TAKE CARE OF ALL THE KIDS IN HERE...
I'M AFTER THREE BRATS... I'M SURE YOU KNOW THE ONES I MEAN...
INSPECTOR!
I THINK I'VE GOT ONE OF 'EM!
WELL DONE, RECRUIT! HE LOOKS LIKE OUR BLONDIE...
PIPE DOWN, YOU MAD OLD HAG!
LEAVE HIM ALONE! THAT'S MY LAD! HE'S NOTHIN' TO DO WITH--
BILLY, ISN'T IT? MY NAME'S INSPECTOR BRADDOCK...
YOU AND ME ARE GOING--

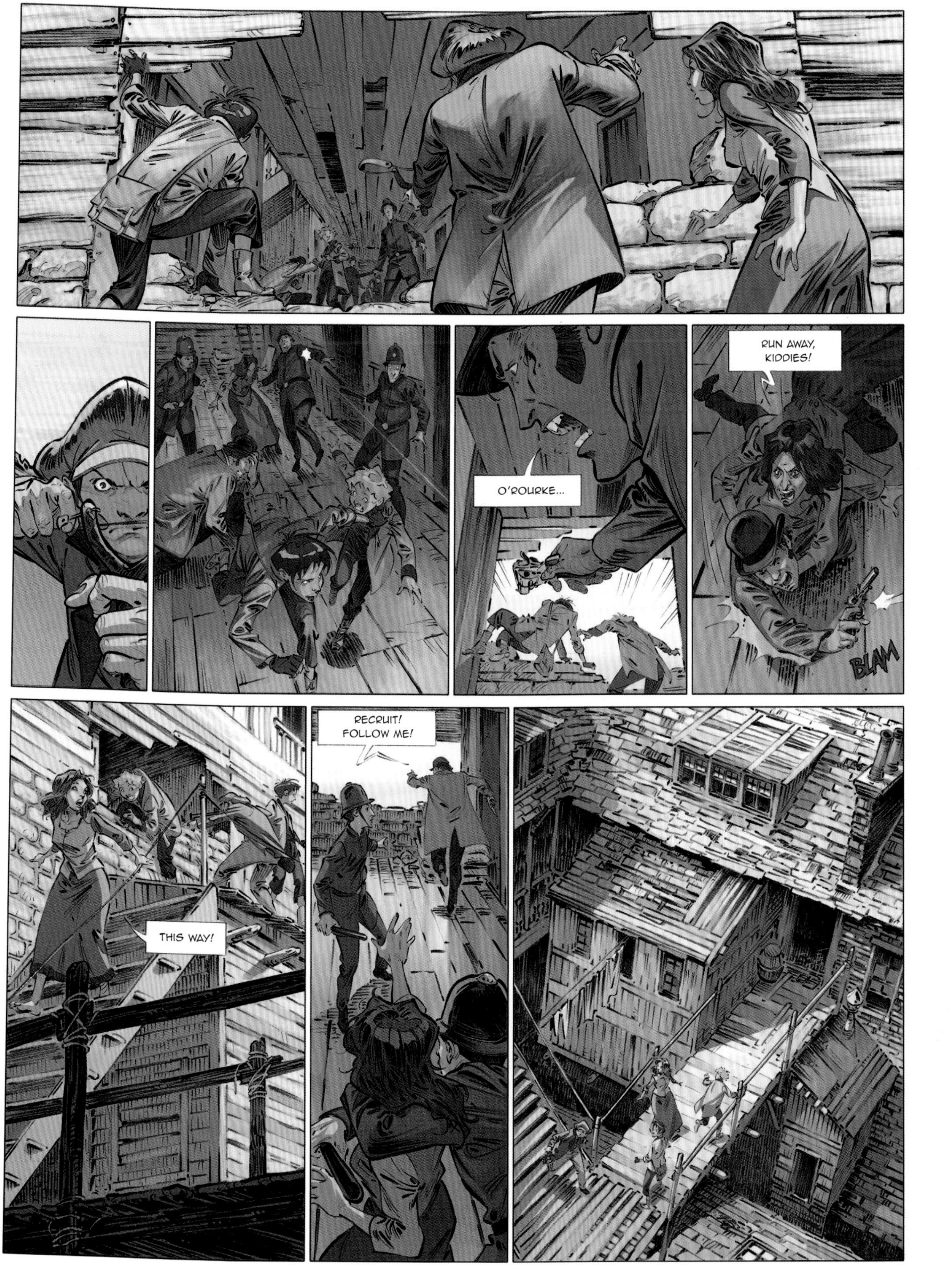
O'ROURKE...
RUN AWAY, KIDDIES!
BLAM
THIS WAY!
RECRUIT! FOLLOW ME!

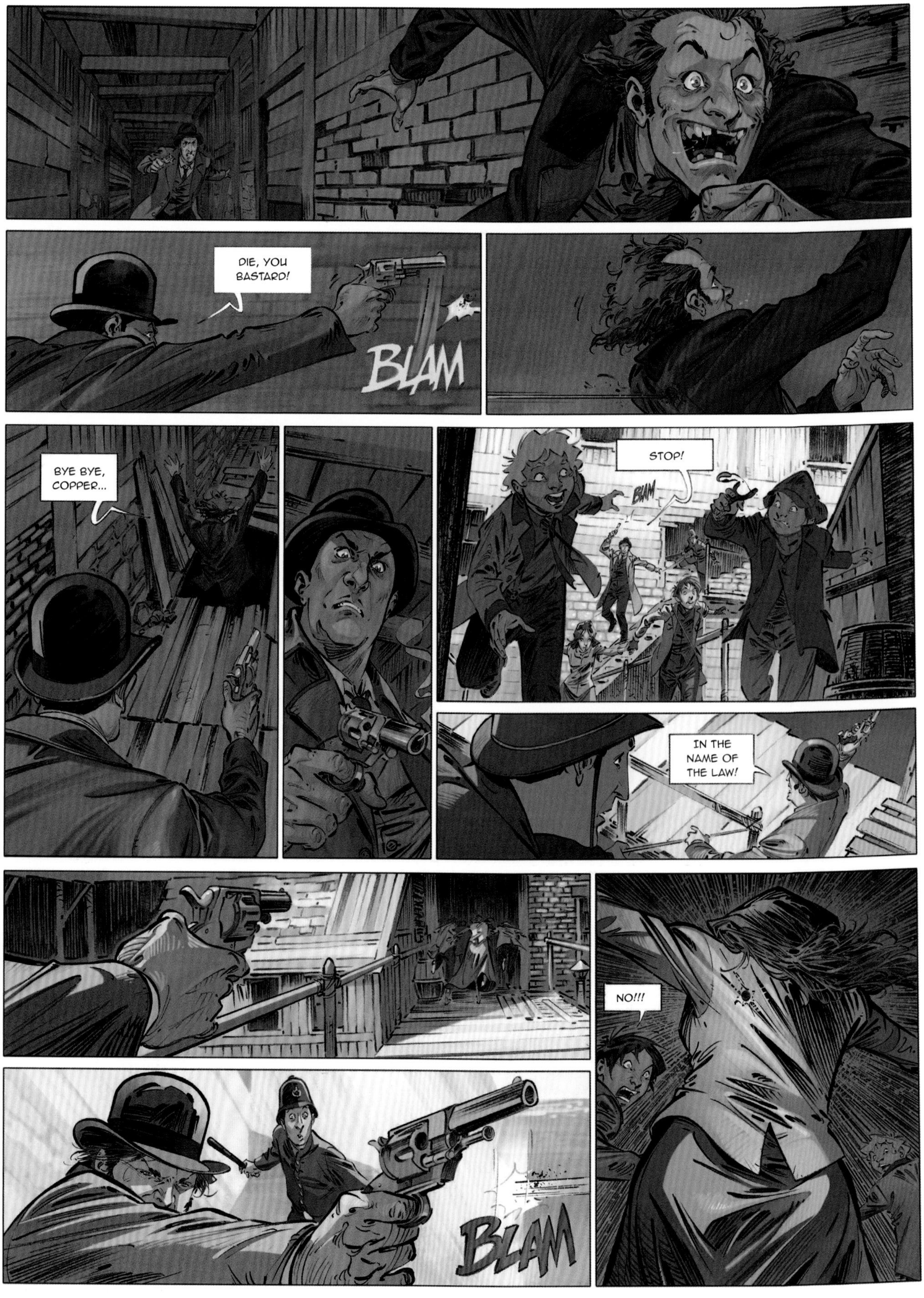
DIE, YOU BASTARD!
BLAM
BYE BYE, COPPER...
STOP!
BLAM
IN THE NAME OF THE LAW!
NO!!!
BLAM

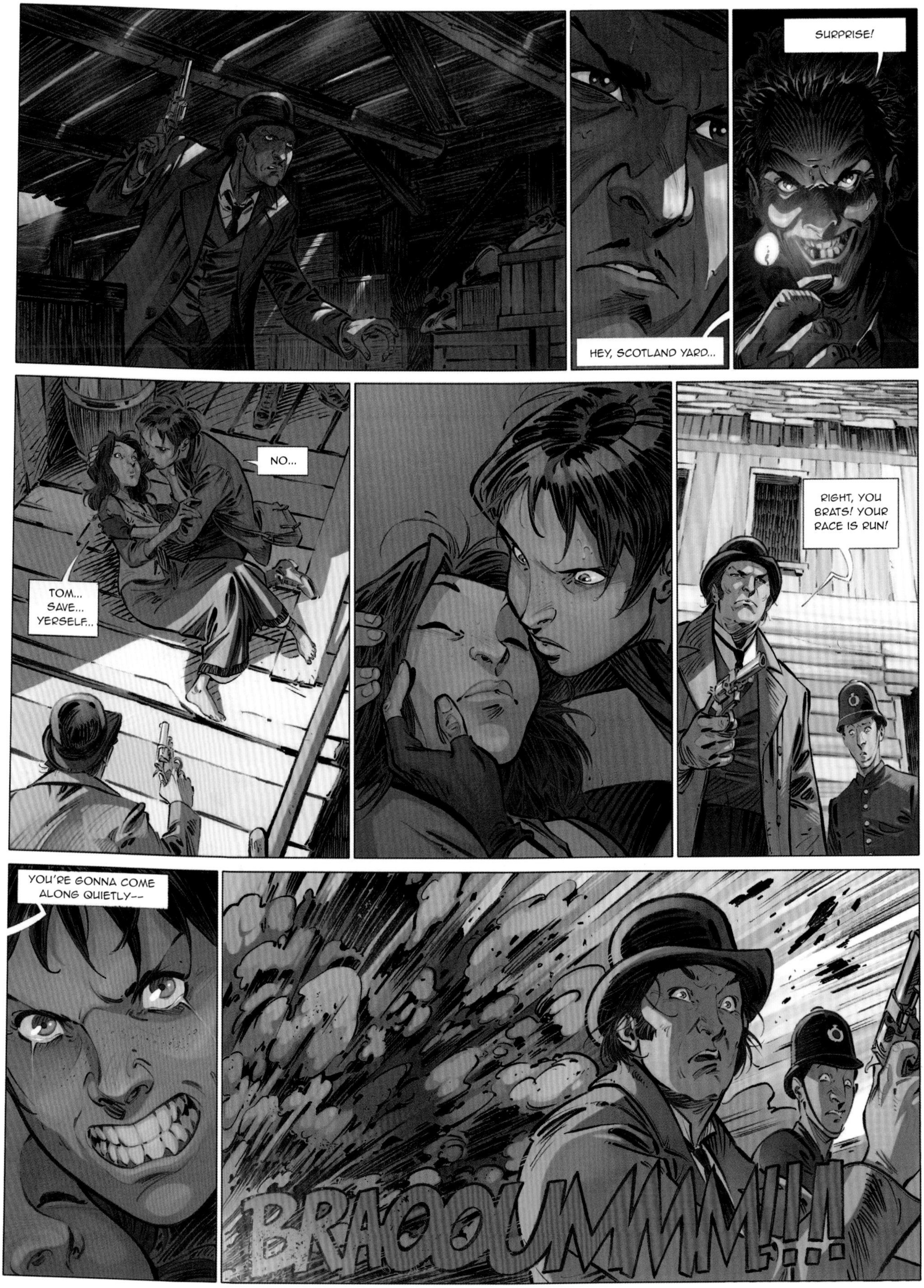
HEY, SCOTLAND YARD...
SURPRISE!
NO...
TOM... SAVE... YERSELF...
RIGHT, YOU BRATS! YOUR RACE IS RUN!
YOU'RE GONNA COME ALONG QUIETLY--
BRAOOUMMM!!!

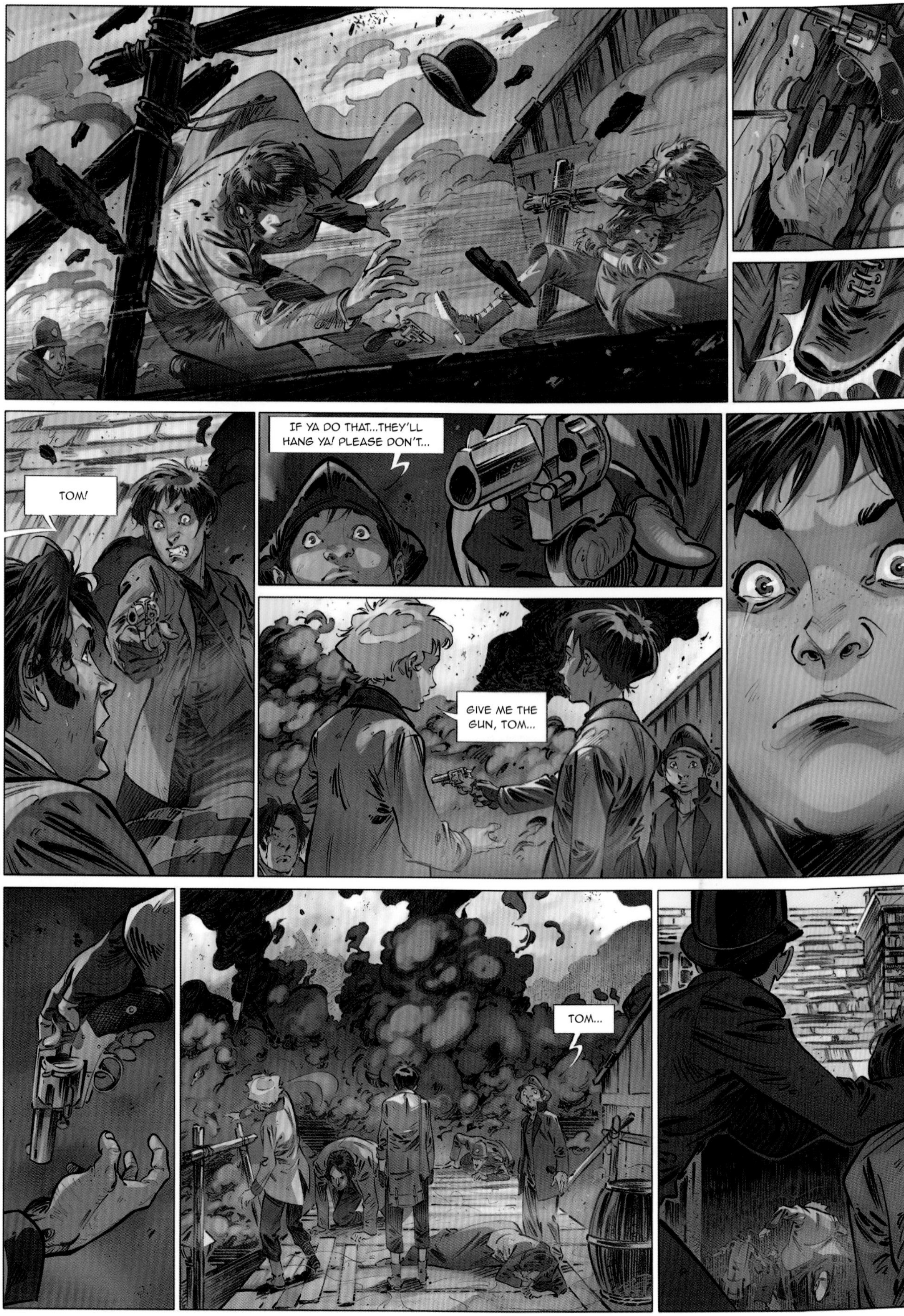
TOM!
IF YA DO THAT...THEY'LL HANG YA! PLEASE DON'T...
GIVE ME THE GUN, TOM...
TOM...

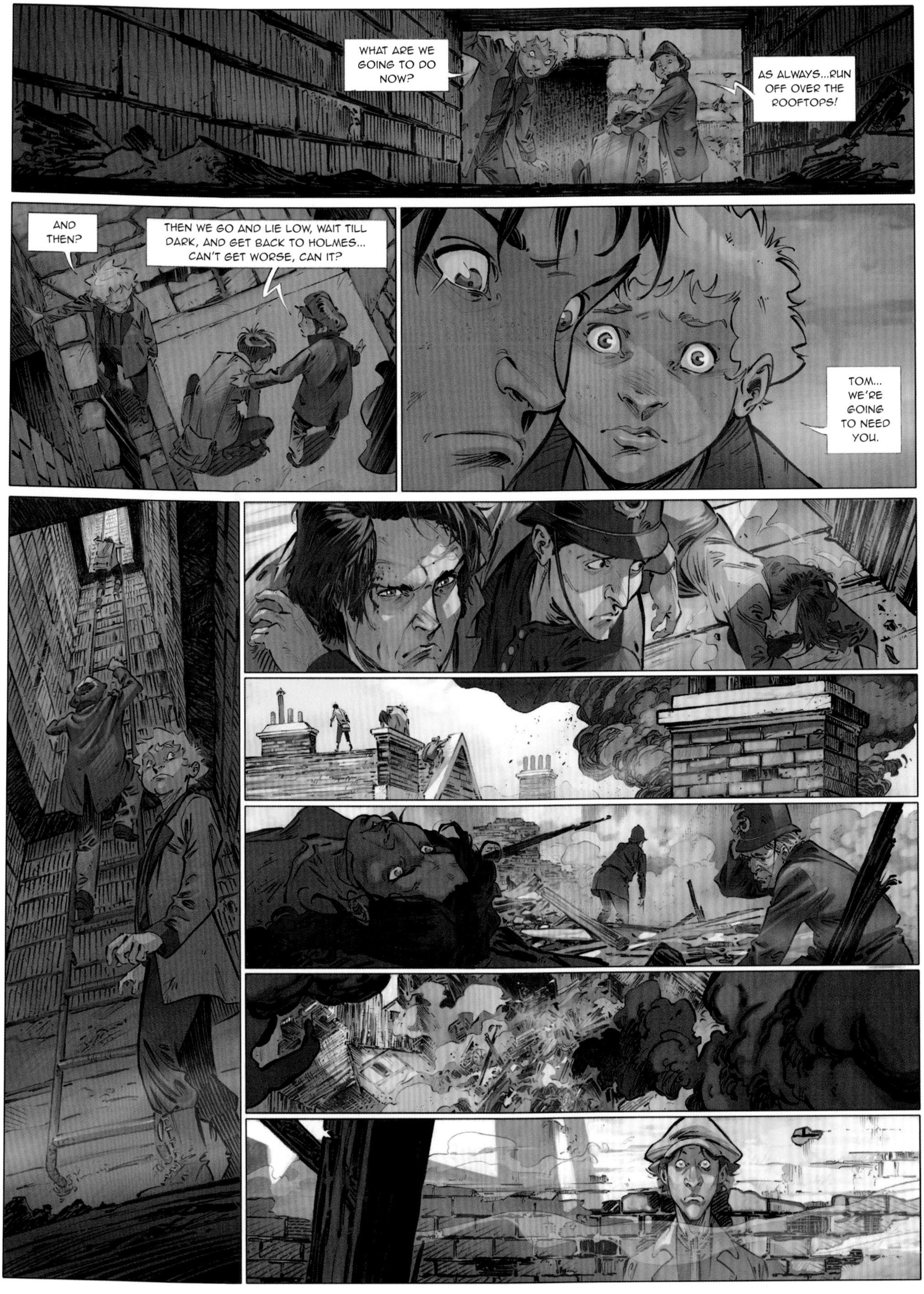
WHAT ARE WE GOING TO DO NOW?
AS ALWAYS...RUN OFF OVER THE ROOFTOPS!
AND THEN?
THEN WE GO AND LIE LOW, WAIT TILL DARK, AND GET BACK TO HOLMES... CAN'T GET WORSE, CAN IT?
TOM... WE'RE GOING TO NEED YOU.

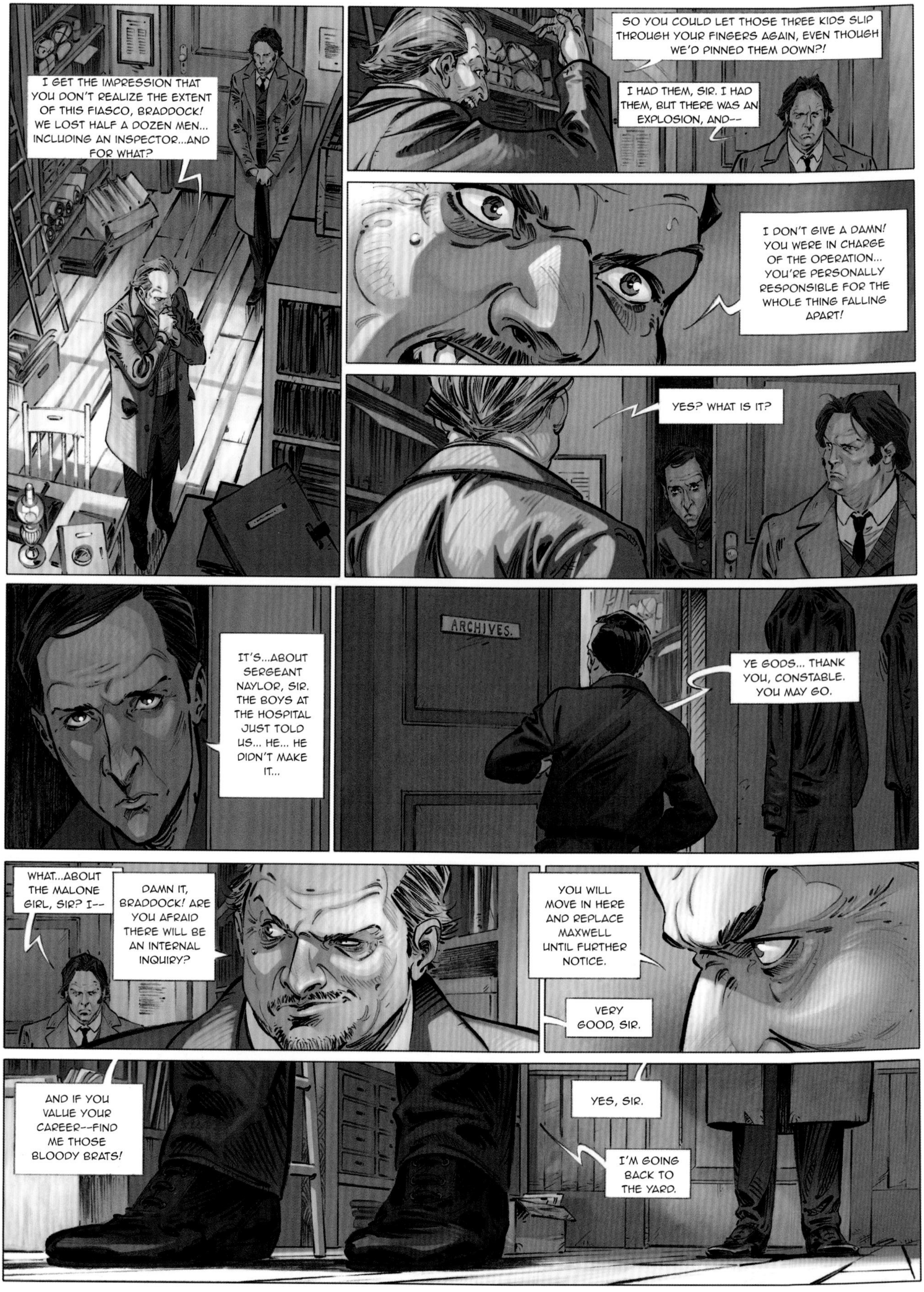

I GET THE IMPRESSION THAT YOU DON'T REALIZE THE EXTENT OF THIS FIASCO, BRADDOCK! WE LOST HALF A DOZEN MEN... INCLUDING AN INSPECTOR...AND FOR WHAT?
SO YOU COULD LET THOSE THREE KIDS SLIP THROUGH YOUR FINGERS AGAIN, EVEN THOUGH WE'D PINNED THEM DOWN?!
I HAD THEM, SIR. I HAD THEM, BUT THERE WAS AN EXPLOSION, AND--
I DON'T GIVE A DAMN! YOU WERE IN CHARGE OF THE OPERATION... YOU'RE PERSONALLY RESPONSIBLE FOR THE WHOLE THING FALLING APART!
YES? WHAT IS IT?
IT'S...ABOUT SERGEANT NAYLOR, SIR. THE BOYS AT THE HOSPITAL JUST TOLD US... HE... HE DIDN'T MAKE IT...
ARCHIVES.
YE GODS... THANK YOU, CONSTABLE. YOU MAY GO.
WHAT...ABOUT THE MALONE GIRL, SIR? I--
DAMN IT, BRADDOCK! ARE YOU AFRAID THERE WILL BE AN INTERNAL INQUIRY?
YOU WILL MOVE IN HERE AND REPLACE MAXWELL UNTIL FURTHER NOTICE.
VERY GOOD, SIR.
AND IF YOU VALUE YOUR CAREER--FIND ME THOSE BLOODY BRATS!
YES, SIR.
I'M GOING BACK TO THE YARD.

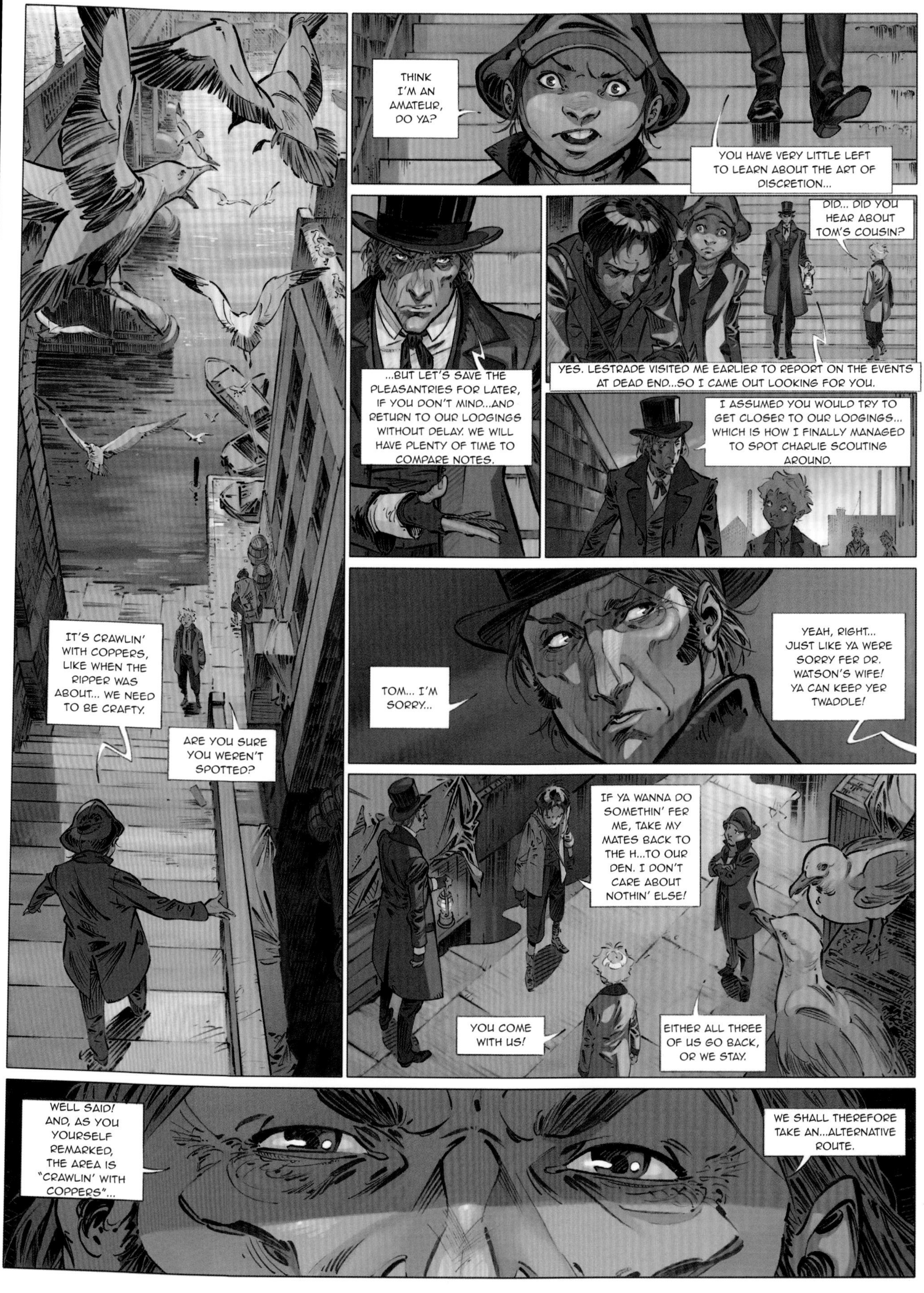
IT'S CRAWLIN' WITH COPPERS, LIKE WHEN THE RIPPER WAS ABOUT... WE NEED TO BE CRAFTY.
ARE YOU SURE YOU WEREN'T SPOTTED?
THINK I'M AN AMATEUR, DO YA?
YOU HAVE VERY LITTLE LEFT TO LEARN ABOUT THE ART OF DISCRETION...
...BUT LET'S SAVE THE PLEASANTRIES FOR LATER, IF YOU DON'T MIND...AND RETURN TO OUR LODGINGS WITHOUT DELAY. WE WILL HAVE PLENTY OF TIME TO COMPARE NOTES.
DID... DID YOU HEAR ABOUT TOM'S COUSIN?
YES. LESTRADE VISITED ME EARLIER TO REPORT ON THE EVENTS AT DEAD END...SO I CAME OUT LOOKING FOR YOU.
I ASSUMED YOU WOULD TRY TO GET CLOSER TO OUR LODGINGS... WHICH IS HOW I FINALLY MANAGED TO SPOT CHARLIE SCOUTING AROUND.
TOM... I'M SORRY...
YEAH, RIGHT... JUST LIKE YA WERE SORRY FER DR. WATSON'S WIFE! YA CAN KEEP YER TWADDLE!
IF YA WANNA DO SOMETHIN' FER ME, TAKE MY MATES BACK TO THE H...TO OUR DEN. I DON'T CARE ABOUT NOTHIN' ELSE!
YOU COME WITH US!
EITHER ALL THREE OF US GO BACK, OR WE STAY.
WELL SAID! AND, AS YOU YOURSELF REMARKED, THE AREA IS "CRAWLIN' WITH COPPERS"...
WE SHALL THEREFORE TAKE AN...ALTERNATIVE ROUTE.

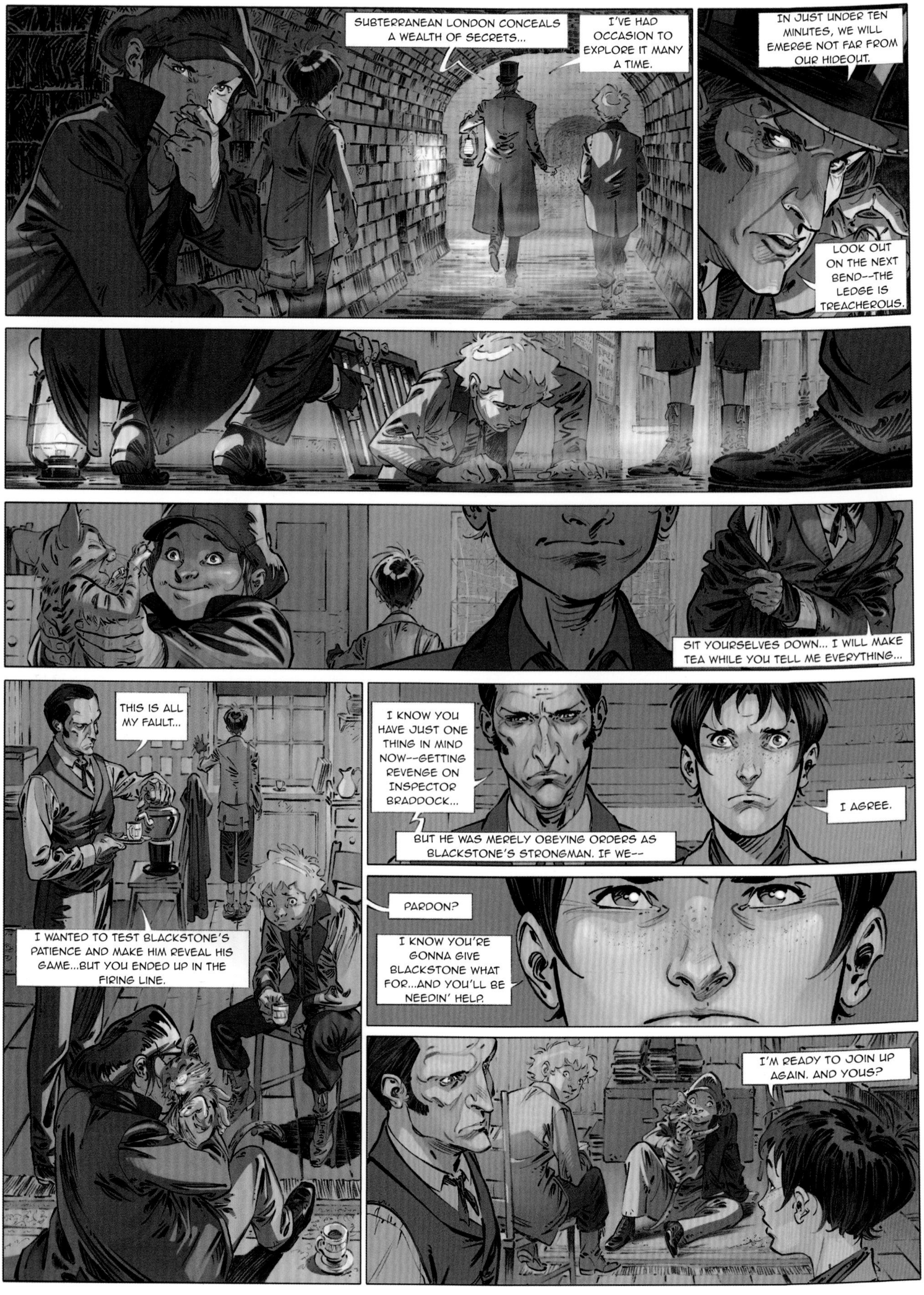
SUBTERRANEAN LONDON CONCEALS A WEALTH OF SECRETS...
I'VE HAD OCCASION TO EXPLORE IT MANY A TIME.
IN JUST UNDER TEN MINUTES, WE WILL EMERGE NOT FAR FROM OUR HIDEOUT.
LOOK OUT ON THE NEXT BEND--THE LEDGE IS TREACHEROUS.
SIT YOURSELVES DOWN... I WILL MAKE TEA WHILE YOU TELL ME EVERYTHING...
THIS IS ALL MY FAULT...
I WANTED TO TEST BLACKSTONE'S PATIENCE AND MAKE HIM REVEAL HIS GAME...BUT YOU ENDED UP IN THE FIRING LINE.
I KNOW YOU HAVE JUST ONE THING IN MIND NOW--GETTING REVENGE ON INSPECTOR BRADDOCK...
I AGREE.
BUT HE WAS MERELY OBEYING ORDERS AS BLACKSTONE'S STRONGMAN. IF WE--
PARDON?
I KNOW YOU'RE GONNA GIVE BLACKSTONE WHAT FOR...AND YOU'LL BE NEEDIN' HELP.
I'M READY TO JOIN UP AGAIN. AND YOUS?

WELL DONE! "MUCH ADO ABOUT NOTHING," AS THE BARD WOULD SAY...

IT'S ONLY A SETBACK! I––

I'VE BEEN PATIENT ENOUGH. IT'S TIME WE APPLIED MY METHODS. SINCE THE BLASTED DOCTOR DECIDED TO TAKE A HOLIDAY, I SHALL DEAL WITH MYCROFT HOLMES.

I GUARANTEE THAT WILL DRAW THE BROTHER OUT OF HIS LAIR...

BUT HE PROBABLY ADVISED WATSON TO LEAVE LONDON.

WE MUST ACT ON THE ASSUMPTION THAT MYCROFT HOLMES KNOWS EVERYTHING.

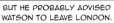

ANOTHER REASON TO ERASE HIM...

OUT OF THE QUESTION! IF YOU KILL HIM NOW, YOU'LL GIVE HIS BROTHER WHAT HE'S BEEN WAITING FOR––THE CHANCE TO INCRIMINATE YOU IN A MURDER. NO, WE MUST KEEP A COOL HEAD AND PROCEED METHODICALLY.

WE WILL DEAL WITH HIM...BUT NOT BEFORE HIS BROTHER IS ELIMINATED. MEANWHILE, AND UNTIL FURTHER NOTICE, MYCROFT HOLMES IS UNTOUCHABLE.

NO ONE IS UNTOUCHABLE, BLACKSTONE. NOT EVEN YOU...

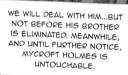

HAVE YOU FORGOTTEN WHAT HAPPENED TO KEENE?

NO, COLONEL... BUT AS FAR AS I'M CONCERNED, I HAVE TAKEN PRECAUTIONS...

I HAVE COMPILED A DOSSIER ON MY...PARALLEL ACTIVITIES WITH PROFESSOR MORIARTY'S ORGANIZATION. HIGHLY DETAILED...

THE SECTION COVERING YOU IS MOST ENLIGHTENING...

SHOULD A TRAGIC ACCIDENT BEFALL ME, OR WERE I TO VANISH MYSTERIOUSLY, THE DOSSIER WOULD LAND STRAIGHT ON MY SUPERIOR'S DESK...

DID YOU REALLY THINK I'D BE SO CARELESS, COLONEL?

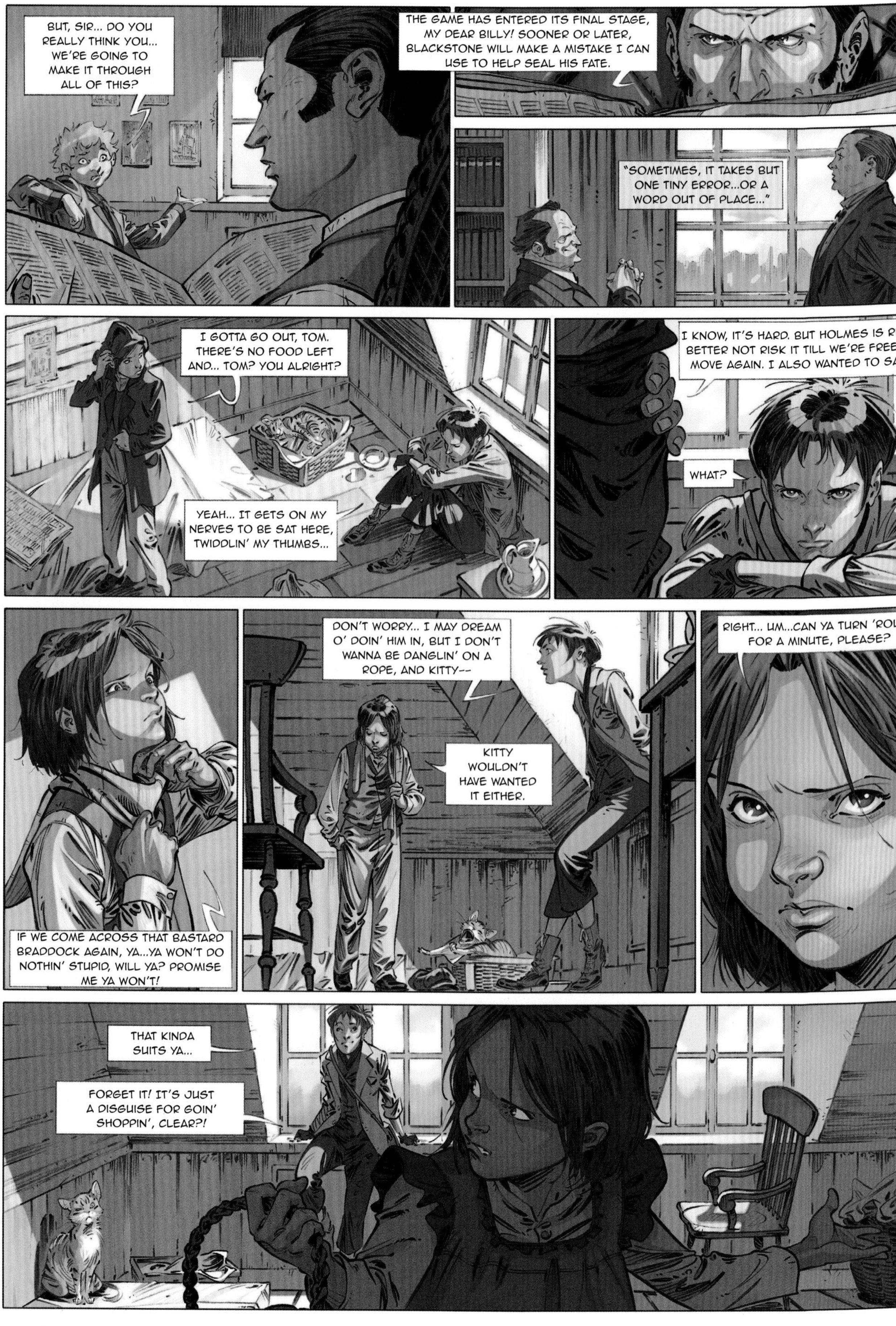
BUT, SIR... DO YOU REALLY THINK YOU... WE'RE GOING TO MAKE IT THROUGH ALL OF THIS?
THE GAME HAS ENTERED ITS FINAL STAGE, MY DEAR BILLY! SOONER OR LATER, BLACKSTONE WILL MAKE A MISTAKE I CAN USE TO HELP SEAL HIS FATE.
"SOMETIMES, IT TAKES BUT ONE TINY ERROR...OR A WORD OUT OF PLACE..."
I GOTTA GO OUT, TOM. THERE'S NO FOOD LEFT AND... TOM? YOU ALRIGHT?
YEAH... IT GETS ON MY NERVES TO BE SAT HERE, TWIDDLIN' MY THUMBS...
I KNOW, IT'S HARD. BUT HOLMES IS RIGHT. BETTER NOT RISK IT TILL WE'RE FREE TO MOVE AGAIN. I ALSO WANTED TO SAY...
WHAT?
IF WE COME ACROSS THAT BASTARD BRADDOCK AGAIN, YA...YA WON'T DO NOTHIN' STUPID, WILL YA? PROMISE ME YA WON'T!
DON'T WORRY... I MAY DREAM O' DOIN' HIM IN, BUT I DON'T WANNA BE DANGLIN' ON A ROPE, AND KITTY--
KITTY WOULDN'T HAVE WANTED IT EITHER.
RIGHT... UM...CAN YA TURN 'ROUND FOR A MINUTE, PLEASE?
THAT KINDA SUITS YA...
FORGET IT! IT'S JUST A DISGUISE FOR GOIN' SHOPPIN', CLEAR?!

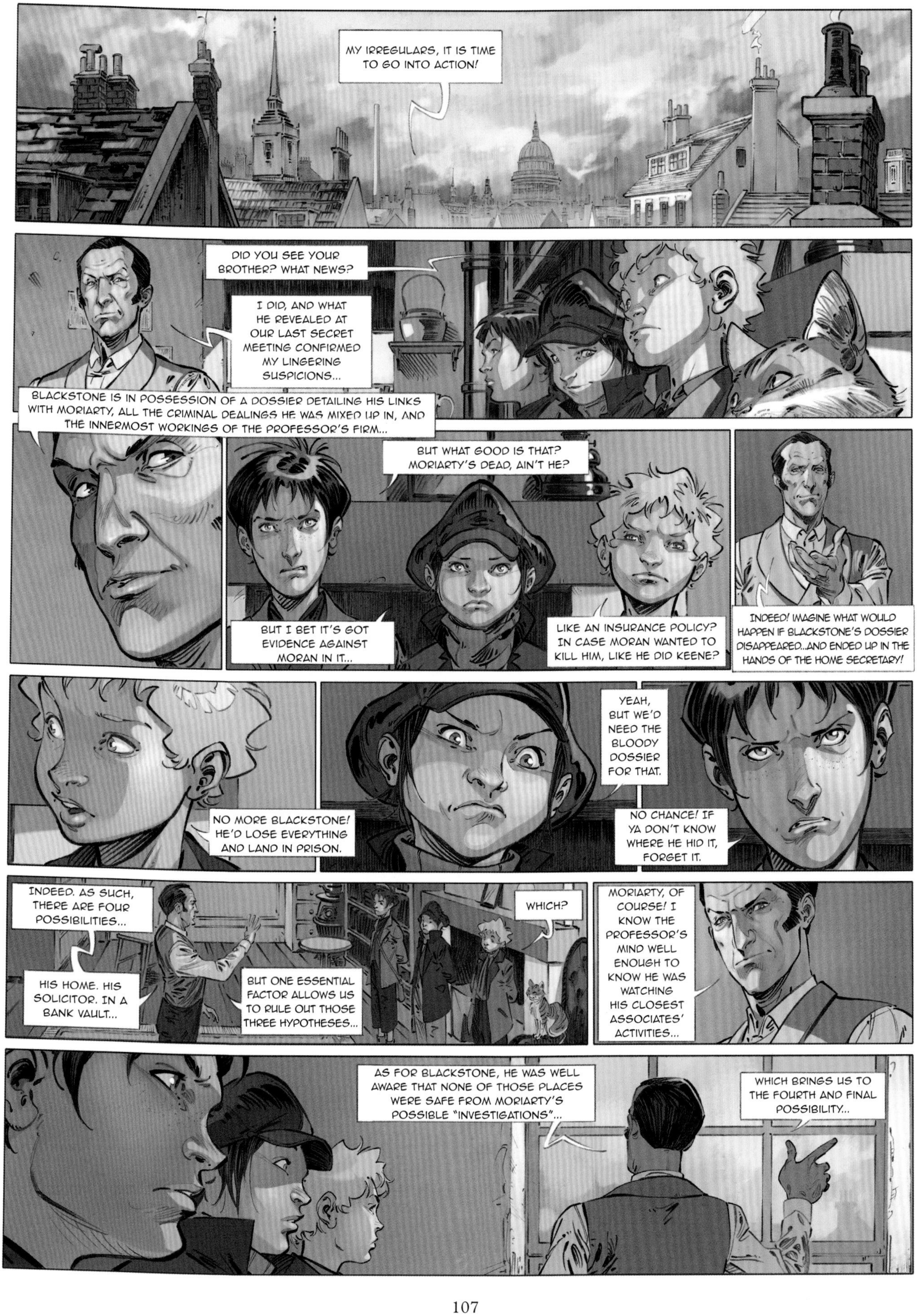
MY IRREGULARS, IT IS TIME TO GO INTO ACTION!
DID YOU SEE YOUR BROTHER? WHAT NEWS?
I DID, AND WHAT HE REVEALED AT OUR LAST SECRET MEETING CONFIRMED MY LINGERING SUSPICIONS...
BLACKSTONE IS IN POSSESSION OF A DOSSIER DETAILING HIS LINKS WITH MORIARTY, ALL THE CRIMINAL DEALINGS HE WAS MIXED UP IN, AND THE INNERMOST WORKINGS OF THE PROFESSOR'S FIRM...
BUT WHAT GOOD IS THAT? MORIARTY'S DEAD, AIN'T HE?
BUT I BET IT'S GOT EVIDENCE AGAINST MORAN IN IT...
LIKE AN INSURANCE POLICY? IN CASE MORAN WANTED TO KILL HIM, LIKE HE DID KEENE?
INDEED! IMAGINE WHAT WOULD HAPPEN IF BLACKSTONE'S DOSSIER DISAPPEARED...AND ENDED UP IN THE HANDS OF THE HOME SECRETARY!
NO MORE BLACKSTONE! HE'D LOSE EVERYTHING AND LAND IN PRISON.
YEAH, BUT WE'D NEED THE BLOODY DOSSIER FOR THAT.
NO CHANCE! IF YA DON'T KNOW WHERE HE HID IT, FORGET IT.
INDEED. AS SUCH, THERE ARE FOUR POSSIBILITIES...
HIS HOME. HIS SOLICITOR. IN A BANK VAULT...
BUT ONE ESSENTIAL FACTOR ALLOWS US TO RULE OUT THOSE THREE HYPOTHESES...
WHICH?
MORIARTY, OF COURSE! I KNOW THE PROFESSOR'S MIND WELL ENOUGH TO KNOW HE WAS WATCHING HIS CLOSEST ASSOCIATES' ACTIVITIES...
AS FOR BLACKSTONE, HE WAS WELL AWARE THAT NONE OF THOSE PLACES WERE SAFE FROM MORIARTY'S POSSIBLE "INVESTIGATIONS"...
WHICH BRINGS US TO THE FOURTH AND FINAL POSSIBILITY...

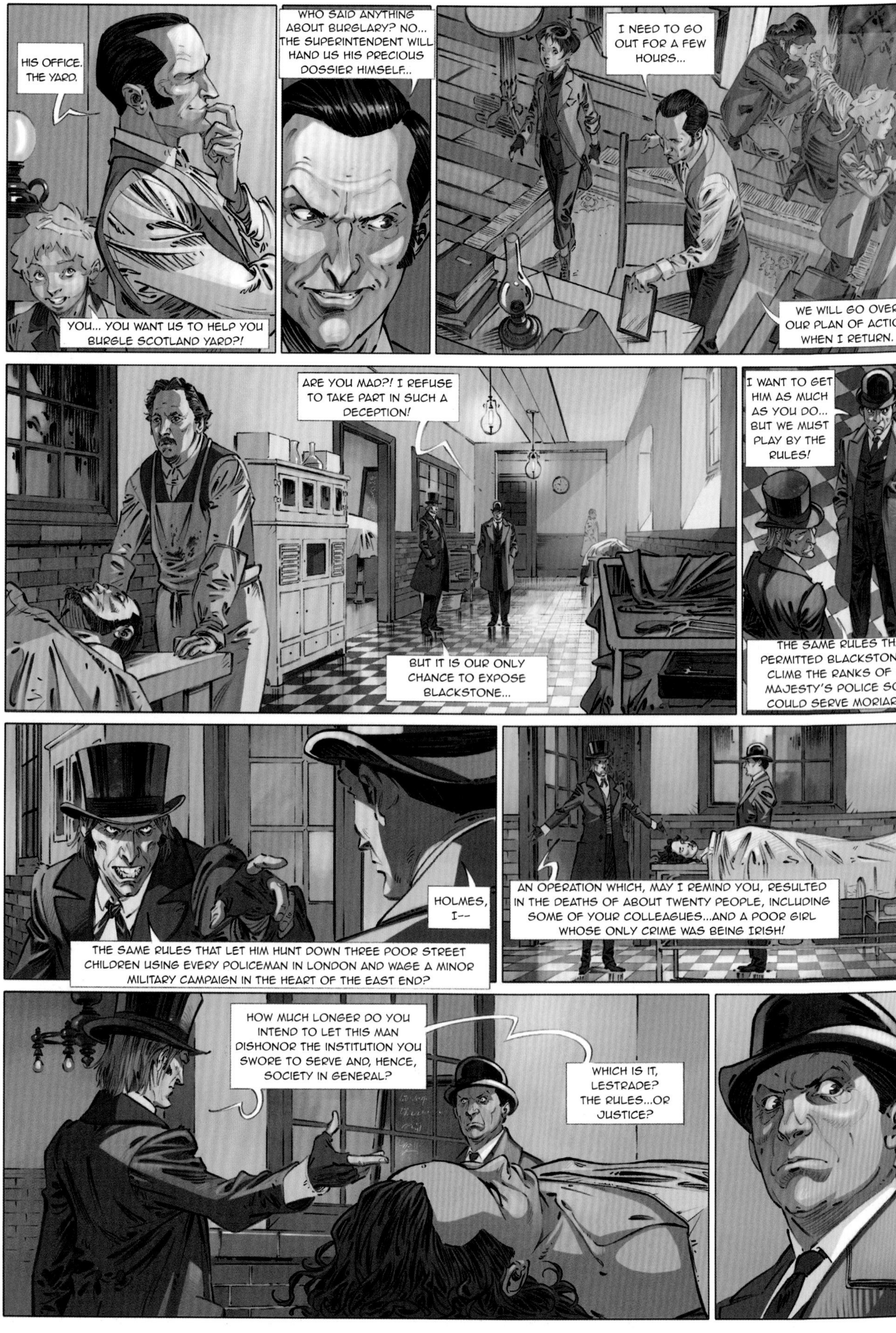
HIS OFFICE. THE YARD.
YOU... YOU WANT US TO HELP YOU BURGLE SCOTLAND YARD?!
WHO SAID ANYTHING ABOUT BURGLARY? NO... THE SUPERINTENDENT WILL HAND US HIS PRECIOUS DOSSIER HIMSELF...
I NEED TO GO OUT FOR A FEW HOURS...
WE WILL GO OVER OUR PLAN OF ACTION WHEN I RETURN.
ARE YOU MAD?! I REFUSE TO TAKE PART IN SUCH A DECEPTION!
BUT IT IS OUR ONLY CHANCE TO EXPOSE BLACKSTONE...
I WANT TO GET HIM AS MUCH AS YOU DO... BUT WE MUST PLAY BY THE RULES!
THE SAME RULES THAT PERMITTED BLACKSTONE TO CLIMB THE RANKS OF HER MAJESTY'S POLICE SO HE COULD SERVE MORIARTY?
HOLMES, I--
THE SAME RULES THAT LET HIM HUNT DOWN THREE POOR STREET CHILDREN USING EVERY POLICEMAN IN LONDON AND WAGE A MINOR MILITARY CAMPAIGN IN THE HEART OF THE EAST END?
AN OPERATION WHICH, MAY I REMIND YOU, RESULTED IN THE DEATHS OF ABOUT TWENTY PEOPLE, INCLUDING SOME OF YOUR COLLEAGUES...AND A POOR GIRL WHOSE ONLY CRIME WAS BEING IRISH!
HOW MUCH LONGER DO YOU INTEND TO LET THIS MAN DISHONOR THE INSTITUTION YOU SWORE TO SERVE AND, HENCE, SOCIETY IN GENERAL?
WHICH IS IT, LESTRADE? THE RULES...OR JUSTICE?

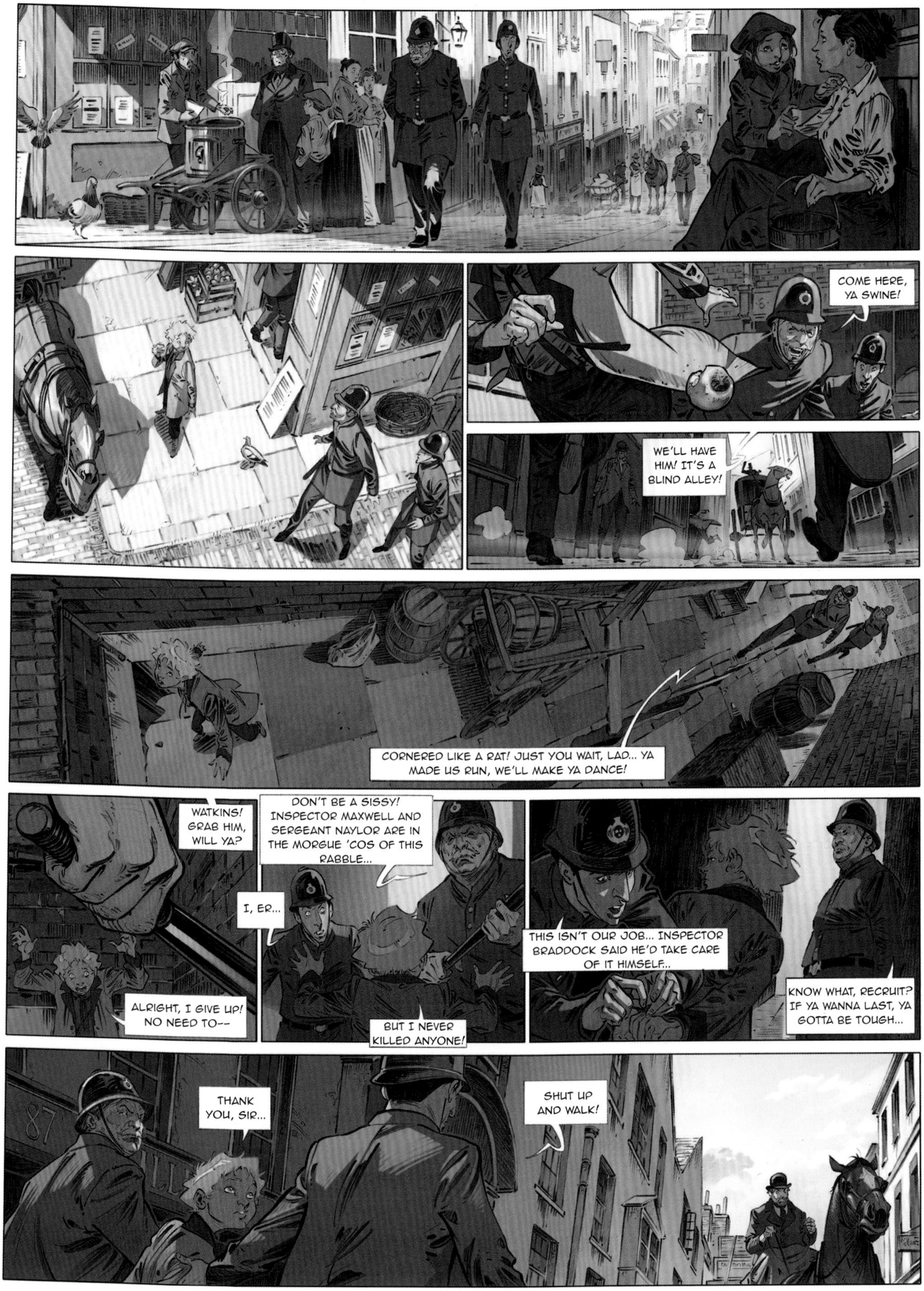
COME HERE, YA SWINE!
WE'LL HAVE HIM! IT'S A BLIND ALLEY!
CORNERED LIKE A RAT! JUST YOU WAIT, LAD... YA MADE US RUN, WE'LL MAKE YA DANCE!
WATKINS! GRAB HIM, WILL YA?
ALRIGHT, I GIVE UP! NO NEED TO--
DON'T BE A SISSY! INSPECTOR MAXWELL AND SERGEANT NAYLOR ARE IN THE MORGUE 'COS OF THIS RABBLE...
I, ER...
BUT I NEVER KILLED ANYONE!
THIS ISN'T OUR JOB... INSPECTOR BRADDOCK SAID HE'D TAKE CARE OF IT HIMSELF...
KNOW WHAT, RECRUIT? IF YA WANNA LAST, YA GOTTA BE TOUGH...
THANK YOU, SIR...
SHUT UP AND WALK!

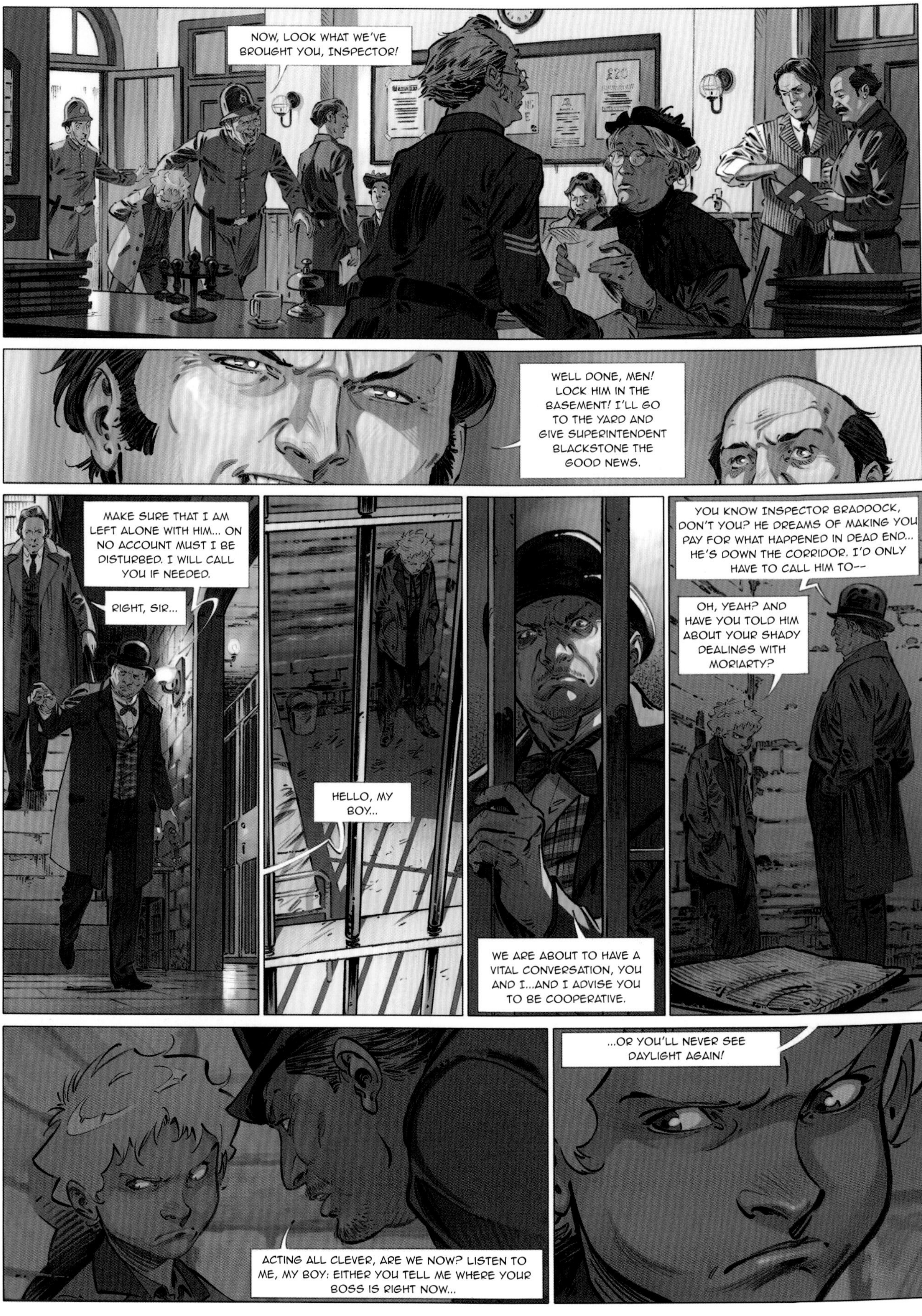
NOW, LOOK WHAT WE'VE BROUGHT YOU, INSPECTOR!
WELL DONE, MEN! LOCK HIM IN THE BASEMENT! I'LL GO TO THE YARD AND GIVE SUPERINTENDENT BLACKSTONE THE GOOD NEWS.
MAKE SURE THAT I AM LEFT ALONE WITH HIM... ON NO ACCOUNT MUST I BE DISTURBED. I WILL CALL YOU IF NEEDED.
RIGHT, SIR...
HELLO, MY BOY...
WE ARE ABOUT TO HAVE A VITAL CONVERSATION, YOU AND I...AND I ADVISE YOU TO BE COOPERATIVE.
YOU KNOW INSPECTOR BRADDOCK, DON'T YOU? HE DREAMS OF MAKING YOU PAY FOR WHAT HAPPENED IN DEAD END... HE'S DOWN THE CORRIDOR. I'D ONLY HAVE TO CALL HIM TO--
OH, YEAH? AND HAVE YOU TOLD HIM ABOUT YOUR SHADY DEALINGS WITH MORIARTY?
ACTING ALL CLEVER, ARE WE NOW? LISTEN TO ME, MY BOY: EITHER YOU TELL ME WHERE YOUR BOSS IS RIGHT NOW...
...OR YOU'LL NEVER SEE DAYLIGHT AGAIN!

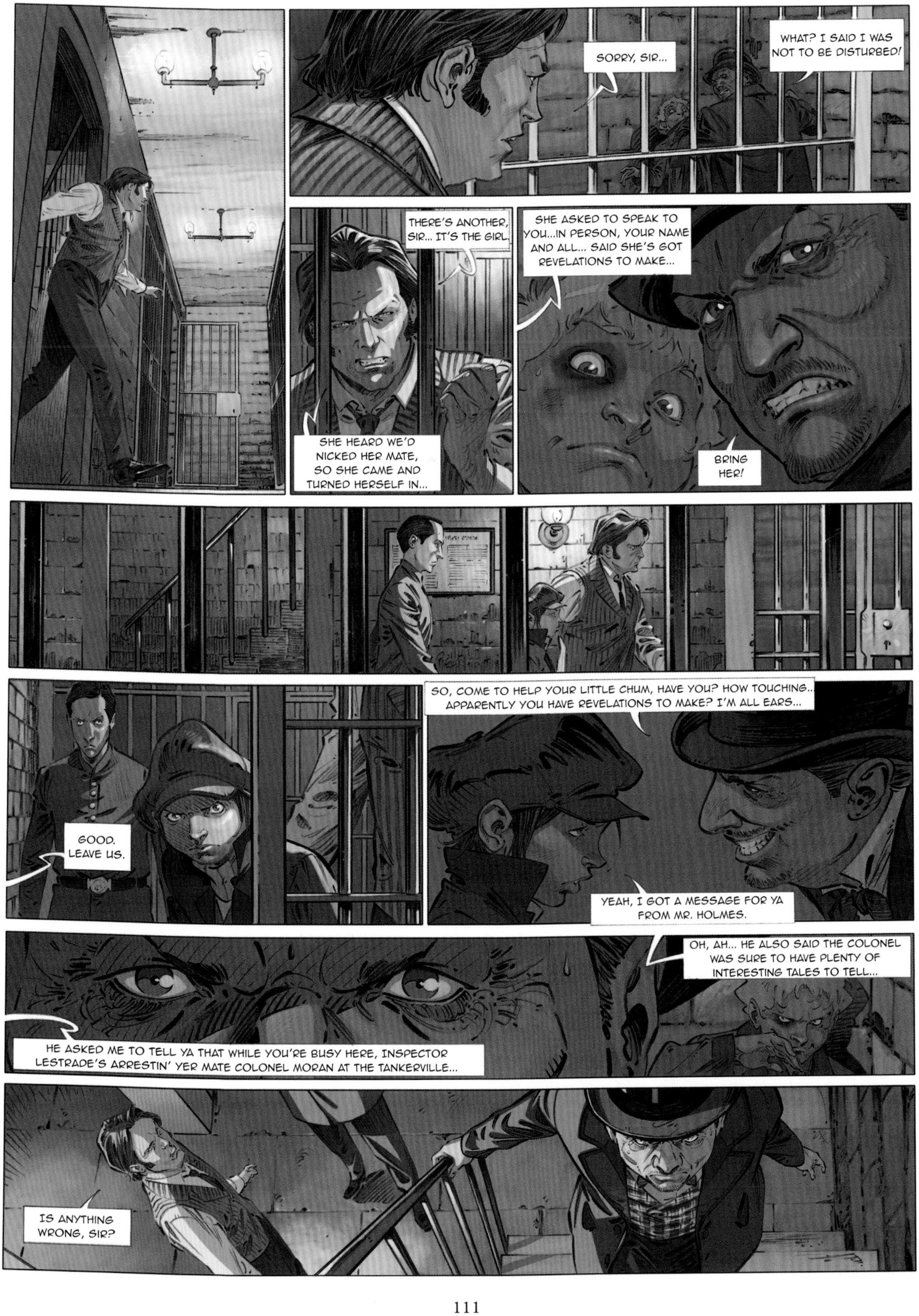
SORRY, SIR...
WHAT? I SAID I WAS NOT TO BE DISTURBED!
THERE'S ANOTHER, SIR... IT'S THE GIRL.
SHE HEARD WE'D NICKED HER MATE, SO SHE CAME AND TURNED HERSELF IN...
SHE ASKED TO SPEAK TO YOU...IN PERSON, YOUR NAME AND ALL... SAID SHE'S GOT REVELATIONS TO MAKE...
BRING HER!
GOOD. LEAVE US.
SO, COME TO HELP YOUR LITTLE CHUM, HAVE YOU? HOW TOUCHING... APPARENTLY YOU HAVE REVELATIONS TO MAKE? I'M ALL EARS...
YEAH, I GOT A MESSAGE FOR YA FROM MR. HOLMES.
HE ASKED ME TO TELL YA THAT WHILE YOU'RE BUSY HERE, INSPECTOR LESTRADE'S ARRESTIN' YER MATE COLONEL MORAN AT THE TANKERVILLE...
OH, AH... HE ALSO SAID THE COLONEL WAS SURE TO HAVE PLENTY OF INTERESTING TALES TO TELL...
IS ANYTHING WRONG, SIR?

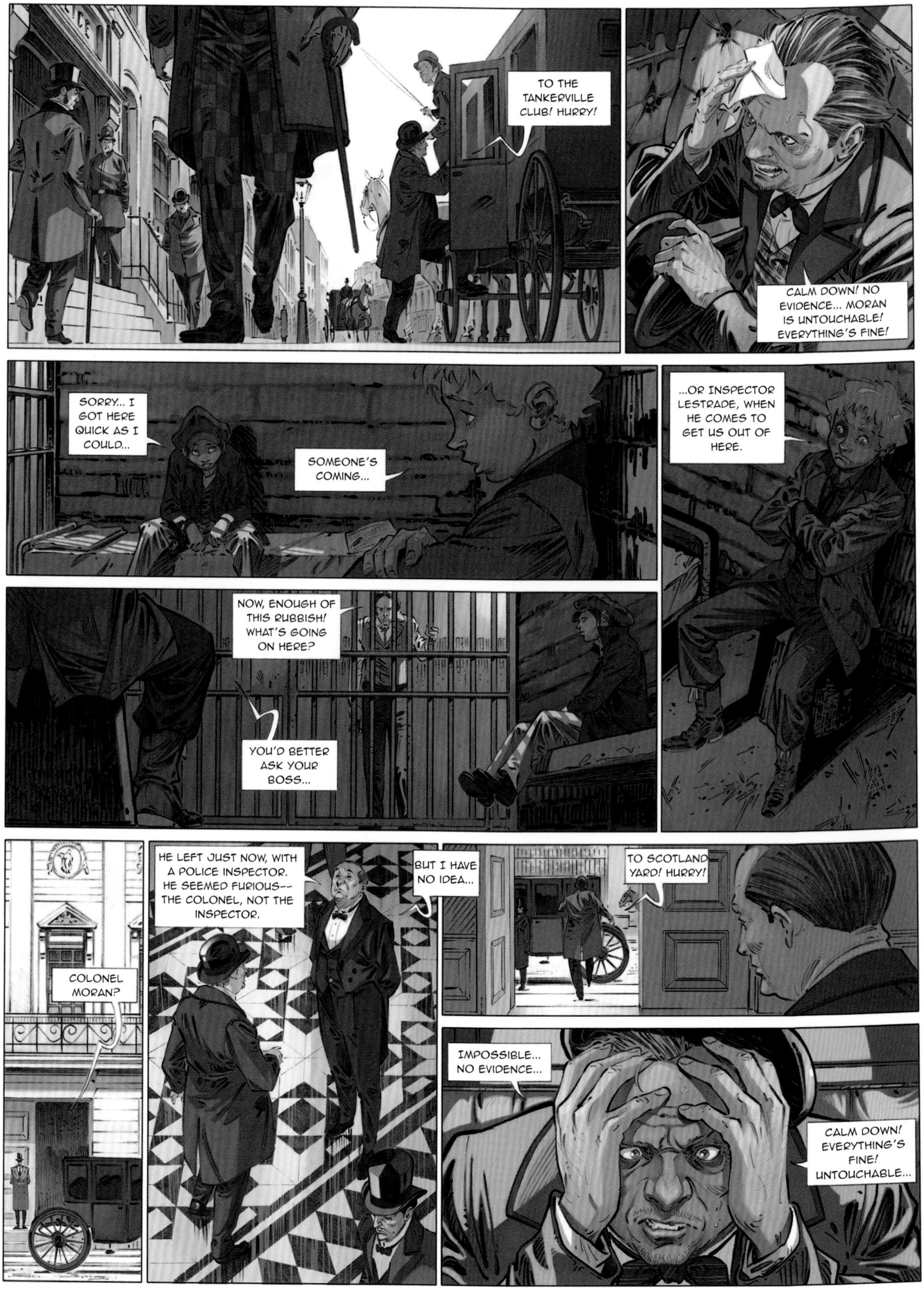
TO THE TANKERVILLE CLUB! HURRY!
CALM DOWN! NO EVIDENCE... MORAN IS UNTOUCHABLE! EVERYTHING'S FINE!
SORRY... I GOT HERE QUICK AS I COULD...
SOMEONE'S COMING...
...OR INSPECTOR LESTRADE, WHEN HE COMES TO GET US OUT OF HERE.
NOW, ENOUGH OF THIS RUBBISH! WHAT'S GOING ON HERE?
YOU'D BETTER ASK YOUR BOSS...
COLONEL MORAN?
HE LEFT JUST NOW, WITH A POLICE INSPECTOR. HE SEEMED FURIOUS-- THE COLONEL, NOT THE INSPECTOR.
BUT I HAVE NO IDEA...
TO SCOTLAND YARD! HURRY!
IMPOSSIBLE... NO EVIDENCE...
CALM DOWN! EVERYTHING'S FINE! UNTOUCHABLE...

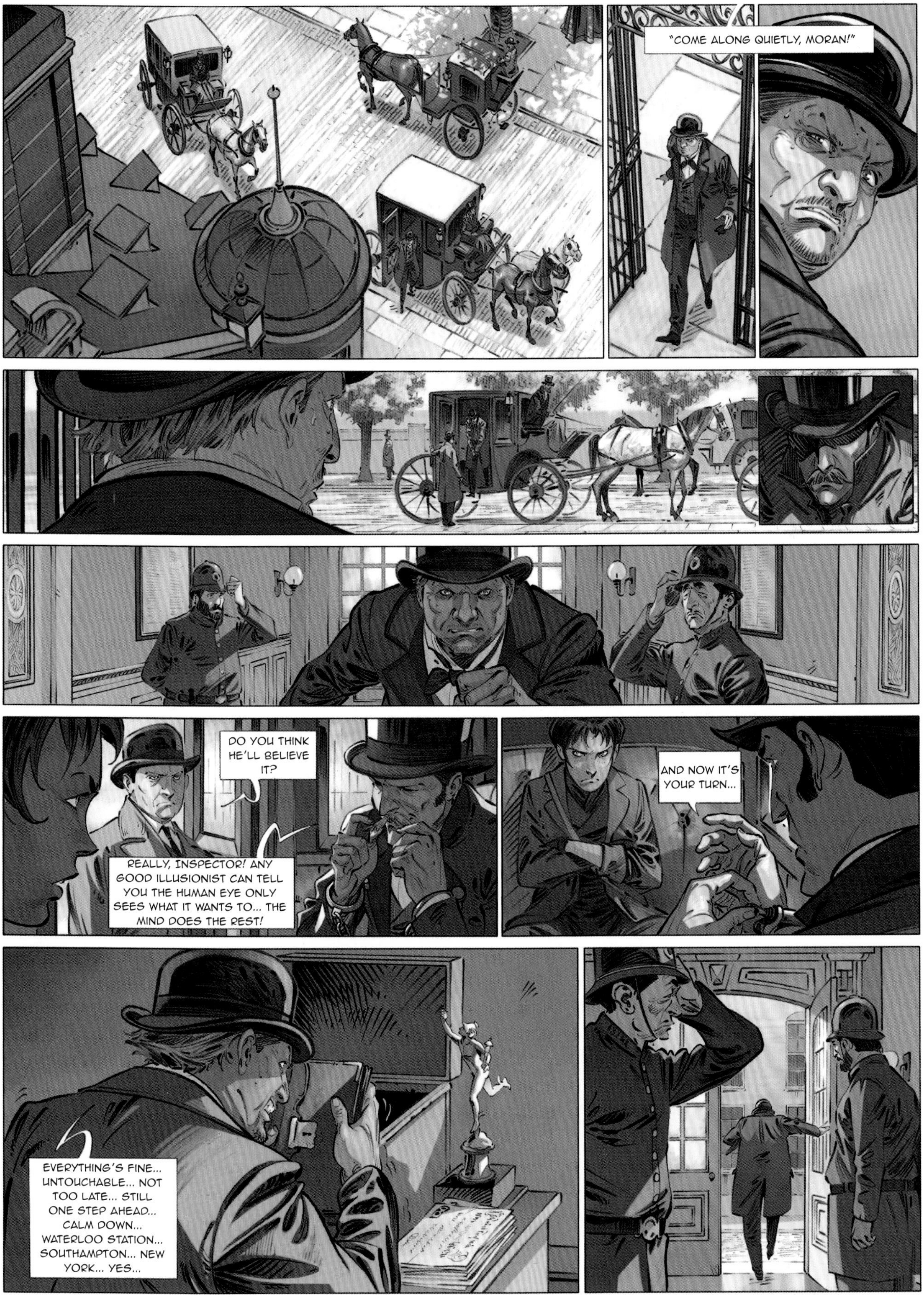
"COME ALONG QUIETLY, MORAN!"
DO YOU THINK HE'LL BELIEVE IT?
REALLY, INSPECTOR! ANY GOOD ILLUSIONIST CAN TELL YOU THE HUMAN EYE ONLY SEES WHAT IT WANTS TO... THE MIND DOES THE REST!
AND NOW IT'S YOUR TURN...
EVERYTHING'S FINE... UNTOUCHABLE... NOT TOO LATE... STILL ONE STEP AHEAD... CALM DOWN... WATERLOO STATION... SOUTHAMPTON... NEW YORK... YES...

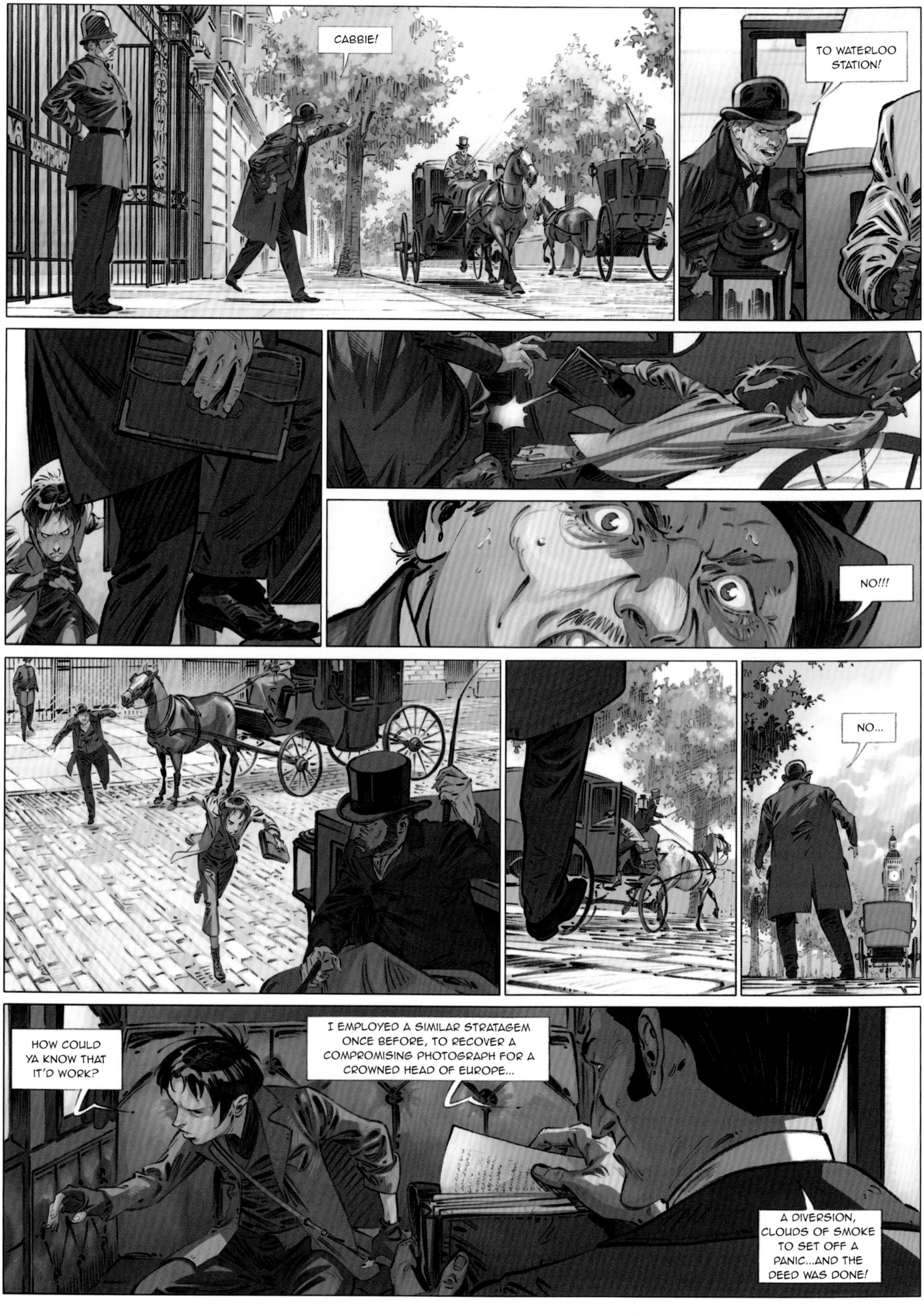
CABBIE!
TO WATERLOO STATION!
NO!!!
NO...
HOW COULD YA KNOW THAT IT'D WORK?
I EMPLOYED A SIMILAR STRATAGEM ONCE BEFORE, TO RECOVER A COMPROMISING PHOTOGRAPH FOR A CROWNED HEAD OF EUROPE...
A DIVERSION, CLOUDS OF SMOKE TO SET OFF A PANIC...AND THE DEED WAS DONE!

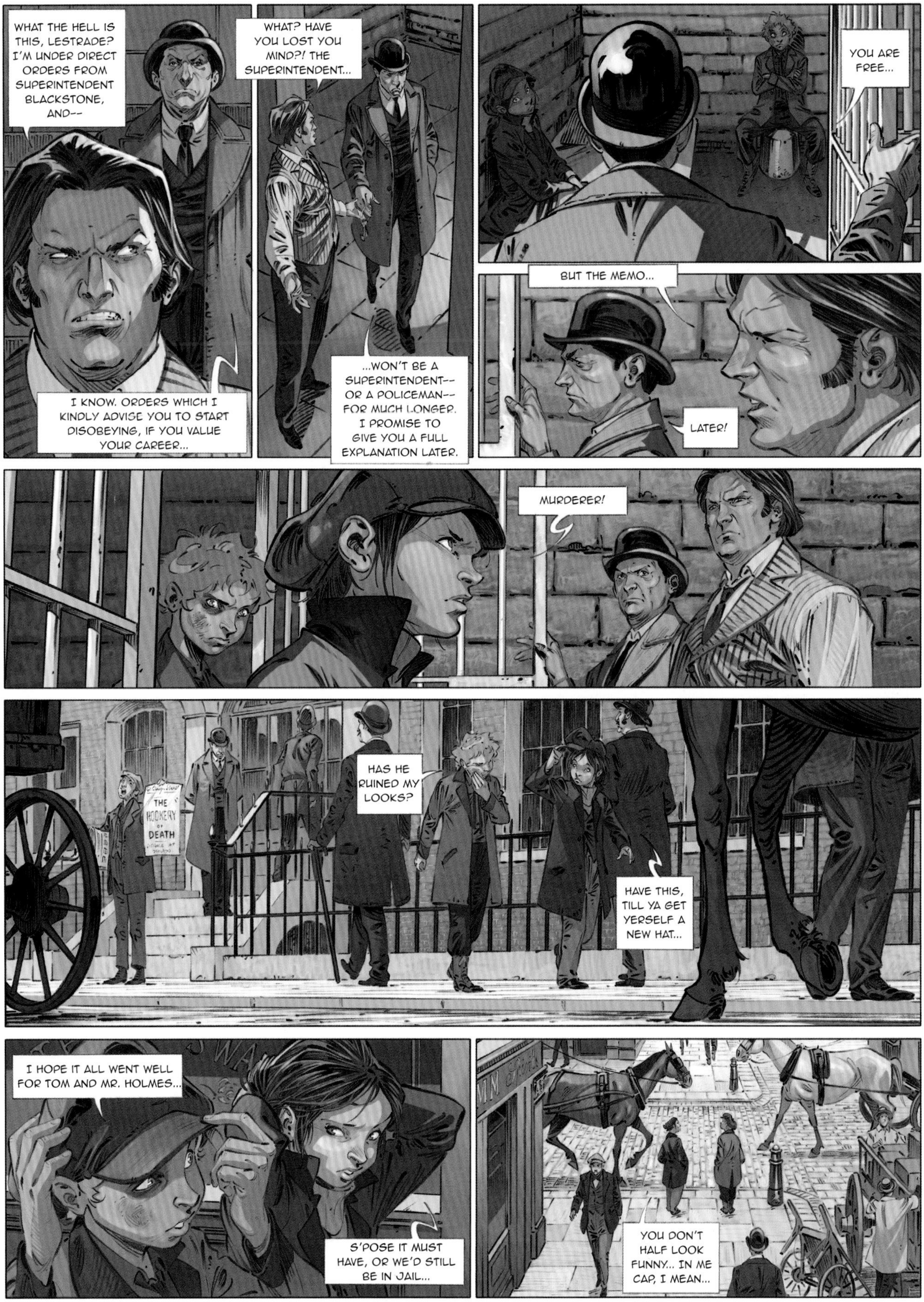
WHAT THE HELL IS THIS, LESTRADE? I'M UNDER DIRECT ORDERS FROM SUPERINTENDENT BLACKSTONE, AND--
I KNOW. ORDERS WHICH I KINDLY ADVISE YOU TO START DISOBEYING, IF YOU VALUE YOUR CAREER...
WHAT? HAVE YOU LOST YOU MIND?! THE SUPERINTENDENT...
...WON'T BE A SUPERINTENDENT-- OR A POLICEMAN-- FOR MUCH LONGER. I PROMISE TO GIVE YOU A FULL EXPLANATION LATER.
YOU ARE FREE...
BUT THE MEMO...
LATER!
MURDERER!
HAS HE RUINED MY LOOKS?
HAVE THIS, TILL YA GET YERSELF A NEW HAT...
I HOPE IT ALL WENT WELL FOR TOM AND MR. HOLMES...
S'POSE IT MUST HAVE, OR WE'D STILL BE IN JAIL...
YOU DON'T HALF LOOK FUNNY... IN ME CAP, I MEAN...

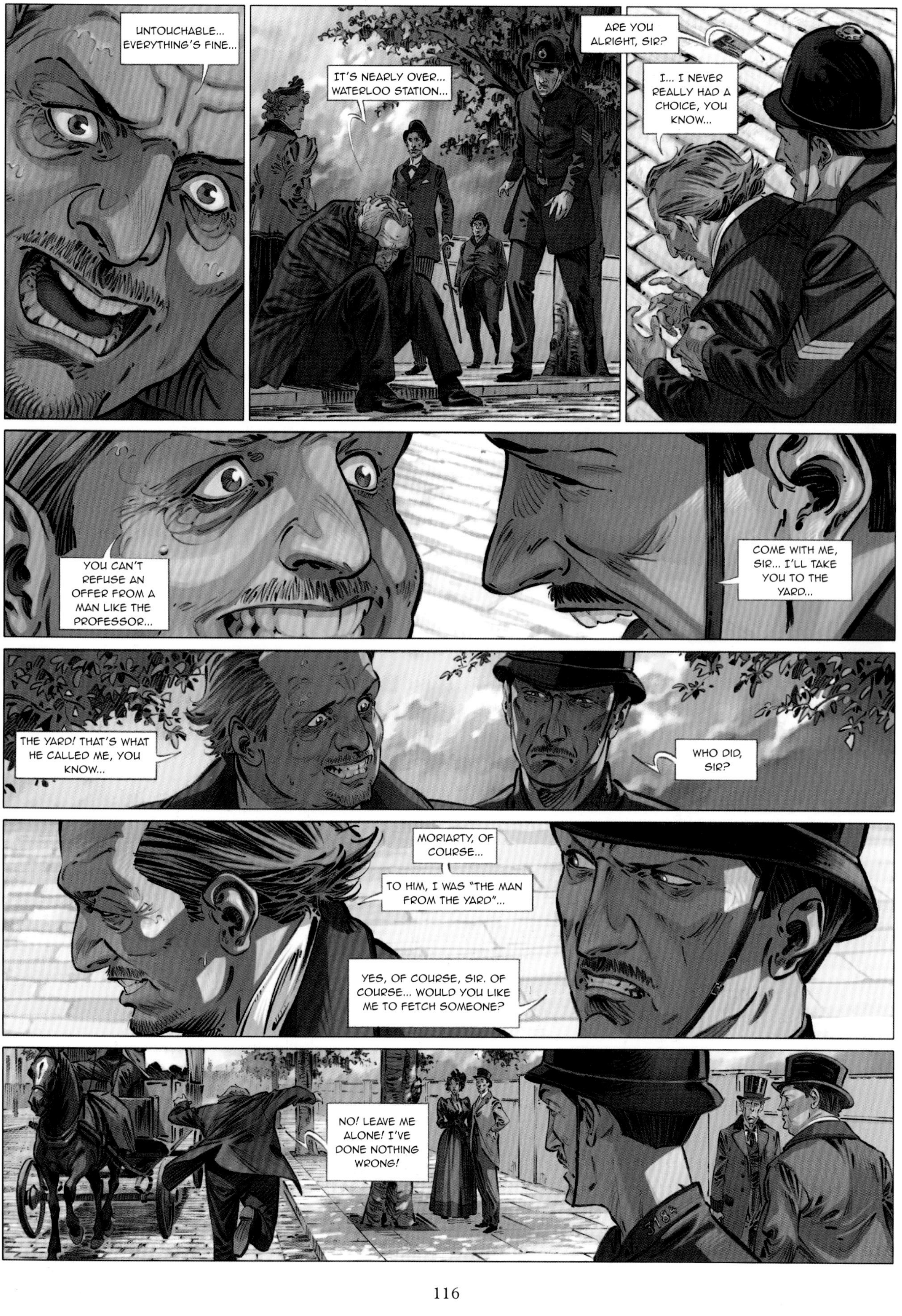
UNTOUCHABLE... EVERYTHING'S FINE...
IT'S NEARLY OVER... WATERLOO STATION...
ARE YOU ALRIGHT, SIR?
I... I NEVER REALLY HAD A CHOICE, YOU KNOW...
YOU CAN'T REFUSE AN OFFER FROM A MAN LIKE THE PROFESSOR...
COME WITH ME, SIR... I'LL TAKE YOU TO THE YARD...
THE YARD! THAT'S WHAT HE CALLED ME, YOU KNOW...
WHO DID, SIR?
MORIARTY, OF COURSE...
TO HIM, I WAS "THE MAN FROM THE YARD"...
YES, OF COURSE, SIR. OF COURSE... WOULD YOU LIKE ME TO FETCH SOMEONE?
NO! LEAVE ME ALONE! I'VE DONE NOTHING WRONG!

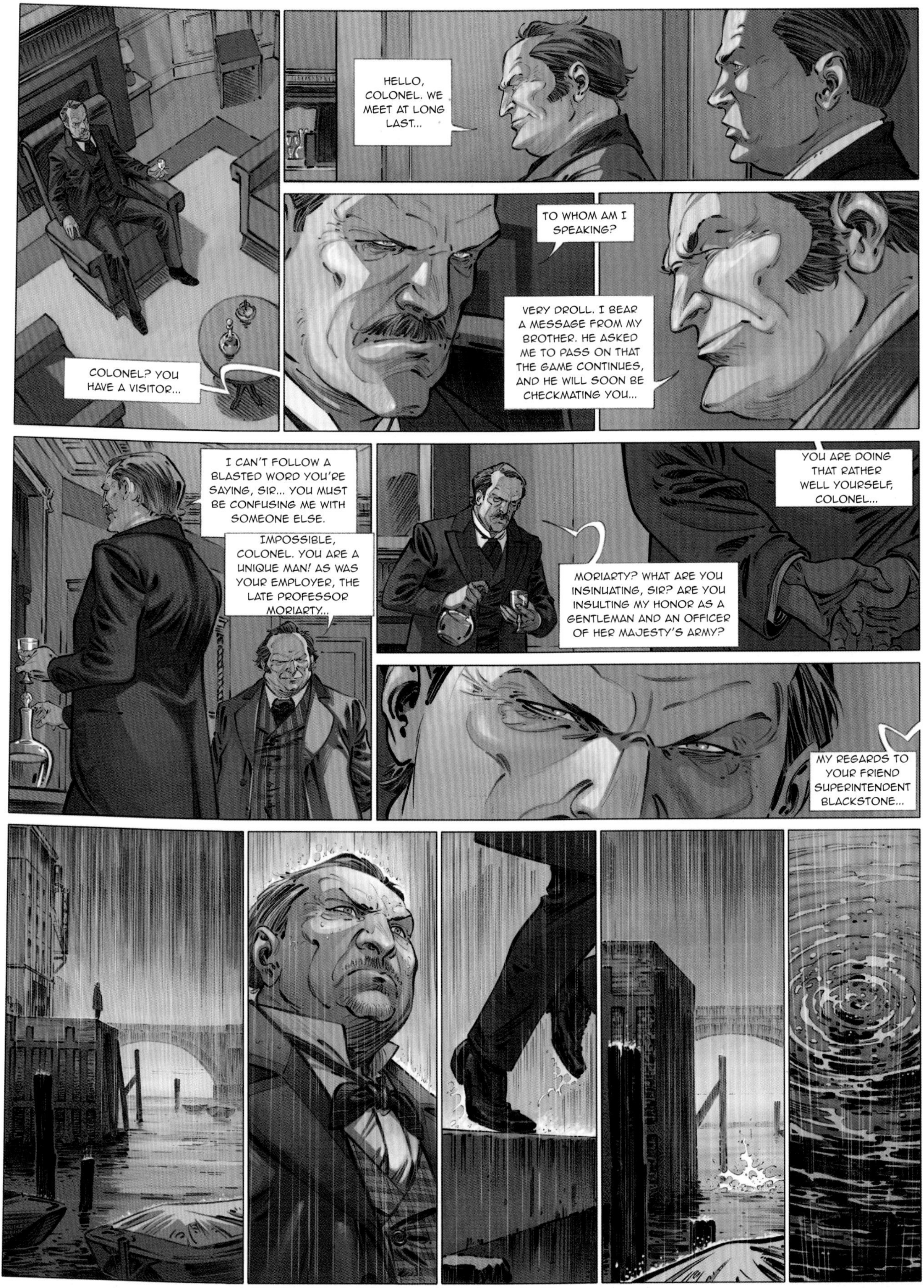
COLONEL? YOU HAVE A VISITOR...
HELLO, COLONEL. WE MEET AT LONG LAST...
TO WHOM AM I SPEAKING?
VERY DROLL. I BEAR A MESSAGE FROM MY BROTHER. HE ASKED ME TO PASS ON THAT THE GAME CONTINUES, AND HE WILL SOON BE CHECKMATING YOU...
I CAN'T FOLLOW A BLASTED WORD YOU'RE SAYING, SIR... YOU MUST BE CONFUSING ME WITH SOMEONE ELSE.
IMPOSSIBLE, COLONEL. YOU ARE A UNIQUE MAN! AS WAS YOUR EMPLOYER, THE LATE PROFESSOR MORIARTY...
MORIARTY? WHAT ARE YOU INSINUATING, SIR? ARE YOU INSULTING MY HONOR AS A GENTLEMAN AND AN OFFICER OF HER MAJESTY'S ARMY?
YOU ARE DOING THAT RATHER WELL YOURSELF, COLONEL...
MY REGARDS TO YOUR FRIEND SUPERINTENDENT BLACKSTONE...

IT'S SICKENING... I WAS CALLED TO THE YARD TODAY...

THEY EXPLAINED THAT, DUE TO BLACKSTONE'S "TRAGIC DEATH" AND CERTAIN "POLITICAL AND PUBLIC OBLIGATIONS"...

...THE DOSSIER SENT TO YOU BY AN INFORMANT MUST REMAIN CONFIDENTIAL, AM I CORRECT?

A SUPERINTENDENT UNDER MORIARTY'S CONTROL?! THE YARD CLEARLY COULDN'T ALLOW SUCH A SCANDAL, MY DEAR LESTRADE!

SO THEY WERE AT PAINS TO POINT OUT... THAT MEANS THERE WILL BE NO MORAN SCANDAL, EITHER...

QUITE LOGICAL! PUTTING THE COLONEL ON TRIAL WOULD GIVE HIM A CHANCE TO EXPOSE THE TRUTH ABOUT BLACKSTONE...

MORAN IS A MURDERER, BUT HE'LL GET AWAY SCOT-FREE!

IT IS OUR DUTY TO TRY...BUT THE GAME IS NOT OVER YET.

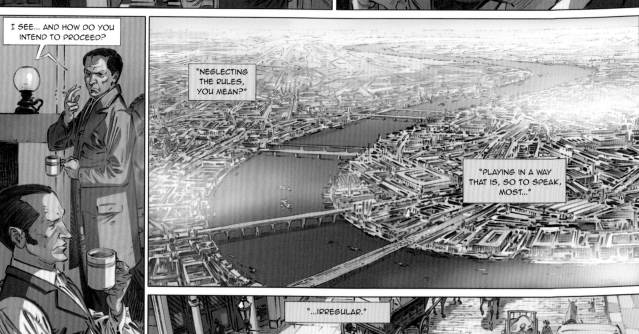

I SEE... AND HOW DO YOU INTEND TO PROCEED?

"NEGLECTING THE RULES, YOU MEAN?"

"PLAYING IN A WAY THAT IS, SO TO SPEAK, MOST..."

THERE IS ONLY ONE WAY TO BEAT SUCH MEN, LESTRADE... YOU KNOW IT AS WELL AS I DO.

"...IRREGULAR."

END OF CHAPTER 6

118

www.insightcomics.com

Find us on Facebook:
www.facebook.com/InsightEditionsComics

Follow us on Twitter:
@InsightComics

Follow us on Instagram:
Insight_Comics

Original Title: Les Quatre de Baker Street vol. 5
Authors: J.B. Djian, Olivier Legrand, David Etien

© Editions Glénat 2014 — ALL RIGHTS RESERVED

Original Title: Les Quatre de Baker Street vol. 6
Authors: J.B. Djian, Olivier Legrand, David Etien

© Editions Glénat 2015 — ALL RIGHTS RESERVED

Library of Congress Cataloging-in-Publication Data available.

ISBN: 978-1-68383-106-8

Publisher: Raoul Goff
Associate Publisher: Vanessa Lopez
Senior Editor: Mark Irwin
Managing Editor: Alan Kaplan
Editorial Assistant: Holly Fisher
Production Editor: Elaine Ou
Production Manager: Alix Nicholaeff

Insight Editions, in association with Roots of Peace, will plant two trees for each tree used in the manufacturing of this book. Roots of Peace is an internationally renowned humanitarian organization dedicated to eradicating land mines worldwide and converting war-torn lands into productive farms and wildlife habitats. Roots of Peace will plant two million fruit and nut trees in Afghanistan and provide farmers there with the skills and support necessary for sustainable land use.

Manufactured in China by Insight Editions

10 9 8 7 6 5 4 3 2 1